## ALSO BY PAUL NEWELL

### Shocking Tales
*from Victorian Portsmouth Vol I*
ISBN 978-1-905597-81-9

Stories from Portsmouth's Victorian newspapers between 1838 and 1900. Graphic descriptions of tales of woe and the scandalous, darker side of city life. Great examples of the sensational and shocking style of journalistic reporting which was so prevalent at the time.

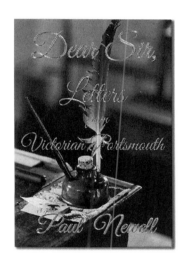

### Dear Sir,
*Letters from Victorian Portsmouth*
ISBN 978-1-905597-91-8

This compilation of 'Letters to the Editor' highlights the gripes of the people of Portsmouth in Victorian times and gives us a chance to meet the 'serial complainers' of the day.

Was it the outrage of mixed bathing? The shocking state of the roads? The smell of the slaughter houses? Or were they just interested in who had the oldest parrot?

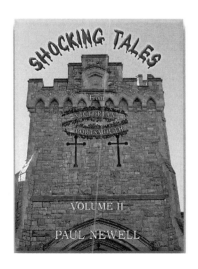

### Shocking Tales
*from Victorian Portsmouth, Vol II*
ISBN 978-1-905597-94-9

Revel in the shocking and sensational once again as we return to the shady back streets of Portsmouth to meet the villainous and the desperate; to learn of life's hardships and the punishments experienced by those who transgressed the law – all as reported at the time.

Life in Victorian Portsmouth was anything but easy for the majority and, it would seem, they would do anything to survive!

# A Victorian Portrayal
of Ghosts
and the
Unexplained

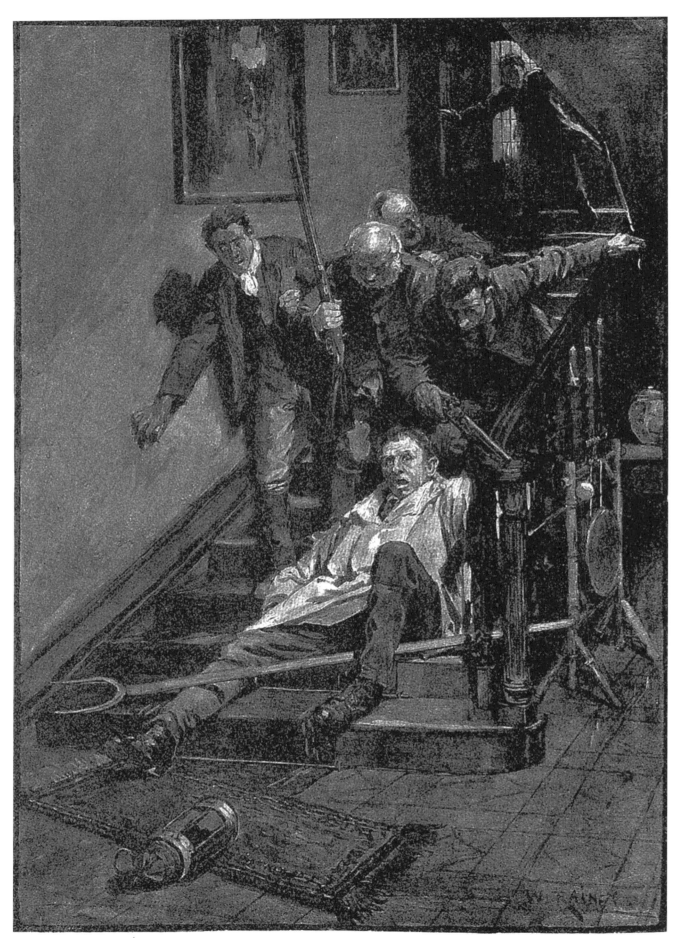

THE PSYCHICAL RESEARCH SOCIETY

# A Victorian Portrayal of Ghosts and the Unexplained

## by
## Paul Newell

*Moyhill* Publishing

First Published in 2019 by Moyhill Publishing.
ISBN 9781905597956

A CIP catalogue record for this book is availablefrom the British Library.

Printed in UK.

Transcripts and Images have been created by myself with thanks to
the The British Newspaper archive (www.britishnewspaperarchive.co.uk),
or from my own private collection.

Book Design and Production by *Moyhill* Publishing.
Cover Design by *Moyhill* Publishing.

The papers used in this book were produced in an
environmentally friendly way from sustainable forests.

*Moyhill* Publishing,
1965 Davenport House, 261 Bolton Rd, Bury, Gtr. Manchester BL8 2NZ. UK

*This book is dedicated*

To my family and generations to come.

# Contents

# Contents

# Contents

# A VICTORIAN PORTRAYAL OF GHOSTS AND THE UNEXPLAINED

SO HOW DID THE VICTORIANS PORTRAY GHOSTS AND THE UNEXPLAINED? AS A SOCIETY, THE VICTORIANS CRAVED THE SENSATIONAL AND FED OFF THE STORYLINES OF THE LOCAL NEWSPAPERS TO SUCH AN EXTENT THAT, IN SOME CASES, MASS HYSTERIA ENSUED. THEREFORE, IT IS NO SURPRISE THAT TALES OF GHOSTS, HAUNTED HOUSES AND THE GENERALLY UNEXPLAINED CAPTURED THE IMAGINATION; AND THESE STORIES WERE CIRCULATED THROUGHOUT THE BRITISH ISLES.

WHILST IT IS TRUE TO SAY THE VICTORIAN ERA WAS RICH WITH GHOST STORIES AND WRITERS, IT WAS A TIME WHERE SCEPTICISM GREW, FAKE SÉANCES WERE BEING EXPOSED AND SCIENCE WAS BECOMING MORE PREVALENT. THE PSYCHICAL RESEARCH SOCIETY WAS EVEN CREATED TO INVESTIGATE THE SUPERNATURAL AND DEBUNK TALES OF KNOCKINGS AND HAUNTINGS. IN RURAL AREAS, HOWEVER, THE FEAR OF SUPERSTITIONS AND THE SUPERNATURAL REMAINED AS IT HAD FOR CENTURIES BEFORE.

THIS COLLECTION OF "REPORTS" IS TAKEN AND TRANSCRIBED VERBATIM FROM NEWSPAPERS OF THE TIME TO SHOW HOW THE VICTORIANS ACTUALLY PORTRAYED THESE SPOOKY EVENTS. IN MANY CASES THE PERPETRATORS OF SOME "GHOSTLY" DEED WOULD BE THOSE "PESKY KIDS" IN THE NEIGHBOURHOOD, BUT SOME OF THE STORIES WILL, I AM CONFIDENT, SEND A SHIVER DOWN YOUR SPINE, OR AT THE VERY LEAST ENTERTAIN YOU. SOME OF THE ILLUSTRATIONS ADD TO THE SENSATIONAL STYLE OF REPORTING.

SO, TURN THE PAGES AND DISCOVER WHO OR WHAT WAS DISTURBING THE SLEEP OF THE VICTORIANS AND MIND YOU CHECK UNDER THE BED BEFORE YOU GO TO SLEEP!!

# 1840 – MOST EXTRAORDINARY CASE OF GROSS SUPERSTITION.

We have frequently heard of the superstitions of the Irish peasantry, but we believe we may with safety affirm that a case which displayed greater ignorance and cruelty than the one about to be detailed, never came before the public eye. When first we heard the circumstances connected with it, we really could not give credence to them. Although we were well aware of the unenlightened state in which the peasantry of this country are kept, still we could not for a moment conceive that in the 19th century, in the present day, when we hear so much about "moral reformation," there could be found a body of persons so dead to every sense of religion, so sunk in the depths of the grossest superstition, so devoid of the commonest feelings of humanity, as to have recourse to the practices which will appear in the investigation, which we this day lay before our readers.

The facts of the case, which will appear more fully in the evidence, are simply these:—

A man of the name of James Mahony, who lives on the demense of Heywood, the property of Mr. Charles Riall, had a son of the age of six or seven, a most delicate child. It appears that the boy had been confined to bed for two years with an affection of the spine, and, being a very intellectual child, and accustomed to make the most shrewd remarks about everything he saw and heard passing around him, his parents and the neighbours were led to the conclusion that he was not the son of his father, but that he was fairy!!

Under this impression, a consultation took place at the house of Mahony, and the result was, that the intruder from the "good people" should be frightened away; and, accordingly, on Tuesday night last, the poor dying child was threatened with a red hot shovel and ducking under a pump if he did not disclose where the real John Mahony was and so successful were the actors in their scheme devised for the expulsion of the fairy, that the feeble child, after being held near the hot shovel, and also having been taken a part of the way to the pump, told them he was a fairy, and that he would send back the real John Mahony the next evening if they gave him that night's lodging. This occurred on Tuesday night last, and the child was dead the next morning.

When our active stipendiary magistrate, Mr. William Nash, heard of the matter, he immediately had four persons named Pierce Whelan, James and Henry Beresford, and James Mahony, taken into custody, as being implicated in the unprecedented affair; and on yesterday an inquest was held on the body before Mr. William Ryan, coroner.

Patrick Pigott sworn.—I am a servant of Mr. Riall's. At half past 8, the kitchen and housemaid told me John Mahony was dying. I was in the kitchen at the time. It was on Tuesday night last. They said they were coming down to Mahony's house, and asked me to come, and I said, "I would." I then went with them. When we came into the house, the child was sitting on the floor in a chair, a little distance from the fire. Some of the men were putting questions to the child all the time. They were asking him was he John Mahony, and whether it was the right person was in it. I heard the child answering and saying he was not, that he was taken by a man and woman, that he had pain in his back, and that he was left in the place of John Mahony. He was then asked where the right John Mahony was, and he said he was in a farmer's house, and that he wore a corduroy coat and trousers, and a green cap. I saw a shovel on the fire, and heard a man threatening he would put him on the shovel if he did not send back the right John Mahony. He said he would send him back between 4 and the next evening. When I was going away, the men were giving him up, and stopping putting questions to him. I was not in the house when he was brought to the pump. I did not see the shovel taken off the fire while I was there. They were blowing the fire and threatening to put him on it. The child did not appear at all alarmed, and wished to be put on the shovel! As far as opinion goes, I think the child thought they were in earnest. I could not point out any person in particular putting the questions to the child.

To a juror,—The child did not appear in any immediate danger.

Andrew Heffernan sworn.—I live in the Irishtown, in Clonmel. I am a carpenter. On Tuesday night when I came in to James Mahony's house, I saw the child stripped in a chair, he had only his linen on him. The chair was near the fire. I heard James and Harry Beresford questioning him. James Beresford said, if he did not send home Johnny Mahony he would put him on the shovel that was on the fire. The child said, to give him that night's lodging and he would have the right Johnny Mahony back the next evening. I saw the shovel taken off the fire. It was laid in the middle of the floor. I saw the child taken out of the chair by two persons. I heard James Beresford and Pierce Whelan threaten to put the child on the shovel. The persons who had the child held him over the shovel, but did not touch him with it. They said if he did not tell the truth they'd put him on it. The child then said it was one Cummins took the right Johnny Mahony and left himself in the grove at Heywood; I did not see the child taken outside the door, but I heard talk about his being taken to the pump. The child did not appear frightened; I told the mother he was dying. I heard him say "to burn him." The shovel was hot enough to scald him. I left the house at half past nine. I was not there the entire time. It was all over when I left, and the child was in bed. Ned English and James Mahony were in the house, and Mrs. Tynan and Mrs. Mahony. Whelan and the Beresfords came in with me. Several others were also in the house. I left Ted English and Mahony in the house.

To Mr. Nash. – There was great threatening to drive the fairy out of the house. When I said the child was dying, the mother took it in her arms and put it in bed. My opinion is, that James Beresford and Pierce Whelan had the child between them. I am sure of Whelan, but cannot say whether it was James or Harry Beresford who had the child with him. The reason I thought the child was dying was, that there was a long time between every word said. I did not think the child would live three minutes.

Matthew Tynan sworn—On Tuesday evening, Anne Mahony came to me crying, and asked me to go with her to her husband, that her son John Mahony was telling his father a great deal of news. I went with her, and when I got to the house I saw a shovel on the fire. I heard the father say he'd put the child on the shovel if he did not tell where the real John Mahony was. The father held the child over the shovel, I saw a second attempt to put the child on the shovel. I don't know who did it. I went away, I was so disgusted with the questions they were putting to the child. They asked him was he a fairy, and he said he was. I think the threats were calculated to frighten the child. I heard the father say, "For God's sake, let him alone now," as if he was tired of asking him questions.

James Mahony (father of the child) examined—I told the child I would take him to the pump when he said he was a fairy. He told me to burn him on the shovel—the devil a bit frightened he was. The reason I frightened the child was, that everyone that came in said he was a fairy. That was what induced me to threaten to put him on the shovel. When I said, "are you fairy?" he answered, "I am." I did not see anyone put him on the shovel. I took him part of the way towards the pump, and said, I'd drown him. He then asked me to burn him. I merely did that to frighten him. I heard him say next morning, before he died, to his mother, "to turn him." He asked for a smoke before he died. He often smoked for half an hour.

James Ryan (grandfather to the deceased) sworn.—I was at the house of Mahony this night. I did not see a single person injured nor would I bear to see any Christian born injured. I did not see the child put on the shovel, nor would I let him. He did not appear at all frightened.

Mr. Nash.—Such a case of ignorance, cruelty, and superstition, should be exposed before the world.

James Ryan, in continuation. – The child often said to me he was not a fairy, that it was himself was there!

Doctor John Smith deposed that the child was in a very debilitated state for some time before his death; that he laboured under a curvature of the spine, and that the debility produced by the affection caused death.

Mr. Nash.—If anything was done that could cause excitement —when that excitement had subsided—a greater degree of debility may be superadded which would accelerate death.

The investigation here closed, and the Jury, after deliberating for about 20 minutes, returned a verdict of—"Died by the visitation God."

*Bristol Times and Mirror.*

## 1841 – A GHOST! A GHOST!!

A correspondent has favoured us with the following *true tale*, which shows, as he says, "that those in the country are as fond of the miraculous as the goodly towns-folk."

Much confusion, in our hitherto quiet little village of Plymtree has been occasioned of late by the appearance of a ghost! Most ancient houses are deemed "troublesome" and such has been long considered the case with Hayne House, in the above parish, about the precincts of which, after many years of absence, the ghost has once again appeared. Only a few nights since, a gay young shoemaker, the rural lover of many a village maiden, was passing the iron gates of Hayne, "whistling for want of thought," when, behold, standing in his path the dreaded spectre appeared.

"An awful guest, it stood, and with an action of command, beckoned the Cobbler with his wan right hand."

The love ditty of this gallant knight of wax was at an end, as, with jaws distended he could only stand and gape. The execrable shape glided past, disappearing as suddenly as it had come. A night or two after this, a certain maiden, tripping it lightly onward, saw this phantom looking on her with pale and ireful glance. Well, the news soon ran from mouth to ear, and on again; and many a tale was told of the direful goblin's walk. "What d'ye mean asked one. "Did 'er speak?" enquired another. No! No! (*Certes* we have heard, that ghosts, like the ladies, "never speak till spoken to.") No! They only knew they saw something.

Nights passed on, and nothing more was seen, though much was said to have been heard for one evening, a pretty seamstress, with gown "tucked up," felt while passing on in a pucker; she heard a sound, stopped and then "to run the faster tried." What could it be? There again. Oh! How foolish was I, – as I'm alive, 'tis only my thimble jingling in my bag.

Again people say within these last few nights a brave basket maker saw some "awful form" having "three fiery heads;" but further of its shape it seems this man did not wait to look upon, for putting his best leg foremost, cried, "I'm off," and left the vision far behind. A fiery hand is sometimes seen—and sometimes people meet there, each other, and both turn back, "as each from every pore distil a clammy dew."

But now these tidings have now spread throughout the neighbourhood, many persons, lads and lasses, with many old dupes as well, resort to the haunted spot, in hopes of being honoured by a visit from the ghost! Several, however, come from more distant parishes, to see,—"nothing," blustering big of what they would do. Truly the gentleman who inhabits Hayne must wish the ghost would be pleased to depart upon his voyage across the Styx ; for the screeching of foolish women, combined with the bravado and hallowing of fellows, who by themselves would run away, convert the grounds into an asylum for the weak intellect.

In this parish it is lamentable to see that many persons will not go to church on a Sunday and hear a good sermon, yet will they spend the evening of that day, by idly loitering, staring after what never existed, save the cranium of their own imagination, evaporating perhaps, with many, from the fumes of certain copious draughts of exhilarating fluid.

*Plymouth Gazette.*

# 1841 – STRANGE KNOCKINGS.

For some few days past, Windsor and its immediate neighbourhood have been in a state of considerable excitement in consequence of a house known as "Wants Cottage," standing alone, surrounded by its grounds at Clewer, about a mile from the town, having been reported, from the extraordinary noises which have been heard there, to be "haunted."

The house is occupied by Mr. and Mrs. Wright (who have for some years past retired from business), their two daughters, and a female domestic. The noises which have been heard and which are continued at intervals throughout the day and night, resemble those which would be caused by a person rapidly striking his knuckles against the panel of a door for two or three seconds. In order to attempt to unravel the mystery, every magistrate of the county, clergymen and the most influential residents of the neighbourhood have visited the house, the whole of whom have been present during the time the extraordinary noises have been repeated, and strange they have evidently proceeded from a door leading from the kitchen, close to which the patties have stationed themselves, they have been unable to throw the least light upon the affair.

The sound clearly proceeds from the door I have described, and can only be in any way imitated upon that door only, by striking the knuckles hard and rapidly upon the centre of the panel. Mr. Riley and Lord Clement Hill stationed themselves in the hall within three yards of this door, and, as soon as the knocking commenced, rushed to the spot within a second afterwards, but not a soul was near it, and the whole of the family were in a different part of the house.

The knocking is so loud that it is heard by the inmates of houses four or five hundred yards off. Such is the alarm these strange and, at present, unaccountable noises have caused throughout the neighbourhood, that a lady named Roberts, who resides some distance from Mr. Wright, and whose house is divided from his by two public roads, has given notice to her landlord that she will quit today', and Mr. Wright's staff who are represented to be in that state of mind, are making preparations to leave the house immediately.

The whole of the machinery of the water closet has been removed, the flooring taken up, and excavated, under the impression that the noise might have proceeded from foul air in the pipes or drains, or from some other cause connected with this part of the interior of the house, but the noise still continues as before, at intervals, and today and yesterday it was even more violent and loud than ever. In order to ascertain how hard the door of the closet was struck, a small piece of wood was laid upon the projecting portion of the panel and after the knocking had ceased this had fallen on the floor, and so on Sunday last, still more clearly to ascertain the strength, Wright's son, who had arrived that morning, fastened up the door by means of a piece of wire, and after the noise had ceased, the wire, upon examination, was found broken, and the door forced inwards.

At that time the door was broken off its hinges, and placed at the back of the closet, but the knocking was precisely the same as before. The landlady of the house (Mrs. Stokes), has arrived from town, and has since caused every event to be instituted, but without the least hopes at present of unravelling the extraordinary mystery.

It should be observed that at three or four times when the knocking took place there were five persons, and sometimes more sent from Windsor and elsewhere, who were determined, if possible, to detect the cause, and who were totally unconnected with the family residing in the house, but they were still left in ignorance of its origin and with not the means of accounting for it.

On Saturday, a gentleman volunteered to sit up with Mr. Wright the whole of that night. This offer, at the suggestion of the magistrates, was accepted. The rest of family retired to rest at the usual hour, and up to six o'clock the next morning no noises were heard, but in the course of Sunday they were more violent than ever.

Many ignorant persons, of course, ascribe the noises to some supernatural agency, and a tale is now current that some person left that neighbourhood some time back in a "very mysterious manner," and that "no doubt a murder was committed near the spot." However this may be, gentlemen of high standing in the county (magistrates clergymen, and others) have visited the house during the past week, and certainly, to say the least, they are all exceedingly puzzled at the extraordinary noises they ha.ve heard within three or four yards of the spot where they had positioned themselves. This singular affair continues to excite the most intense interest, and to be wrapped in the greatest mystery.

*Standard.*

# 1843 – CAPTURE OF A GHOST.

It is said that ghosts are not unfrequently inspired with a considerable share of puissant valour. A singular act of bravery on the part of a disembodied spirit has just come under our observation, and at the season of Christmas, as stories of ghosts and goblins are the order of the day, it may not prove altogether unacceptable. At any rate, it may dispel the idea with which wiseacres occasionally solace themselves, that ghosts are altogether harmless.

A widow lady, who resides in the parish of St. Martin, has of late been visited by a ghost of rather a mischievous character. Inhabiting a lonely dwelling, with no protection save that afforded by a servant girl little more than just entered into her teens, the lady, with her two children, during the last four weeks have had their nocturnal slumbers frequently disturbed by the escapades of an evil spirit. Precisely as the clock had struck what the Scotch poet has styled " The wee short hour ayont the twal," and which, from its contrast with the previous twelve distinct sounds upon the hammer, is said to inspire, even in the strongest minds, a feeling of mysterious apprehension, a loud knocking at the door was heard. Nor was the feeling of awe inspired on the occasion unstrengthened by any extraneous circumstance; for on the third evening of the occurrence of the mysterious knockings, the disturbed lady, having summoned up sufficient courage to look out from the window, beheld a figure, apparently in white, making its escape from the gateway. The occurrence made a rather powerful impression on the lady's mind, for it was the first time she had ever seen a denizen of the world of spirits.

For ten successive nights the same sounds were repeated, every night the strength of the knocking gradually increasing! The ghost evidently thought that the depth of the slumbers of the inmates prevented them from hearing its efforts at obtaining an audience, for no notice whatever was taken of its mysterious proceedings. It was necessary, therefore, to alter his line of tactics, and the line which the ghost now adopted was of a somewhat novel nature. Instead of now knocking at the door every night, it at length began to throw stones at the windows, and on one evening demolished no less than three panes of glass in the windows of the drawing room. This, however, was not to be endured much longer, and, even at the risk of coming in contact with an inhabitant of the lower world, it was at length determined to give battle to the spirit.

The lady having communicated the circumstance to a gentleman who resides with his family about a quarter of a mile distant, a watch on Thursday evening last was set upon the premises. The gentleman referred to, armed with a good stout cudgel, took his station at the corner of the building, about ten paces from the spot from which the ghost was wont to hurl its missiles, while at the opposite corner stood his man-servant, armed in a somewhat similar fashion to his master. Precisely at the usual hour the figure clothed in white was seen to enter at the gateway, and having slowly made its way to within a few feet of the house, deliberately lifted a handful of pebbles and threw them at the window. This feat performed, the ghost was about to depart, but the gentleman and his fellow-watchman, not having their spirits completely prostrated, sallied forth and intercepted its progress. The yell of horror which the spirit now uttered was awful in the extreme, and throwing itself at the feet of the gentleman, it besought in piteous tones his pardon. The white sheet in a moment was thrown from the back of the now embodied spirit, and a bona fide human woman actually stood before them.

A confession soon followed, and it was discovered that the ghost had determined to frighten the poor lady to death, in consequence of having been recently discharged from her service for theft.

*Morning Post.*

# 1843 – GHOSTS BE HANGED!

No such things in nature; all laid long ago, before the wood pavement. What should they come for? The colliers may rise for higher wages, and the chartists may rise for reform, and Joseph Sturge may rise for his health, and bread may rise, and the rising generation may rise; but that the dead should rise only to make one's hair rise, is more than can credit. Suppose yourself a ghost. Well, if you come out of your grave to serve a friend, how are you to help him? And if it's an enemy, what's the use of appearing to him, if you can't pitch into him."

*Hull Packet.*

---

# 1845 – AN ABSURD RUMOUR.

An absurd rumour having got abroad that for the last few nights a ghost appeared in white, and among other ghostly qualifications, the power not only of ubiquity, but of invisibility at will, was to be seen wandering about Chapel field. A number of the curious in such matters assembled on Tuesday and Wednesday evenings, in the expectation of seeing it. Neither were they disappointed (if their own statements can be believed), for between eleven and twelve o'clock an apparition was observed coolly to walk through a wall at the east side of the field, cross the road, hop over the wooden palisades, and glide along the grass, under the old elm trees that waved mysteriously at the time, and pass into one of the ancient towers, which was, as usual, wrapped in impenetrable gloom. A whole army of little boys, and a pretty fair sprinkling of children of a larger growth, are said to have witnessed this interesting exploit.

After the apparition had thus unaccountably disappeared, the little boys grasped their sticks, exchanged incoherent expressions of wonder and alarm, and appeared indignant that the ghost had not boldly advanced among them and given battle. A council of war was then held, and it was determined to ascend, *en masse*, the grassy eminence which the old tower is situate, and either take the building by storm or make the ghost capitulate on honourable terms. With this intention the whole body—now about four hundred with a gallant intrepidity alike creditable to themselves and worthy the heroic cause in which they were embarked, moved in formidable precision along the field, across the gravel walk, and actually up the ascent, and finally stood, with palpitating hearts, under the old tower itself. Alas, however, for the lovers of the marvellous – no ghost, not even the wave of a white garment, or even the smell of brimstone, could be traced. It is true a few vagrant and unhappy rats scampered away, and in their hurried exit almost frightened to death the front rank of the detachment; but beyond that fact nothing could be seen or heard. After lingering about an astonishing length of time to no purpose, these daring spirits retired, much crest-fallen at the unsuccessful termination of the evening's adventures.

*Norwich Mercury.*

---

# 1845 – CLAIMED TO BE A WITCH.

A singular and interesting trial took place at Tain on Monday last, showing that superstition is not yet wholly dispelled. William Grant, a fisherman at Portmahomack, conceiving that the wife of Walter Munro, a fisherman there, possessed the power of witchcraft, and that her supernatural influence was directed against himself, went into her husband's house on the 3rd August last, and with his pocket knife deliberately inflicted a gash on her forehead. The prisoner admitted the assault, but that considered himself justified on account of the provocation he had received.

The prosecutor refused to accept such a plea and the case went to trial, when the jury found Grant guilty, and he was sentenced to three months' imprisonment in Dingwall jail. The declaration made before the Sheriff by the prisoner was a very curious and original statement. He attributed the loss of his new nets and the want of success in the herring fishing, to the woman's "dark dealings in sorcery," and the rest of the crew were not willing to go out with him while he was under the curse of the witch!

In consequence of this, he took the opportunity, on the night in question, to cut her "above the breath," believing that with the first drop of blood brought out by such a process the devil would come out along with it, and that the woman would be deprived of the power of harming him! It would seem that a superstitious notion of this sort is prevalent among the Highland people; but the "cut" is generally made by a pin or needle. In the absence of these, the prisoner used his knife, by which there was an effusion of blood for several hours, until the doctor arrived from Tain, and also confinement to bed for five weeks.

The Sheriff addressed the prisoner at considerable length, in which he dwelt on the recklessness of his conduct in assaulting an old woman who was unable to defend herself; and also exposing the groundless superstition which prompted him to such an act of cruelty. It is to be hoped that the punishment of Grant will have a salutary effect on the fishermen and villagers, of whom, it is said, a great proportion entertain the same superstitious belief in witchcraft.

*Glasgow Citizen.*

---

# 1845 – HIGHLAND SUPERSTITIONS.

We find much more superstition among the Highlanders than among any other nation. But this peculiarity can be well accounted for. The peculiar aspect of their country, in which Nature appears in her wildest and most romantic features.—presenting, at a glance, sharp and rugged mountains, with dreary wastes, wide stretched lakes, and rapid torrents, over which the thunders and lightning, and rains and tempests, exhaust their terrific rage,—wrought upon the creative powers of the imagination; and, from these appearances, the Highlanders were naturally led to ascribe every disaster to the influence of superior powers, in whose character malignity towards the human race was the only feature.

Another great characteristic was their seclusion from other nations; but now their communication with the rest of the island is open, and the introduction of trade and manufactures has destroyed that leisure which was formerly dedicated to hearing and repeating the superstitions of ancient times. Many have now learned to leave their mountains, and seek their fortune in a milder climate; and though a certain *amor patriae* may sometimes bring them back, they have, during their absence, imbibed enough of foreign manners to despise the customs of their ancestors. Bards have been long disused, and the spirit of genealogy has completely subsided. Men are now less devoted to their chiefs; and consanguinity is, among them, little regarded. When property is established, the human mind confines its views to the pleasure it produces. It does not go back to antiquity, or look forward to succeeding ages. The cares of life increase, and the actions of other times no longer amuse, Hence it is, that the taste for their ancient poetry and superstitions, is at a low ebb among the Highlanders. They have not, however, thrown off all the good qualities of their brave ancestors. Hospitality still subsists, as well as a laudable civility to strangers. Friendship is inviolable, and revenge less blindly followed than formerly.

We are well aware that the superstitions which are still so prevalent in the Highlands of Scotland, were handed down by tradition, which, if could be depended upon, is only found among a people from all times free of intermixture with foreigners. We are to look for these among the mountains and inaccessible parts of a country,—places, on account of their barrenness, uninviting to an enemy, or whose natural strength enabled the natives to repel invasions. Such are the inhabitants of the mountainous parts of Scotland. We, therefore, find that they differ greatly from those who possess the more fertile parts of the country. Their language is pure and original, and their manners are those of an ancient and unmixed race of men. Conscious of their own antiquity and valour, they long despised others. As they lived in a country only fit for pasture, they were free of that toil and business which engrossed the attention of a commercial community. Their sole amusement was in hearing or repeating their songs and traditions, and these always referred to the antiquity of their nation and the exploits of their forefathers.

It is no wonder, therefore, that there are more remains of antiquity to be found among them than among any other people in Europe. But the character of the Highlanders, of late, has undergone a material change and now, instead of roving through unfrequented wilds, in search of subsistence by means of hunting, they apply themselves to agriculture. We cannot but admire the sprightliness and sublimity, in these ages of superstition, of their imagination; but as the world advances, the understanding gains ground upon the imagination,—the understanding is more exercised, the imagination less.

The early history of the Highlanders presents us with a bold and hardy race of men, filled with a strong attachment to the native glens. Having little intercourse with the rest of the world, they acquired a peculiar character, and retained or adopted habits and manners differing greatly from those of their Lowland neighbours. Firmness and decision, fertility in resources, ardour in friendship, and a generous enthusiasm, were the results of such a situation, such modes of life, and such habits of thought. Thus, their exercises, their amusements, their motives of action, their prejudices, and their superstitions, became permanent and peculiar.

Among them the most dangerous and most malignant creature was the kelpie or water horse, which was said to allure men to his subaqueous haunts, and there devour them. Sometimes he would swell the lake or river, in which he had his abode, beyond its usual limits, and overwhelm travellers in the flood. The shepherd, as he sat upon the brow of a rock, on a summer evening, often fancied he saw this animal dashing along the surface of the lake or browsing on its banks.

The wrisks, which were supposed to be of a condition somewhat intermediate between that of men and spirits, were like the brownies of England, and could be gained over by kind treatment, to perform the work of the farm. It was believed that many families had a wrisk for this purpose. No weaver was considered to want one. The wrisks were supposed to live dispersed over the Highlands, each having his own recess; but they were said to hold stated meetings on certain days, in some large cave. Those of Caithness met in a large grotto, in a hill, in the parish of Latheron, called Conerick. On the days of assembly no one would dare go out of doors. They were said to come from every part of the country, each company headed by its piper.

The Daoine Shith, men of peace or Daoine Matha, good men, as they are sometimes called, were supposed to live under grassy eminences and cairns, where, during the night, they celebrated their festivities to the light of a large fire, which was always kept burning, although no fuel was added, and danced to the softest music imaginable. The Daoine Shith, who are the fairies of the Highlands, were supposed to be clothed in green, and that they took offence when any of the mortal race presumed to wear their favourite dress. Tradition reports that they have often allured some of the human race into their subterraneous retreats, consisting of the most splendid apartments, and that they have been regaled at the most sumptuous banquets, and with the most delicious wines. Their females far exceed the daughters of men in beauty.

A woman, says a Highland tradition, was conveyed in the days of yore, into the secret recesses of the men of peace. There she was recognised by one who had formerly been an ordinary mortal, but who had, by some means, become associated with the Shiths. This acquaintance, still retaining some portion of human benevolence, warned her of her danger, and advised her, if she valued her liberty, to abstain from eating or drinking with them for a certain space of time. She complied with the counsel of her friend and when the period assigned had arrived, she found herself again upon the earth, restored to the society of mortals.

Another tradition says, a young man, roaming one day through the forest, observed a number of persons, all dressed in green, issuing from one of those round eminences, which are generally called fairy hills. Each of them, in succession, called upon a person by name, to fetch his horse. A steed immediately appeared; they all mounted and sallied forth into the regions of the air. The young man ventured to pronounce the same name. A caparisoned steed was immediately at hand; he mounted, and soon joined the fairy choir. He remained with them for a year, going about with them to fairs and weddings, and feasting, though unseen by mortal eyes, on the victuals that were exhibited on those occasions. They had, on one day, gone to a wedding, where the cheer was abundant. During the feast, the bridegroom sneezed. The young man, according to the usual custom, said, "God bless you." The fairies were offended at the pronunciation of the sacred name, and assured him, if he dared to repeat it, they would punish him. The bridegroom sneezed a second time, and he repeated his blessing. The fairies were enraged, and tumbled him from a precipice; but he found himself unhurt, and was restored to the society of mortals.

The Shiths, or men of peace, are supposed to have a design against new born children, and women in child-bed, whom, it is still believed, they sometimes carry off into their recesses. To prevent this abduction, women, when in this state, were closely watched, and were not left alone, even for a single moment, till the child was baptized, when the Shiths are supposed to have no more power over them. The Shith, it is still believed, have a great propensity for attending funerals, weddings, and public entertainments, and, it is believed, that, though invisible to mortal eyes, they are busily engaged in carrying away the substantial articles and provisions, in place of which they substitute shadowy forms; and so strong was the belief in this mythology, even till a recent period, that some persons are old enough to remember, that some individuals would not eat anything presented on the occasions alluded to, because they believed it to be unsubstantial and hurtful.

As the Shiths, who are said to be of both sexes, are always supposed to present on all occasions, though invisible, the Highlanders, whenever they allude to them, do so in terms of respect. This popular superstition, relating to the Daoine Shith, is supposed, with good reason, to have taken its rise in the times of the Druids, or rather to have been invented by them, after the overthrow of their hierarchy, for the purpose of preserving the existence of their order, after they had retreated for safety to caves, and the deep recesses of the forest. This idea receives some corroboration from the Gaelic term Druid'eachd, which the Highlanders apply to the deceptive power, by which the men of peace are thought to impose upon the senses of mankind, founded on the opinion entertained of old, concerning the magical powers of the Druids, who found it easy to excite the belief of their supernatural powers, in the minds of the vulgar.

A prevailing superstition still exists, that women, by some secret charm or influence, could withdraw and appropriate to their own use, the increase of their neighbour's cow's milk, and it is believed that the milk so charmed, does not produce the ordinary quantity of butter. To bring back the fruit, it is usual to take a little of the rennet from all the suspected persons, and to mingle it with some milk, which, then, is restored to its proper state. Trouts are supposed to take away the increase of milk, when the dishes, in which the milk is kept, have been washed in a stream or rivulet, in which trouts are, and the only remedy in such case, is to take a live trout, and pour some milk into its mouth.

To remove any contagious disease from cattle, they used to extinguish the fires in neighbouring townships, after which they forced fire with a wheel, or by rubbing one piece of dry wood upon another, with which they burned juniper in the stalls of the cattle, that the smoke might purify the air about them. When this was performed, the fires in the houses were rekindled from the forced fires. This practice was had recourse to, about twenty eight years ago, in Dorery, Caithness, with no success, to the great surprise of the people.

The Highlanders had other superstitions which it would be too tedious to mention, such as Dessil, Deassoil, Taish, &c.

*John O'Groat Journal.*

# 1846 – SUPERSTITION IN SHETLAND.

The extent to which superstition influences the minds of the Shetlanders is scarcely conceivable. At the very time I write (August 3rd) an example of this has been making what you publishers call, I think, the "round of the press." No fewer than four hundred fishermen from the west coast of Caithness, who had travelled towards the Moray Firth IN quest of employment at their annual labour of herring fishing, in order to enable them to earn as much money as will support them throughout the winter, have been deterred from engaging in their wonted occupation, and nearly frightened out of their wits, by the prediction of an old woman, foretelling that an awful storm would arise and destroy both men and boats. This silly rumour was held by those ignorant Highlanders to be sufficient warning not to jeopardise their lives; and accordingly many of them prepared to retrace their steps to the cheerless boothies they had just left. The greater part of them, it is said, returned home, whilst the more stout hearted, believing themselves safe from the impending danger in Banff and Morayshire, wandered about the towns and villages, endeavouring to find employment by land. The old wife who has caused all this mischief was committed to prison, with a view to have her punished according to her deserts; but, in the meantime, it is estimated that on the beach at Wick nearly fifty boats have been thrown idle in consequence, involving a loss of some £5,000, attributable solely to the desertion of these foolish men, who have gone back to their families to rusticate in a state of half starvation, the victims of their own blind delusions.

*Illustrated London News.*

# 1846 – THE NOCTURNAL VISITOR.

A ghost! We have this week a ghost story to relate. Yes, a ghost story—a real ghost story, and a ghost story without, yet, any clue to its elucidation.

Where do you think has this ghost made his appearance? Not of course in a modern house—no ghost of good taste would think of coming to any tenement that was not time-honoured—that had not a charter at least of 200 years; and what edifice more fit for his supernatural reception than the ancient residence of the Calendars— the Vicarage House of All Saints, Bristol, adjoining and almost forming a part of that church?

Of this house, the abode of the ancient fraternity, and from which there was one time a window looking into the church, there is an account in the interesting and very agreeable work lately published by the respected Vicar of the parish —the History of the Calendars; there is also some allusion to it in Barrett's Bristol, where it is described as situate "at the south-western part of the church, and in fact projecting into the sacred building. After the dissolution of the Calendars it was converted into a Vicarage House, and it is still called that name, though the incumbents have for many years ceased to reside there. The present occupants are Mr. and Mrs. Jones, the sexton and sextoness of the church, and one or two lodgers, and it is to the former and their servant maid that the strange visitor has made his appearance, causing such terror by his nightly calls, that all three have determined on quitting the premises, if indeed they have not already carried their resolution into effect. What makes the whole affair the more unaccountable and extraordinary is the official quality of the persons affected by the fright. Had it been a commonplace family, unconversant with grave matters, a very simple incident, coupled with the ancient and monastic character of the building, might be sufficient to create alarm and terror; but here are people—sexton and sextoness—whose vocation lies in solemn churches, and amongst the silent tombs, who, in the way of business, must every day have something do with skulls and grey mouldering bones, and who might be almost said to be on such familiar terms with at least the outward emblems of the invisible world, as to be able to shake hands with a ghost without any great perturbation— terrified out of their house by a nightly visitor, scared to such an extent as to determine to take down their tester and four-post bedsteads, "being certain," to use Mrs. Jones's own words to their landlord, "that they shall die if they sleep another night in the house."

Mr. and Mrs. Jones's description of the disturbance as given by the landlord, on whom they called in great consternation, is as distinct as any ghost story could be. The nocturnal visitor is heard walking about the house when the inhabitants are in bed; and Mr. Jones, who is a man of by no means nervous constitution, declares he has several times seen a light flickering on one of the walls. Mrs. Jones is equally certain that she has heard a man with creaking shoes walking in the bedroom above her own, when no man was on the premises (or, at least, might to be), and "was nearly killed with the fright." To the servant maid, however, was vouchsafed the unenvied honour of seeing this restless night visitor: she declares she has repeatedly had her bedroom door unbolted at night, between the hours of twelve and two clock—the period when such beings usually make their promenades-by something in human semblance; she cannot particularise his dress, but describes it as something antique, and of a fashion "lang syne gane,"and to some extent corresponding to that of the ancient Calendars, the former inhabitants of the house. She further says, he is a "whiskered gentleman" (we give her own words), which whiskered gentleman has gone the length of shaking her bed, and, she believes, would have shaken herself also, but that she invariably puts her head under the clothes when she sees him approach.

Mrs. Jones declares, she believes the appearance of the whiskered gentleman, and she had made up her mind, the night before she called on her landlord, to leap out of the window (and it is not a trifle that'll make people leap out of a window), as soon as he entered the room. The effect of the "flickering light" on Mr. Jones was quite terrific, causing excessive trembling, and "the complete doubling up of his whole body into a round ball like."

*Bristol Times.*

———◦◦◦———

# 1848 – MRS. PARTINGTON ON GHOSTS.

"Do you believe in ghosts, Mrs Partington?" was asked of the old lady somewhat timidly. "To be sure I do (replied she), as much as I believe that bright fulminary will rise the yeast tomorrow morning, if we live and nothing happens. Two apprehensions have sartinly appeared in our own family. Why, I saw dear Paul, a fortnight before he died, with my own eyes, just as plain as I see you now and though it turned out afterwards to be a rosebush with a nightcap on it, I shall always think to the day of my desolation that it was a forerunner sent to me. T'other one came in the night when we were asleep, and carried away three candles and a pint of spirits that we kept in the house for an embarkation.

Believe in ghosts, indeed! I guess I do; and he must be a dreadful styptic as doesn't."

*Derbyshire Courier.*

———◦◦◦———

# 1849 – THE ORTON GHOST.

In order to lay before our readers the fullest particulars of the strange and mysterious doings of the invisible ghost at Cowper House, Orton, we append the following accounts, gleaned from the two last numbers of the *Kendal Mercury*. We stated in the *Chronicle* of the 12th inst., that the ghost had been "laid' by a Penrith policeman; but, from subsequent details in various newspapers, it appears that the statement was premature. The place had been visited by a policeman, and others, from Penrith, by whom it was afterwards stated, on the word of the servant girl (about 13 years of age), to be nothing more than a hoax, got up by the mistress of the house and herself, for the avowed purpose of inducing Mr. Gibson, the husband, to leave the premises. This statement, as will be seen below, has since been contradicted by the Gibsons and the girl herself; and we leave the matter to our readers to decide for themselves in whose declaration they will place the most reliance. The following particulars are from the *Kendal Mercury* of the 12th instant:-

The excitement connected with the wonderful disturbances occurring at Cowper's House, during the past three or four weeks, remains unabated, and our statement, last week, that the whole had been discovered to be a gross imposition, practiced by the mistress and her servant girl for some unassigned reason, was premature. No sooner had our paper been issued from the press on Saturday, than messengers came to us from Orton, stating that the ghost had again made its appearance, and that the conduct of the constables had been most shameful. Our natural love of the marvellous, and our desire to ascertain for ourselves what degree of truth there was in the wonderful stories we had heard, induced us to make a personal visitation of the spot on Monday, and we herewith detail the result of our enquiry for the enlightenment of our readers.

Cowper's House is a miserable bleak farm house, situated at Gaitagill, on the top of a hill chiefly composed of moor and swamp, about three miles from Orton, and about a mile from Tebay Railway Station. We arrived there about seven o'clock on Monday morning, and found Mr. Gibson and his family at home, with whom our party entered into conversation respecting the marvellous occurrences that had created so much sensation far and near. They were very communicative, and gave the readiest and most straightforward answers to every question that was put to them. The conversation, after a while, naturally turned upon the conduct of the constables, and they expressed the utmost indignation at their outrageous demeanour.

Our party, we may promise, consisted of five individuals, two of them residents at Orton, men of most unimpeachable character in every point of view, one Kendalian, who had been staying several days in Orton, engaged in superintending the fitting up of some new houses in the village, ourselves, and a companion who had come with us from Kendal. In a few minutes the servant girl made her appearance, with one of the children in her arms; and on being interrogated, gave precisely the same account of the behaviour of the constables, as we heard from the master and mistress, and as she had given to other parties. One of the Orton gentlemen here produced a written document, drawn up from statements made on the previous Saturday by the respective parties, and after reading it carefully over, asked them if they were willing to put their names to it. They consented at once, and the others present added their names as attesting witnesses. The document is subjoined.

The visit of the Penrith constables seems to have quieted the ghost for a while, but it soon plucked up courage again, and on Saturday afternoon, the flyleaf of a table was raised, the sliding foot drawn out, and a dish from a plate rack hard by placed upon it. The plate was removed to its place by the same invisible agency, and the table restored to its original condition. All this occurred when not a soul was in the room.

On Sunday evening, also, sundry mysterious knocks were heard, though they could not have been of a very alarming nature, as the wife, on being asked if the ghost had exhibited since Saturday, said it had not, and it was only when her husband reminded her, that she spoke of these sounds. This appears to have been the last performance. The inmates profess that they have no fear. We took careful stock of the premises, and could easily have detected any collusion on the part of the inmates.

Hundreds of persons have visited the spot, not only from the immediate neighbourhood, but from distant places, some even from Glasgow and Edinburgh. In the immediate neighbourhood, implicit belief prevails in the reality of the supernatural appearances. High and humble, rich and poor, gentle and low born, all are in the same mind, and seem almost to resent the slightest expression of scepticism.

April 17th, the first day of the strange appearances, was the fifth anniversary of the death, by drowning, of Gibson's uncle, a man of some wealth, and his wraith has been often seen, not only by neighbours, but by the family themselves. It was suggested by one of our party, that the whole was an ingenious scheme to levy contributions; but so far as we can learn, the visitors do not generally think themselves bound to give money, as they cause no trouble or cost to the inmates, who are not, so far as we can learn, either needy or greedy people. Another theory is, they want to get a better farmhouse; but the fact that the ghost "skifted" with them to Byebeck refutes that supposition, so that all is as dark as before.

Mr. Lipsett, the superintendent of the Kendal police, also visited the spot, though not in his official capacity, on Wednesday last. His ghostship, would not exhibit his tricks in his presence. He asked the inmates if they would allow him to stay two or three days there, as he would gladly remain for the purpose of gratifying his curiosity; but they declined on the plea of want of accommodation, though he declared himself willing to be satisfied with an armchair, and referred him to the Cross Keys, promising to summon him at the first opportunity. Such an arrangement was obviously unsatisfactory, and he was obliged to leave as wise as ourselves.

Mrs. Gibson's Statement: – "On Thursday, four men came into the house as near to two o'clock as I can remember, when Mr. Torbeck, of Kirkby Stephen, was the first to enter. They conversed together, and appeared to be acquainted. About four o'clock my husband returned from Orton fair, and shortly afterwards Mr. Scott and the others came in. Mr. Scott took a chair, and drew a book from his pocket, observing that he had come, like many more, through curiosity, to ascertain the truth of what he had heard, having found such excitement prevailing both in Westmorland and Cumberland, and that he wanted to get to the bottom of the matter, and to unravel the mystery. He then said to my husband, "You must tell us what you think upon the subject?" Who replied, "What can I think, or any person else, who has witnessed any of these unaccountable movements? It is an entire mystery to me." He threw up his head, saying scornfully, "A mystery indeed." He then said, "Would you be as kind as to tell us when and how it began?" My husband said he was not at home at the time, but I could tell them, whereupon I told them all I could possibly recollect answering every question they put to me. But Mr. Scott, being impatient, stopped me abruptly, "That'll do." He then asked my name and the girl's, and said, "Will you be so kind as to take the child from the servant girl, and allow her to go out with me for about five minutes?" He brought the child to me and took hold of the girl's arm, another man taking hold on the other side, when she, being frightened, screamed out, as any young girl might have done in such a case."

William Gibson states:- Upon hearing the girl's screams I immediately ran out and seized hold of her, to release her from their grasp. They both let go and I asked them what they meant by treating the girl in that rude manner, telling them it was very strange for them to come here and act in such a way, and if they wanted her to go with them, they ought to have treated her more kindly, and not attempted to take her by force. I also told the girl not to be alarmed, and wished her to tell the truth, and nothing but the truth. They then both took hold as before, and she walked between them round the house to the barn door. When they came in again, Scott said to me, "We have found out the mystery now, your wife and girl have done it." I said, "I'll not believe you. He replied, "The girl has confessed." I then said to the girl, "Ann, did you say that you did it?" She replied, "They made me say it." Upon this, Thomas Bousfield, a friend to who was present, said, "They have frightened her to it." As soon as he had said this, Mr. Scott told him to hold his peace, as he had nothing to do with it. Then turning to me he said, "We have now got to the bottom of the matter. Your wife, and the girl as her instrument, have occasioned all the disturbances. The girl has confessed, and your wife will confess also before we leave the house." When we said this, Mrs. G., being afraid they would seize her, went out, and went to Mr. Bousfield's (the nearest house). Mr. Scott and I were disputing about the girl's statement and I told him that I would neither believe him nor any of his company, as I could believe my wife and the girl before any of them. I also said that I could not resist the evidence of my senses. What I myself had seen and heard I could believe.

I then pointed to the links attached to the crane over the fireplace which I had seen wrenched off and thrown upon the floor, when I took them up and replaced them, tying them with a string, after which they were frequently shaken, but never came off so long as the string remained. Next, I pointed to the pan upon the fire, saying I had seen the lid, made of cast iron, taken off the pan and thrown across the floor. I also pointed to the heavy armchair in the corner (no person being near it) and thrown upon its back, where it remained until I replaced it in its usual position. Mr. Scott remarked that a person might do that without being very near it. Upon which I said, "Stand there, where you are now and bring that chair out of the corner, as I have described, and then I will believe you." He held his head down, and gave me no answer. I then said, "You are a strange set of men to come here and act as you have done, attempting to cause disturbances in the family, and to make me and my wife disagree on account of the scandalous proceedings. He said it was a great pity that a girl like that should be in such a family and be ruined. I think he said the name of her father, and noted it down, saying he, would send him a letter and inform of this, that he might take her away immediately. He also said, "I have come here this day to deliver her from this destruction," and observed that we should have no more of these disturbances.

Ann Lindsay, (the servant-girl,) says, – "Mr. Scott said to me, 'Was it not you and your mistress who caused all the disturbances in the house?' I said, 'No, it was not.' He said, 'Yes, but it was you; if you won't say that you did it, I will immediately take you to gaol.' I said, 'No, I could not say so.' He then pulled out an instrument, which he told me was a knife having two blades, and if I did not say that I and Mrs. Gibson had caused the disturbances, he would, in an instant, cut my throat.' He said might he not go in, and tell the master that we had done it all; that Mrs. Gibson had done three parts of it, and I the rest, for 5s. reward?' I replied, 'you may go and tell him, if you think, but we did not do it.' I then ran away into the house, and one of them hit me with a stick before I got in, as they followed close after me.

Signed "William Gibson, Agnes Gibson, Ann Lindsay."

*(From the Kendal Mercury of May 19.)*

The excitement caused by the "Orton ghost" continues unabated, and though, as we stated on Saturday, its' exhibitions had since the visit paid by our reporter, been on a very limited scale, it seems to have commenced its operations during the past week, with increased vigour. On Monday morning last our informant relates, Mr. Mattison, of Sockbridge Hall, near Penrith, a highly respectable farmer under the Earl of Lonsdale, visited Cowper's House in company with his brother-in-law, Mr. Thomas Atkinson of Orton. They found the family at home, and there were also in the house Mr. Robert Farrer and Mr. J. Robertson, joiners, of Orton, who had been there overnight. Nothing remarkable had occurred previous to their getting up; but shortly after breakfast, as Farrer was passing the cow house, he saw the bull standing outside of the building, greatly to the dismay of Mr. Gibson, who, coming up shortly after, along with Robertson, declared that the bull had been tied up in the byre, and no human being could have entered and unbound it. Mr. Mattinson, his companion and Robertson, on again entering the house, saw a water dish moved from behind them which dropped near the feet of the former. The small oak table in the keeping room was moved a few inches, and an umbrella was thrown down from the partition close to which it had been placed. The drawer in the oak dining table next moved out of its place and dropped on the floor without scattering any of the articles which it contained. Mr. Mattinson also observed the little oak table move, with the water dish and milk bowl upon it, though neither of them was thrown down or broken. In the course of the morning, also, the turf flew out of the fire in different directions on the floor.

On Tuesday, Mr. John Garnett Holmes, of Old Hall, Orton, paid a visit to the spot. He appears to have been the most persevering of all the visitors, for he stayed on the premises from nine in the morning till seven at night. His patience, though well-nigh exhausted, was at length fully rewarded. Just as he was on the point of returning home, the fender bounded upwards, striking the child in Mrs. Gibson's arms, and creating no little alarm. A large stone was also broken in two by coming against the partition, and three chairs were moved from their position and thrown upon their backs. These statements have been handed to us, with the signatures of the parties concerned. Everything connected with this extraordinary affair remains as much a mystery as ever; and though speculation is afloat, and an infinite variety of solutions has been suggested, not one of the visitors seems to have made any approach to the detection of the imposture, for such it undoubtedly is.

The statement which we published last week from Mr. and Mrs. Gibson, and the servant girl, has given rise, as we expected it would, to counter statements. The two following documents which we have received, we here subjoin, as in impartiality we are bound to do:-

To the Editor of the *Kendal Mercury*.
Sir,

We beg leave to state that we have seen, with surprise and indignation, an article in the *Kendal Mercury* of the 12th inst., headed "Orton Ghost," and signed "William Gibson, Agnes Gibson, and Ann Lindsay," which we declare, in substance to be false. And in that part of the article which reflects on the conduct of Mr. Scott, the high constable of Penrith, towards the girl, Ann Lindsay, every word of which is a gross and scandalous falsehood, not one word of which is true. Mr. Scott used no threats to the girl in question, his bearing and conduct towards her were the very reverse, – it was kind and conciliatory. No knife or weapon of any kind whatever was exhibited to her; neither did he make any promise to her of reward money, or anything else, whereby to draw forth the statement which she made. He particularly cautioned her to tell the truth. The only observations he made to her were the following:- "He asked her age and if she knew where she would go to if she told a lie" which she answered to his satisfaction. He then said to her, "Do you know what will become of you if you speak the truth?" which question she properly answered. Mr. Scott then said, "Very well, now tell us the truth, and nothing but the truth, about the tricks which have been played off in the house," when she said, "I rocked the cradle, thew down the pail, struck at the partition and numerous other tricks." Question, "When persons were in the house?" She answered, "Yes, when persons were in the house." Mr. Scott then asked her if any person beside herself had to do with it, when she answered, without hesitation, "Her mistress had." She was asked, "Had anybody else besides," when she answered, after being in deep thought for a moment, "I think – I think master had not." We all of us then went into the house; the girl walking quietly beside Mr. Scott.

In justice to Mr. Scott, we will thank you to insert the foregoing in your next publication,
And, we are your faithful servants,
Benjamin Slee, Keeper of the House of Correction, Penrith.
John Bird, Superintendent of the Rural Police (East Ward), Appleby, Westmorland.

To the Editor of the *Kendal Mercury*.
Sir,

We were not a little surprised at seeing an article in your last week's paper, reflecting on the conduct of the constables who visited Cowper' house. We will briefly say (as the subject is not interesting to any but the most ignorant), the statements made by the Gibson's is totally false, and the girl's, on the conduct of Mr. Scott, only shows what she is capable of doing. Her story, also, is a tissue of falsehood from beginning to end.
John Rayson, Assistant Overseer.
John Lancaster, grocer and tea dealer.

Sir,

On the 3rd inst., being at Orton fair, I was led, like many others, to call at Cowper's house, more through curiosity (yet with a view to detect) than any belief I had in supernatural beings. I got there between three and four, p.m. My party consisted of Mr. Bird, superintendent of the rural police, Appleby, and two other gentlemen from that neighbourhood, and one from Penrith. On arriving there, we found Mr. Slee, keeper of the House of Correction, Penrith, and three more gentlemen from that town. This party had been there for upwards of an hour before us. We now amalgamated and made one party. Gibson had been to Orton, and he arrived simultaneously with us. We may now state that Cowper's house, occupied by Gibson, is a miserable looking place, situate on the top of a high bleak hill, almost inaccessible to any but horsemen and foot. You approach the inside of the house by and through a zigzag passage. The inside of the house is miserable and gloomy-looking, and we all agreed that never was there a house better calculated to carry on tricks of legerdemain with success than the one In question, if skilfully performed. We were, indeed, all surprised that greater feats of deception had not been practised, which proved to demonstrate that the actors in the case in question are but new beginners in the art of magic.

We may be allowed to state here, that the accounts which have gone forth to the public are grossly exaggerated statements – in fact, not a twentieth part are true. The tricks which have really, and, in fact, been performed by this artful girl, with the child in her arms, and which Mrs. Gibson related to us, are most ridiculous, and are nothing more than what might be readily accomplished by an expert person. How, indeed, the five persons whose names first figured in the *Mercury*, which gave the account of the wonderful supernatural performances of the ghost, should have been gulled by the artifices of a girl of 13 is most extraordinary. No other five persons In the United Kingdom (excepting those who may be found located on the fell sides in the parish of Orton) could have been so shamefully deceived. As one of the party of the five is the parish doctor, it is supposed that he had used chloroform to his four partners, and that, while putting them under its agency, he himself had become affected, and that whilst the whole of them were in a state of stupor, but partly recovering, the ghost (seeing his men) went to work in good earnest, and performed all the tricks like magic, and with wonderful agility. This is the only reasonable way to account for these persons having been gulled by a girl of 13 years of age. Get enlightened, and let us hear no more of the "Worton Boggle."

On our proceeding to detail to Mr. Gibson, how grossly he had been deceived by the servant girl, and that she had made a voluntary confession, (not extorted from her, as stated in your paper of last week, by threats and the gift of money) that she and her mistress had done it all, he became greatly excited, and could not be pacified. Why he became so, the public shall be the judge. Had he been otherwise, and kept himself calm and quiet, all the mysterious tricks with which his wife has furnished to the public who have been there, including the tricks done when the five wise men before mentioned were in the house, should have been then and there performed, and performed not by hobgoblins nor by mysterious spirits from the vast deep, but by the assistance of the servant girl, or, if you like, by the servant girl alone, while nursing the child. In fact, the tricks which have been done are legerdemain tricks badly performed. Let visitors who may be led to Cowper's house through curiosity, keep a sharp lookout after the servant girl, the mistress, and the master, if you like; for, since he has been told the way to find out the boggle, and he will not, persons will now begin to suspect that he also has a hand in the deception. Some of the more enlightened inhabitants of the parish have paid a visit to Cowper's house, and have detected the girl. Since I have not their authority to publish their names, I send them to you privately.

Yours truly,
M. SCOTT.

### WORTON BOGGLE.

Wey, Gwordie, lad, has te nut been up to Worton,
T' see the queer tricks that's at Cowper House duin;
Fwolk say that the ghost of an auld witchcraft doctor
Turns aw wrong seyde up iv'ry day about nuin.
A carvin knife jamp at a parson when prayin';
He up an' meade off leyke the shot ov a gun:
His walkin' stick rush'd boldly out o' the cworner,

And, join'd by his hat, quickly efter him spun.
The cistern began to rwoar out leyke a Ranter,
Tha clock knock'd the girt rammin keale pot aboot,
The snap teables clink'd off a Westmoerlan' whornpipe,
An' t'brush gev the kettle a bang on the snout;
The warmin' pan ran rovin' mad t' the pump trough,
The pwoker hopp'd lishly about on the chairs,
T'auld wife's Sunday hat went leyke leetnin up't chimley,
An' t' coppy stull jam leyke a cat up the stairs.

The auld heir-loom kurn walk'd int' haw quite compos'dly,
And danc'd Cross the Buckle and Leatherdy Patch;
An' t' auld kitchen fender waltzed roun' like a madman,
Then lap wi' the shovel and broom through the thatch.
Twea bacon flicks fell wi' a clash on the floorin',
And roll'd roun' the house leyke twea biln' drunken men;
The auld cwoley dog crap snunder the ash grate,
An' t' salry tom cat why naebody's seen 't sen.

The caff beds com rolling down stairs in confusion,
An' t' auld carv'd yok wardrobes fell flat o' the fluir;
Young Jwohn's hairy trunk flew reet into the dairy,
And aw the milk vessels bang'd out at the duir.
The worn out cheese press was dung owra wi' a bowster,
The seape dish rush'd out o' the house in a crack,
A wood box threw knives leyke an Indian juggler,
An' t' dishes and plaetes danc'd leyke mad on the rack.

Big piles through the roofin' cam droppin leyke hailstone,
And brattles leyke thunder were frequently heard,
Till in drop'd frae Penrith sly Scott, Slee, and Rayson,
When t' auld "whorny" gentleman niver yence stirr'd.
The truth suin crap out – t'was but witchcraft pretension,
The sarvant lass split how the stwory was rais'd.
The mistress suin cut down the field leyke a reacer,
Far leykest of ought just a woman gone craz'd.

Now ye whe put faith in sic trash teales o' witchcraft,
Luik back to the reign of that king – what's his neame?
When deeth was the fate of aw see leyke balievers;
An' monie a breet chap t' the gallows was taen.
Ye bigots o' Worton, an' other bit hamlets,
Be asheamed o, your conduct – I think its full teyme-
For whea wad hae thowt t' hear tell a' see nonsense
In the year eighteen hundred, forty, and nine?

*Preston Chronicle.*

## 1850 – THE BLACK GHOST.

The neighbourhood of St. Owen's Gate is become famous for tales of ghosts which are said to wander about in that classic region, "making night hideous." Here haunted of late the quadrupedal ghost which well-nigh affrighted the supernumerary police constable out of his wits, and here, reports says, have been seen ghosts of all sizes, colours, and shapes.

The scene of our present story is "Turk's Alley." Among the denizens of this alley, lives John ___, no matter what for our tale, who deals in crockery ware and keeps donkeys. Sometime during the night of Monday last, John was awakened hearing his donkeys going down the yard. He immediately got out of bed, and like Saul went in search of his asses. He overtook them, and was taking them back to the stables whence they had strayed, when a black figure "grabbed" at him (as John elegantly expresses himself) with his arms or paws, whichever they may have been. John hurried back to bed with all haste, and, putting his head under the bed clothes, shook like an aspen leaf till the bed fairly rattled underneath him. His wife inquired the cause, and John told her the tale of the "black ghost" which had tried to "grab" him.

His better half reproached him for cowardice, and insinuated that the "black ghost" or the "gentleman in black," whichever it might be, was merely a phantom of his imagination conjured by imbibing too much of the juice of "Sir John." John persisted that it was a real ghost he had seen, and, consequently, his better half sallied out to ascertain if there were indeed a ghost. She speedily returned and reported that she too had seen "something black," and was soon in a swoon.

A female neighbour was called in to render her assistance, and she, likewise, heard a "knocking on the table." More of the neighbours were alarmed and went in search of the "black ghost," but to their eyes he remained invisible, and the general opinion is that the "black ghost" and the knocking on the table were mere phantoms of imagination.

*Hereford Times.*

## 1851 – AN UNWELCOME VISITOR.

Much gossip has been occasioned at Weston-Super-Mare by a ghost story. John Clark, a gardener, living in small house near the Infant School, declares that his family, and two labouring men lodging at his house, were all in bed on Sunday night last, when, between eleven and twelve o'clock, strange noises were heard below by all of them, resembling the rattling of chairs and tables, &c. The noise having subsided, the inmates of the house, with the exception of Clark, went to sleep. Clark states that he was wide awake, and heard footsteps coming up the stairs, and presently a man entered the room, and coming up to the bed side, placed his hands on Clark's face, drew down his arms, and grasped him very tight by his two hands; he held him in this situation for a short period, when the hands of the nocturnal visitor appeared to get gradually smaller, till they became as small as a young child's when his hold relaxed, and the apparition disappeared.

Clark says it appeared to be a man about five feet six inches in height, with very black curly hair, and rather stout; that when he was holding him he placed his face very near his, and that he felt his breath very hot, as were also his hands. Clark says he tried to speak and move, but had no power to do either, but immediately his visitor left he jumped up in bed and gave an alarm. He was terribly frightened, and could not close his eyes. He got up, and went to his work on Monday morning, but such was the effect of the shock he received that he became very ill, and was obliged to leave his work and go to bed.

On Thursday he told this tale to a man named Tripp, who lived in the same house three years previous to Clark's occupying it, and from Tripp he received the cheering assurance that he must expect frequent visits from this unwelcome guest, as during the three years he had lived in the house he had appeared to him upwards of a dozen times nearly in a similar way, his last visit being about six weeks before he left the house; the other persons in the house could always hear the chairs and tables rattling downstairs on those occasions, but the visitor never made his appearance to anyone but himself.

The men both say the doors and windows were all found secure in the morning, and the furniture in the same position as when left the previous evening.

*Bath Chronicle.*

## 1851 – THE DOCTRINE OF VAMPIRES.

What is a Vampire?

The word, in good Sclavonic, implies a bloodsucker, and that is the name given in Sclavonia, to those of the unhallowed dead who return to earth to prolong the power beneath the glimpses of the moon, by sucking the life blood of the victims.

What are the signs by which you may know a Vampire?

Moreri states that a certain Vampire was disinterred in the regency of Belgrade, and he gives the following as the principal characteristics by which the fatal quality of the foul fiend was recognized-

I.    His body had not the scent of a corpse.
II.   Decomposition had not touched it, save at the tip of the nose, which was withered and perishing.
III.  The hair and beard had recommenced growing.
IV.   New nails had taken the place of the old ones which had fallen off.
V.    Beneath the outer skin, which was white and peeling, a new skin had begun appear.
VI.   The face, the hands, the feet, in short the whole body, were as well-disposed as they were in life.
VII.  Blood, fresh and liquid, was found in his mouth. It was believed that this was the blood of the victims of the monster.

"What becomes of the victims who are thus sacrificed to the unhallowed appetites of these monsters?" Immediately after they have had the Vampire-tooth in their throats, and their life blood has swilled his unearthly jaws, they die, and become Vampires in their turn! Horrible! The world would become peopled with these terrible monsters? No! happily there is means of annihilating them!"

What is it?

The method is extremely simple. You have only to drive a stake through the heart of the Vampire—to burn his body and cast his ashes to the wind.

"Are Vampires distinguished by sex?" "Alas! they are both masculine and feminine. The male Vampires exercise their terrible passion upon the women. The female Vampires, who are called Goules, attack men only."

The Rev. Father Augustin Calmer, Benedictine Monk and Abbe of Senones, in Lorraine, has given a history of these terrible monsters, with whose doings he was tolerably familiar. The following is one of the facts which he narrates:-

A certain Peter Plogojowits lived in Kisolova, a village in Hungary. He died, and had been buried ten weeks, when he returned to the village, and appeared by night to several of the inhabitants, during their sleep. The gripe of his terrible teeth was found in their throats, and in less than twenty four hours they were all dead. Thus there perished, in the space of eight days, nine persons, both old and young. The widow of this same Plogojowits declared also that he had returned to her since his death, and demanded his old shoes. This frightened her so much that she withdrew from the village, and went to live in another place afar off. These facts being all established, beyond the reach of doubt or cavil, the villagers determined to drag the wretched corpse from the grave, and burn this diabolical Plogojowits to ashes.

They therefore addressed the Military Commander of the district, and the Cure of the place, for permission to proceed therein. The Officer and the Cure both raised all the objections they could, to turn the villagers from the execution of their design. But they were firmly persuaded that this Plogojowits was a Vampire, and they were equally determined to rid themselves of his terrible infestations. If their reasonable request were not complied with, they swore, to a man, that they would abandon the village, and wander abroad, to find a home where they might.

The Officer of the emperor and the Officer of the church, seeing that they could not stop these determined Hungarians from unearthing this terrible Plogojowits, and taking vengeance on him, went to the village of Kisolova, and caused the body to be disinterred. There, in all verity, they found on the corpse all the indications which we have established beforehand. The body exhaled no deathly odour —the limbs were lithe and lissom, and extended in an easy and natural manner. In every respect, save at the tip of the nose, there was evidence of life and freshness. That organ alone was a little dry, mouldy, and withered at the tip. The hair and beard were growing, fresh blood was found in the mouth, and the villagers satisfied themselves that the blood of their compatriots had been drunk by the monster.

The officer of the emperor and the reverend priest could not gainsay these facts which stood before their eyes. The people were seized with a lively burst of indignation. They ran and got a sharp pointed stake —they plunged it into the bosom of the terrible Peter Plogojowitz and blood—fresh vermillion blood— spouted out from the chest, and flowed from the mouth and the mouldy nose of the Vampire. They hurried his body to a scaffold, and then, before God and man, they burned to ashes the cadaverous frame of this unearthly being. These facts cannot be gainsaid, and all Paris is now witnessing, night after night, the drama by M.M. Alexandre Dumas, and Auguste Maquet, which illustrates the history of these monsters. It commences at half past six, and endures till midnight!

*Western Times.*

# 1852 – A "RAPPIST" GHOST IN HULL.

The inmates of a house situate in a lonely lane in Hull, were startled, about a month ago, in the stillness of the night, by a "sharp sudden knocking upon the walls of the room, from some invisible hand." This phenomenon in acoustics was repeated at short intervals for several weeks before it reached the public ear.

During the cold, drizzly nights of last week, a crowd kept watch at the gates of the lonely house, waiting for the sound of his ghostship's knuckles, and discussing the cause of his visitations. A detachment of police keeps order without, and two intelligent detectives were charged with the apprehension of the disturber within.

*Hampshire Telegraph.*

---

# 1852 – WRAITHS.

Instances of people being seen at a distance from the spot on which they are dying are so numerous that in this department I have positively an embarrassment of riches, and find it difficult to make a selection; more especially as there is in each case little to relate – the whole phenomenon being comprised in the fact of the form being observed, and the chief variations consisting in this, that the seer or seers, frequently entertain no suspicion that what they have seen is any other than a form of flesh and blood; whilst on other occasions the assurance that the person is far away, or some peculiarity connected with the appearance itself, produces the immediate conviction that the shape is not corporeal.

Mrs K., the sister of Provost B., of Aberdeen, was sitting one day with her husband, Dr. K., in the parlour of the manse, when she suddenly said, "Oh! there's my brother come; he has just passed the window;" and, followed by her husband, she hastened to the door to meet the visitor. He was however not there. "He is gone round to the back door," said she; and thither they went, but neither was he there, nor had the servants seen anything of him. Dr. K. said she must be mistaken, but she laughed at the idea; her brother passed the window and looked in; he must have gone somewhere, and would doubtless be back directly. But he came not, and the intelligence shortly arrived from St. Andrew's, that at that precise time, as nearly as they could compare circumstances, he had died quite suddenly at his own place of residence. I have heard this story from connexions of the family, and also from an eminent professor of Glasgow, who told me that he had once asked Dr. K. whether he believed in these appearances. "I cannot choose but believe," returned Dr. K., and then accounted for his conviction by narrating the above particulars.

Lord and Lady M. were residing on their estate in Ireland. Lord M. had gone out shooting in the morning, and was not expected to return till towards dinner time.

In the course of the afternoon Lady M. and a friend were walking on the terrace that forms a promenade in front of the castle, when she said. "Oh! there is M. returning," whereupon she called to him to join them. He, however, took no notice, but walked on before them, till they saw him enter the house, whither they followed him, but he was not to be found; and before they had recovered their surprise at his sudden disappearance, he was brought home dead – having been killed by his own gun. It is a curious fact in this case, that while the ladies were walking behind the figure on the terrace. Lady M. called the attention of her other companion to the shooting jacket, observing that it was a particularly convenient one, and that she had the credit of having contrived it for him herself.

A person in Edinburgh, busied about her daily work, saw a woman enter her house, with whom she was on such terms that she could not be but surprised at the visit; but whilst she was expecting an explanation, and under the influence of her resentment at avoiding to look at her, found she was gone. She remained quite unable to account for the visit, and, as she said, "was wondering what had brought her there," when she heard that the woman had expired at that precise time.

Madame O. B. was engaged to marry an officer who was with his regiment in India, and wishing to live in privacy till the union took place, she retired to the country and boarded with some ladies of her acquaintance while awaiting his return. She at length heard that he had obtained an appointment, which, by improving his prospects, had removed some difficulties out of the way of the marriage, and that he was immediately coming home. A short time after the arrival of this intelligence, this lady, and one of those with whom she was residing, were walking over a bridge when the friend said, alluding to an officer she saw on the other side of the way, "what an extraordinary expression of face"! But, without pausing to answer, Madame O. B. darted across the road to meet the stranger – but he was gone! Where? They could not conceive. They ran to the toll keepers at the ends of the bridge to inquire if they had observed such a person—but they had not. Alarmed and perplexed, for it was her intended husband that she had seen, Madame O. B. returned home; and in due time the packet that should have brought himself brought the sad tidings of his unexpected death.

Madame O. B. never recovered from the shock, and died herself of a broken heart not long afterwards.

Mr. H., an eminent artist, was walking arm in arm with a friend, in Edinburgh, when he suddenly left him, saying, "Oh! there's my brother!" He had seen him with the most entire distinctness, but was confounded by losing sight of him without being able to ascertain whether he had vanished. News came, ere long, that at that precise period his brother had died.

Mrs. T., sitting in her drawing room, saw her nephew, then at Cambridge, pass across the adjoining room. She started up to meet him, and, not finding him, summoned the servants to ask where he was. They, however, had not seen him, and declared he could not be there, whilst she as positively declared he was. The young man had died at Cambridge quite unexpectedly.

A Scotch minister went to visit a friend who was dangerously ill. After sitting with the invalid for some time, he left him to take some rest, and went below. He had been reading in the library some little time, when, on looking up, he saw the sick man standing at the door. "God bless me!" he cried starting up, "how can you be so imprudent?" The figure disappeared; and, hastening upstairs, he found his friend had expired.

Three young men at Cambridge had been out hunting, and afterwards dined together in the apartments of one of them. After dinner, two of the party, fatigued with their morning's exercise, fell asleep, whilst the third, a Mr. M., remained awake. Presently the door opened, and a gentleman entered and placed himself behind the sleeping owner of the rooms, and, after standing there a minute, proceeded into the gyp room, a small inner chamber, from which there was no egress. Mr. M. waited a little while, expecting the stranger would come out again; but, as he did not, he awoke his host saying, "There's somebody gone into your room; I don't know who it can be."

The young man rose and looked into the gyp room but there being nobody there, he naturally accused Mr. M. of dreaming; but the other assured him he had not been asleep. He then described the stranger – an elderly man, &c., dressed like a country squire, with gaiters on and so forth. "Why, that's like my father," said the host, and he immediately made inquiry, thinking it possible the old gentleman had slipped out unobserved by Mr. M. He was not, however, to be heard of, and the post shortly brought a letter announcing that he had died at the time he had been seen in his son's chamber at Cambridge.

Mr. C. F. and some young ladies, were not long ago standing together looking in at a shop window at Brighton, when he suddenly darted across the way, and they saw him hurrying along the street, apparently in pursuit of somebody. After waiting a little while, as he did not return, they went home without him, and when he came, they of course arraigned him for his want of gallantry.

"I beg your pardon," he said, "but I saw an acquaintance of mine that owes me some money, and I wanted to get hold of him."

"And did you?" inquired the ladies.

"No," returned he, "I kept sight of him for some time; but I suddenly missed him. I can't think how."

No more was thought of the matter; but by the next morning's post, Mr. C. F. received a letter, enclosing a draft from the father of the young man he had seen, saying that his son had just expired, and that one of his last requests had been that he would pay Mr. C. F. the money that he owed him.

Two young ladies, staying at the Queen's Ferry, arose early one morning to bathe; as they descended the stairs, they each exclaimed, "There's my uncle!" They had seen him standing by the clock. He died at that time.

Very lately, a gentleman living in Edinburgh, whilst sitting with his wife, suddenly arose from his seat, and advanced towards the door, with his hands extended, as if about to welcome a visitor. On his wife's inquiring what he was about, he answered that he had seen so-and-so enter the room. She had seen nobody. A day or two afterwards, the post brought a letter announcing the death of the person seen.

A regiment, not very long since, stationed at New Orleans, had a temporary mess room erected, at one end of which was a door for the officers; and at the other, a door and a space railed off for the messman. One day, two of the officers were playing at chess, or draughts, one sitting with his face towards the centre of the room, the other with his back to it. "Bless me! Why, surely that is your brother!" exclaimed the former to the latter, who looked around eagerly, his brother being then, he believed, in England. By this time the figure having passed the spot where the officers were sitting, presented only his back to them. "No," replied the second, "that is not my brother's regiment; that's the uniform of the Rifle Brigade. By heavens! It is my brother, though," he added, starting up, and eagerly pursuing the stranger, who, at that moment, turned his head and looked at him, and then, somehow, strangely disappeared amongst the people standing at the messman's end of the room. Supposing he had gone out that way, the brother pursued him, but, he was not to be found; neither had the messman, nor anybody there, observed him. The young man died at that time in England, having just exchanged into the Rifle Brigade.

I could fill pages with similar instances, not to mention those recorded in other collections and in history. The case of Lord Balcarres is perhaps worth alluding to, from its being so perfectly well established. Nobody has ever disputed the truth of it, only they get out of the difficulty by saying that was a spectral illusion. Lord B. was in confinement in the castle of Edinburgh, under suspicion of Jacobitism, when one morning, whilst in bed, the curtains were drawn aside by his friend, Viscount Dundee, who looked upon him steadfastly, leaned for some time on the mantelpiece, and then walked out of the room. Lord B., not supposing that what he saw was a spectre, called to Dundee to come back and speak to him, but he was gone and shortly afterwards the news came that he had fallen about that same hour at Killicranky.

Finally, I have met with three instances of persons who are much the subjects of this phenomenon, that they generally see the wraith of any friend that happens to die, and frequently also of those who are merely acquaintances. They see the person as if they were alive, and unless they know him positively to be elsewhere they have no suspicion but that it is himself, in the flesh, that is before them, till the sudden disappearance of the figure brings the conviction. Sometimes, as in the case of Mr. C. F., above alluded to, no suspicion arises, till the news of the death arrives, and they mention, without reserve, that they have met so-and-so, but did not stop to speak, and so forth.

*Aberdeen Herald and General Advertiser.*

## 1854 – THIRTY SEVEN EYES IN PORTSMOUTH.

During the last two nights the neighbourhood of the Jewish synagogue at Portsmouth has been for hours impassable. Crowds have collected despite the efforts of the police, in order to catch a glimpse of a ghost, which it is affirmed, disports its unearthly form in that locality. There is a rather remarkable dissimilarity in the description of its appearance, for while some assert that it is like a Cochin-China cock, with boots and spurs, and fifty tremendous horns, others maintain that it has glaring eyes, thirty seven in number and formidable hoofs, with a wide-awake on its tail, and fire and brimstone issuing from its mouth.

*Portsmouth Guardian.*

## 1855 – FRIGHTENED TO DEATH.

That the popular belief in ghosts is not extinct, even in a large town like Sheffield, is proved by a tragic circumstance of recent occurrence. It was currently reported in Campo Lane, that a ghost, "all in white," had made its appearance in the house of John Favell, who lives in Campo Lane, a little beyond the parish church. The story was genuine thus far, that a young woman, named Harriet Ward, who lodged ay Favell's house, affirmed in the most solemn manner that she had seen an apparition in the cellar kitchen. This assertion was made with such an air of credibility that the other inmates in the house – Favell, his wife, and the wife's sister—could not altogether disbelieve it, though they had no visual evidence of its truth.

Favell had heard strange sounds, however, which he thought might have had their origin in supernatural agency. One evening they felt much concerned on account of the ghostly presence, that, for the sake of greater security, a friend of the family, named Robert Rollinson, who lodged in Court No. 24, South Street, Park, was requested to spend the night at Favell's house. Being neither superstitious nor timid, Rollinson acquiesced. He and the other persons went to bed in due time, and Rollinson reported the following morning that he had seen nothing extraordinary, but towards morning had heard a strange noise that he could not account for. He returned home to breakfast, having first received an invitation for himself and his wife to dine with the Favells. His wife and the family with whom they lodged were very inquisitive about the ghost, but Rollinson assured them that he had seen nothing of it. His wife at once accepted the invitation to dinner, and seemed to regard the apparition story as a pleasant jest. She little knew that within a few hours it would prove her death. She and her husband kept their appointment at Favell's and remained to spend the rest of the day there.

It should here be stated, as a circumstance which may throw some light on this strange affair, that all the parties concerned—except perhaps the ghost, of whose creed nothing is known—were members of the community called Latter-day Saints, whose congregational meetings are held at the Hall of Science, Rockingham Street. To this place Favell and his family and friends repaired, leaving in their house Mrs. Favell's sister, Mrs. Rollinson, and Mrs. Johnson (the person at whose house in South Street, the Rollinson's lodged).

On the return of the party who had gone to the Hall of Science, they were accompanied by several acquaintances, who had heard of the apparition and perhaps felt curious to know more about it. Harriett Ward was eloquent on the subject of the vision, and several of the visitors went into the cellar kitchen to see the ghostly residence, and the precise spot it had been seen. A number of persons had assembled in front of the house, understanding that the ghost was "on view," anxious to have a peep for nothing but Mrs. Favell, feeling annoyed at seeing many individuals prying at the kitchen window, requested her sister to fasten a temporary blind against it with two forks.

The sister, however, had no courage to perform the task, although several individuals had already gone down into the kitchen, preceded by Harriett Ward with a lighted candle. It was this moment that Mrs. Rollinson's disbelief in ghostly manifestations exhibited itself in full force. "Pooh, pooh," she exclaimed, rather impatiently, "Give me the forks, child!" and immediately she descended into the kitchen to hang the blind. She had not been there many moments when, looking in the direction of the stairs down which they had descended, she became suddenly terror-stricken, and seizing the arm of her friend, Mrs. Johnson, with a convulsive grasp, exclaimed in broken accents, "Oh, Mrs. Johnson, I saw something on the steps! Take me away!"

This unexpected incident imparted reality to the occasion, which perhaps few present had expected. Mrs. Rollinson, in an agony of terror, was conveyed up the steps, and immediately afterwards fainted. After a while her consciousness returned, but for a brief interval, and she assured her friends in the most earnest and solemn manner, that she had seen on the stairs a female form, dressed in white apparel, and that it approached and rushed past her. The fact of no one else having seen it made no difference to her. She believed the evidence of her eyesight in that instance as she had been accustomed to do on ordinary occasions, and probably nothing could have shaken her conviction that she had seen a spectre.

Again she relapsed into a state of unconsciousness, in which condition she was removed in a cab to her lodgings, and died the following day. Her death had certainly been caused by the fright received on the previous day, up to which time she was in perfect health and spirits, and her friends concur stating that she was by no means of a timid disposition.

A Coroner's inquest was held, in consequence of the poor woman's sudden death. The hard-headed matter-of-fact jury could make nothing of the ghost story, so they returned a verdict of "Sudden, but natural death."

*Sheffield Times.*

---

# 1857 – A GHOST IN PARLIAMENT.

We are told that there is a ghost in every house, a spectre in every family, and certainly the present Government – that happy family over which Lord Palmerston presides with much patriarchal grace and dignity is no exception to the general rule. In private life and in vulgar houses this unwelcome guest, whenever an opportunity has been afforded of observing his movements, manifests his presence by ugly noises and senseless sounds, by absurd rappings and knockings, by ringing bells and rattling of panes and shutters, by mere hubbub and clatter, in fact, sheer rant and stamping, He rarely speaks, and then not very much to the purpose; he still more rarely shows himself in a visible shape, and then only to a housemaid on the back stairs, who instantly falls down, faints away, and breaks the family teapot or some other precious heirloom, which has been confided to her by an anxious mistress, in the firm faith

that it would be speedily and safely deposited in the ancestral china closet on the second floor.

Well! all this is provoking enough in everyday life and private houses, but what shall we say to public life and the Houses of Parliament? What shall we say to a ghost in these, and what shall we say to an Administration saddled with such an incubus, haunted by such a spectre, and on whose shoulders a perpetual Old Man of the Mountain sits inexorably astride? It is said, but it is the simple truth? The Lord Chancellor—we say it with unfeigned respect for his office—is such a spectre, and such an incubus to the present Government. Year after year he appears on the woolsack in the House of Lords, and—differing from the domestic ghost in this, that he is only too visible—night after night potters and chatters, and hems and haws, and mumbles and fumbles over this bill and that bill, until that venerable assembly is fairly bored and frightened out of its propriety, rejects all the bills in a panic, and rushes to an adjournment, to escape the intolerable apparition of the Old Woman of the Woolsack, who inspires it with such unmitigated disgust.

*The Times.*

---

# 1858 – SECOND–SIGHT & SUPERNATURAL WARNINGS.

All ghost stories have a strange fascination about them; and the various corroborations which certain well-known tales of this class have received in the pages of newspapers, suggest to me a kindred topic, repeating a belief which is said to be peculiar to the inhabitants of mountainous countries. I allude to what is called second-sight; connected with which are certain super-natural warnings with reference to approaching death, to which it is difficult to assign a defined name.

The county of Pembroke is rife with tales of this class; many of them depending upon such trustworthy evidence, to compel the mind to refuse to dismiss them altogether as unworthy of credit; and yet at the same it is difficult to understand the object of such interferences with the ordinary course of events. I might easily, were I so disposed, fill an entire number of this periodical with authentic records (as far as the evidence of the senses may be relied on), which can scarcely be referred to the ordinary theory of coincidences.

From the many stories of the class which I have indicated, I may perhaps be allowed to select a few; for the authenticity of which I can vouch, either from having heard them from the parties whom they actually occurred, or from having been myself an actor in the scene.

Many years ago, seven or eight members of the family of my paternal grandfather were seated at the door of his house on a fine summer evening, between the hours of eight and nine o'clock. The parish church and its yard are only separated from the spot by a brook and a couple of meadows. The family happened to be looking in the direction of the churchyard, when they were amazed by witnessing the advent of a funeral procession. They saw the crowd, and the coffin borne on men's shoulders come down the pathway towards the church, but the distance was too great to enable them to recognise the face of any of the actors in the scene. As the funeral cortege neared the church porch, they distinctly saw the clergyman, with whom they were personally acquainted, come out in his surplice to meet the mourners, and saw him precede them into the church. In a short time they came out, and my relatives saw them go to a particular part of the yard, where they remained for time long enough to allow the remainder of the supposed funeral rites to be performed.

Greatly amazed at what he beheld, my grandfather sent over to the church to inquire who had been buried at that unusual hour. The messenger returned with the intelligence that no person had been buried during that day, nor for several days before. A short time after this, a neighbour died, and was buried in the precise spot where the phantom internment was seen.

My mother's father lived on the banks of one of the many creeks or pills with which the beautiful harbour of Milford Haven indented. In front of the home is a large court, built on a quay wall to protect it from the rising tide. In this court my mother was walking one fine evening, rather more than sixty years ago, enjoying the moonlight, and the balmy summer breeze. The tide was out, so that the creek was empty. Suddenly my mother's attention was aroused by hearing the sound of a boat coming up the pill. The measured dip of the oars in the water, and the noise of their revolution in the rowlocks, were distinctly audible. Presently she heard the keel of the boat grate on the gravelly beach by the side of the quay wall. Greatly alarmed, as nothing was visible, she ran into the house and related what she had heard. A few days afterwards, the mate of an East Indiaman, which had put into Milford Haven for the purpose of undergoing repair, died on board; and his coffined corpse was brought up the pill, and landed at the very spot where my mother heard the phantom boat touch the ground.

Some years ago a friend of mine, a clergyman resident in the city of St David, who was the vicar of a rural parish, had a female parishioner who was a notorious seer of phantom funerals. When my friend used to go out to his Sunday duty, this old woman would accost him frequently with, "Ay, ay, Mr _____, you'll be here of a week day soon, for I a saw funeral last night." Upon one occasion the clergyman asked her, "Well, Molly, have you seen a funeral lately?" "Ay, ay, Mr ___," was the reply, "I saw one a night or two ago, and I saw you as plainly as I see you now; and you did what I never saw you do before." "What was that?" inquired my friend. "Why," replied the old woman, "as you came out of the church to meet the funeral, you stooped down, and appeared to pick something off the ground" "Well," thought my friend to himself, "I'll try, Molly, if I cannot make a liar of you for once."

Some little time after this conversation occurred, my friend was summoned to a burial in his country parish, Molly and her vaticinations having entirely passed from his memory. He rode on horseback, and was rather late. Hastily donning his surplice, he walked out to meet the funeral procession. As he emerged from the church porch, his surplice became entangled in a spur; and he stooped down to disengage it, the old woman and her vision flashed across his recollection. "Molly was right, after all," said he to himself as he rose up and walked on.

In the year 1838, I was on a visit to my parents, who at that time resided on the spot on which mother was born, and where she passed the latter years of her life. Within a short distance of the house stood a large walled garden, which was approached through a gate leading into a stable yard. From underneath the garden wall bubbled a well of delicious spring water, from whence the domestic offices were supplied. It was a custom in the family, in summer time, that the water for the use of the house should be brought in late in the evening, in order that it might be cool; and it was the duty of a servant to go out with a yoke and a couple of pails to fetch the water, just before the time of closing up the house for the night.

One evening the girl had gone out for this purpose. The night was beautifully fine, the moon shining so brightly that the smallest object was distinctly visible. The servant had not been absent many minutes, when she ran into the house without her burden, and, throwing herself into a chair in a state of extreme terror, fainted away. Restoratives having been used she recovered a little, and upon being questioned as to the cause of her alarm, she told us that as she was stooping over the well about to fill one of her pails, she suddenly found herself in the midst of crowd of people, who were carrying a coffin, which they had set down at the gate of the stable yard. As she had received no intimation of the approach of the concourse by any sound of footsteps, she was greatly alarmed; and as the object borne by the throng did not tend to tranquillise her nerves, she took to her heels, leaving her pails behind her.

As no persuasion could induce her to return to the well, I offered to do so for her, and to ascertain the cause of her terror. When I arrived at the stable yard there was neither coffin nor crowd to be seen; and upon asking a neighbour whose cottage commanded a view of the well whether she had seen a funeral go by, she put a stop to any further inquiry by asking me, "Who had ever heard of a funeral at ten o'clock at night?" To which pertinent query I could only reply by stating what the servant professed to have seen.

So the matter rested for a few weeks, when there occurred an unusually high tide in Milford Haven. The water far above the level of the ordinary springs; filling the creek, and flowing into the court into the front of the house, it usually ebbed when it had reached the door. The roadway at the end of the pill was impassable. A person having died on the opposite side of the inlet a few days before this, the funeral took place on the morning of the high tide; and it was impossible to take the corpse to the parish church by the usual route, the bearers crossed the pill in a boat with the coffin, and having laid it down at the gate of our stable yard remained there until the boat could bring over the remainder of the funeral concourse.

In the year 1848, I returned to my home, after an absence of some years. A few days after my arrival, I took a walk one morning in the yard of one of our parish churches, through which there is a right of way for pedestrians. My object was a twofold one firstly, to enjoy the magnificent prospect visible from that elevated position; and, secondly, to see whether any of my friends or acquaintances who had died during my absence were buried in the locality.

After gazing around me for a short time, I sauntered on looking at one tombstone and then at another, when my attention was arrested by an altar-tomb enclosed within an iron railing. I walked up to it and read an inscription which informed me that it was in memory of Colonel ___. This gentleman had been the Law Commissioner for South Wales; and while on one Assistant Poor of his periodical tours of inspection he was struck with apoplexy in the workhouse of my native town and died in a few hours. This was suggested to my mind as I read the inscription on the tomb, as the melancholy event occurred during the period of my absence, and I was only made cognisant of the fact through the medium of the local press. Not being acquainted with the late Colonel ___, and never having seen him, the circumstances of his sudden demise had long passed from my memory, and was only revived by my thus viewing his tomb. I then passed on, and shortly afterwards returned home.

On my arrival my father asked me in what direction I had been walking? I replied, "In ___churchyard, looking at the tombs; and among others I have seen the tomb of Colonel ___, who died in the workhouse. That," replied my father, is impossible, as there is no tomb erected over Colonel ___'s grave.'

At this remark I laughed. "My dear father," said I, "You want to persuade me that I cannot read. I was not aware that Colonel ___ was buried in the churchyard, and was only informed of the fact by reading the inscription on the tomb." "Whatever you may say to the contrary," replied my father, "What I tell you is true; there is no tomb over Colonel ___'s grave.' Astounded by the reiteration of this statement, as soon as I had dined I returned to the churchyard, and again inspected all the tombs having railings round them, and found that father was right.

There was not only no tomb bearing the name of Colonel ___, but there was no tomb at all corresponding in appearance with the one l had seen. Unwilling to credit the evidence of my own senses, I went to the cottage of an old acquaintance of my boyhood, who lived outside of the churchyard gate, and asked her to show me the place where Colonel ___ lay buried. She took me to the spot, which was a green mound undistinguished in appearance from the surrounding graves. Nearly two years subsequent to this occurrence, surviving relatives erected an altar-tomb, with a railing round it, over the last resting place of Colonel ___, and it was, as nearly as I could remember, an exact reproduction of the memorial of my daydream.

I do not attempt to account, on rational or philosophical principles, for any of the occurrences which I have narrated. I have merely made a plain unvarnished statement of facts, leaving it to others to draw their own deductions or inferences therefrom.

Of course the theory of coincidences is an easy mode of severing any Gordian knot; and the *cui bono* argument may serve as an adjunct to the former mode of settling a difficulty. But at the same time the numberless anecdotes of a class similar to those which I have imperfectly endeavoured to relate, all resting upon unimpeachable testimony, must make the thoughtful pause, and ask themselves, in the language our master-poet:-

Can such things be,
And overcome us like a summer cloud
Without our special wonder!

Pavin Phillips.

*Potter's Electric News.*

# 1861 – SOME NOTABLE GHOST STORIES.

Very few men or women of intelligence believe in ghosts now—the hard, practical realities of life have too much interest for them, and visitors from a supernatural world would be altogether out of place in a railroad and cotton spinning age like the present. The day is gone by for these legends of haunted houses which used to be attached to nearly every old country mansion, and even to certain trees, hedges and nooks along the road. Not many years ago, before cheap newspapers and magazines were established for the advantage of the humbler classes, every tale of an apparition was eagerly discussed and readily believed. It is well known that many men of learning were as credulous as the most ignorant, and Dr. Johnson himself firmly believed in ghosts. How strangely absurd some of these stories now appear, which then found a place in grave volumes and expensive works! What will the reader think of the following "yarns," for example, published in 1731?

The scene is laid in Scotland, near a farm house, and the time is night, as a matter of course. The farmer, named William Sutor, was walking about his fields when he heard "an uncommon shrieking noise," proceeding apparently from a grey-coloured dog. Mr. Sutor and his servants thought at first that the animal was a fox, and accordingly set the dogs on its track, but not one would "so much as point his head that way." This was mysterious, and caused the party at the farm to feel a little uncomfortable. A month passed over, when the farmer again happened to be in the same spot at the same hour. This time, "something" passed by him, and in doing so "touched him so smartly on the thigh that he felt a pain all that night." It must have been a smart touch indeed to have caused this, and the farmer could not attend to his turnips and swedes as he ought to have done. At last the dog found its tongue, and spoke – spoke quite plainly. After uttering some mysterious sentences, it said "I am David Sutor's brother, I killed a man more than thirty five years ago, with a dog, and am made to speak out of the mouth of a dog." The talking animal further charged the trembling farmer to bury the bones of the murdered man—eight bones he was to find, and no more. He dug up the place indicated, and found the bones. The grey dog was satisfied and wagged his tail approvingly. And such was the kind of "appearances" which our ancestors saw. We have nothing half so remarkable to appear in our own prosy days.

A writer in a popular magazine, published in December, 1717, defends the ghosts from the attacks which were made upon them about that time and says, "It is pleasant to observe that notwithstanding the endeavours to discredit the being of spirits, there is hardly a person in England (I believe I may say in the world) but hath either heard or seen one himself or been acquainted with those that have." This gentleman's notion of what is "pleasant" must have been a little peculiar. He does not tell us that he ever saw a ghost himself, but doubtless he was prepared with a good story if he had been asked to produce one.

Stories of the following character are very common, and even at the present day there are many who believe in them. A young woman living in Bristol was attacked with smallpox, and lay in a dangerous condition. Her mother was with her, the father, a clergyman, lived twenty miles distant. Her sister was living with her father, and one night this young lady is reported to have "heard the voice of her mother lamenting herself upon the death of her daughter." At breakfast the next morning her father noticed her disturbed look, and asked what was the matter. She hesitated to tell the story, but being much pressed, she gave an account of the affair. The father then acknowledged that he, too, had heard the same "lamenting" sounds. Presently the news came that the daughter in Bristol was really dead. When the mother returned she told her husband that she "lay down in her clothes," after the death of her child, "and dreamed that she was with them at home telling her grief." The editor of the magazine to which this story was originally sent adds a foot note, that all three persons were in a dream, but such dreams are very difficult to account for. Many well-attested instances of a similar kind are on record, and have been generally credited.

The Rev. J. Hughes, of Jesus College, is responsible for a "notable ghost story," which has been many years forgotten. It seems that a Mr. Shaw, a fellow of St. John's College, Oxford, was sitting one night by himself smoking his pipe and reading, when he observed some person opening the door. He recognised the visitor as a fellow collegian, one Mr. Nailor, who had been dead five years. Mr. Shaw desired his friend to sit down, and he did so. "They had," says the clergyman who wrote the account, "a conference of about an hour and a half," in the course of which the "spirit" told Mr. Shaw that he would die very suddenly in a short time. The latter did not seem much disconcerted at this, but asked his supernatural guest to pay him another visit. "No," said he, "I have others to see, who are at a great distance." Mr. Shaw then asked the ghost "how it was with him in the other world!" "He answered," says the reverend narrator, "with a brisk and cheerful spirit," "very well." Mr. Shaw farther said, "are there any of our old friends with you?" and the shadow answered, "Not one." We are told that the next day the "conference" so affected Mr. Shaw that he made his will and expired soon afterwards – the victim, in all probability, of nervous fright arising from a strange dream – for there is no reason to doubt the truth of the story.

Not long ago, narratives quite as remarkable as this were published by a physician, under the authority of Mr. Charles Dickens, and the perfect truth of them all was vouched for. Another account, the truth of which was certified by Dr. Yarborough, Rector of Sewing, Hertfordshire, in the year 1759, is not a little curious. General Sabine, Governor of Gibraltar (from whose lips the Rector heard the story), was lying dangerously ill of a wound, and one night the curtains of his bed were drawn back by an invisible hand. He saw his wife, a lady then in England, and "whom he greatly loved." She "presented herself to his full view, and then disappeared. In a short time after he received the melancholy news that his beloved consort was dead," and that she died about the same hour on which he saw her.

Anecdotes of this kind might be multiplied indefinitely, and they are so strongly authenticated in many instances that some philosophers in the present day have constructed a theory to account for the visitations described. They contend that at the moment of dissolution the soul may have power, by "a strong violation of will," to visit another soul afar off. This is the essence of the theory advocated by the "physician" just alluded to, in the pages of one of our best known periodicals—*All the Year Round*. It is obvious that these accounts are divested of the foolish horrors which were formerly associated with apparitions, and present legitimate ground for calm, thoughtful inquiry. Legends like the "Corsican Brothers" are common in every country, and Sir David Brewster cites numerous examples. The theory of dreams is still in an undeveloped stage, and in a few years thinking men may throw great light upon many things which are now full of mystery.

Perhaps there may be no better advice to those who believe in apparitions of any kind than that offered by Addison:- "If we believe, as many wise and good men have done, that there are such phantoms and apparitions, let us endeavour to establish to ourselves an interest in Him who holds the reins of the whole creation in his hand, and moderates them after such a manner that it is impossible for one being to break loose upon another without His knowledge and permission."

*St. Neots Chronicle and Advertiser.*

# 1861 – THE UPAVON GHOST STORY.

During the past few weeks the inhabitants of Upavon and the surrounding villages have been kept in a state of excitement by mysterious rumours that at Upavon a real ghost had been for some time "making night hideous," by creating extraordinary sounds, &c., at the house of an old lady residing in that parish.

Many and varied were the versions of the affair, but the real facts of the case appear to be these:-

There is residing at Upavon an old lady, 73 years of age, named Miss Rolfe, and her next door neighbour is Mr. John Davis, a respectable plasterer and tiler. As far

back as the 27th of January Miss Rolfe found that a watch which she had in the house had been broken by some unknown hand, and on the following day a window of her house was smashed. No one could imagine by whom the mischief had been occasioned, until the middle of February when to the minds of the inmates the fact at once became apparent that the house was haunted.

It appears that as Miss Rolfe and Sarah Davis, a girl of 15 years of age (daughter of Miss Rolfe's neighbour), were in the kitchen some crockery fell down in a very mysterious manner. Miss Rolfe, in a state of alarm, at once put up her shutters, but whilst so doing, and whilst her back was turned, several other pieces of crockery descended from the shelves and danced themselves to atoms. This was followed by a series of strange noises, altogether so astounding, that the suggestion of Miss Davis, that "a ghost" was about the premises, seemed the only rational solution of the strange vagaries that were being perpetrated. The news of such extraordinary proceedings of course spread like wildfire through the village; and next day nearly all the inhabitants flocked to the house to see the damage which "the ghost" had done, and to testify to the knockings and noises which were still audible.

This state of things continued for two or three days, during which persons of all ranks came to the house, and amongst them the village policeman, Smith, who shrewdly suspected that the "ghost" was no other than the young lady, who had from the first suggested the cause of the mischief, and who had stuck to the suggestion with so much pertinacity that she had succeeded in persuading all the neighbours, even her own father. One or two little matters confirmed the policeman's suspicions; but although a rigid search of the premises was made, no positive result was arrived at, save that poor old Miss Rolfe's household goods, as well as her nerves, were on the eve of dissolution.

One curious fact, however, was discovered—evidently unconnected with ghosts—as ghosts are never known to take to cold water. On examining the well on the premises, a beehive stool, some garden lines, and other things were found; and, convinced in his own mind that no other person than Miss Sarah Davis placed them there, the policeman at once charged her with it. She was accordingly apprehended on Thursday last, and on the next day was taken before the magistrates (T. E. Fowle, Esq., Capt. Heathcote, and the Rev. J. H. Gale), at Pewsey, and charged with being the perpetrator of the wanton mischief which had been occasioned. Mr. Wittey, of Devizes, was retained to unravel the mystery; and Mr. Holloway, Pewsey, to keep the blame where it had long rested—on the shoulders of the ghost. Evidence, however, of so conclusive a nature was offered by Miss Rolfe, Charles Hillier, Police Sergeant Manley, and P.C. Smith, that Mr. Holloway said it would be useless to endeavour to keep up the hoax any longer, and the fair Miss Davis accordingly stood before the Bench as the acknowledged Upavon Ghost.

The magistrates, however, were disposed to take a lenient view of the case, and discharged the girl with a suitable admonition, upon her paying the damages and costs, which amounted to 6l. 8s. 4d. At the close of the enquiry, the Rev. H. Crook, of Upavon, who had taken much interest in the case, made a few remarks upon the notoriety which it had attained, and said he hoped after the satisfactory investigation which it had received, that the people's minds would now be at rest.

*Salisbury & Winchester Journal.*

---

# 1862 – A RAPACIOUS GHOST.

A Limerick priest recently suggested the following practical method of answering an appeal from purgatory—by a ghost! "A woman in the county of Limerick, not far from Emly, buried her husband a few months ago. A knock came to the door some night last month. She asked who was there. A hollow voice answered, "I am your husband whom you buried, and I am very miserable in purgatory till my debts are paid. Sell the two pigs you have and be sure to have the money for me on such a night when I call." The poor woman did as he required, and felt happy at being able to meet his request, whether through fear or love (as he appeared with his shroud and pale face). Between the first and second visit of the ghost, the poor woman went and told her story to the priest; he told her it was all very good, but at the same time to have two policemen in the house when she would be giving the money. Accordingly, after getting the money, the purgatorial and shrouded ghost came, and was arrested by the police and lodged in Limerick Gaol, there to undergo a little more purgatory till his trial comes on. The ghost turned out to be a near neighbour who is godfather to one of her children."

*Kendall Mercury.*

---

# 1862 – PHANTOM MANIA.

London society just now seems inflicted with a general phantom mania. The last new phase of the malady is a ghost story, which has lately obtained extensive currency in what are called the "upper circles," and which claims for its believers two counsel, learned in the law, and the Lord High Chancellor himself! I don't pretend to vouch that the story can pretend to the "ghost" of a foundation for its existence – I merely testify that it is being talked of by everybody, and that the first question asked at most dinner tables is, "Have you heard of Lord Westbury's ghost?"

The story runs thus:-

Lord Westbury lately purchased Hackwood House, an old mansion near Basingstoke, the property of Lord Bolton. Snatching a spare day or two, to obtain a more minute inspection of his investment he took with him two of the gentlemen belonging to his official establishment, both members of the learned profession. On separating for the night the bedroom destined for one of them, was found to be on the opposite side of the hall to those of the other gentlemen; he therefore shook hands and said "Good night" in the hall, leaving the others talking there. He had not been very long asleep before he "felt" himself awoke; but could neither hear nor perceive anything. By degrees, however, he became conscious of something luminous on the side of the room opposite his bed, which gradually assumed the appearance of a woman clothed in grey. He at first thought it was an optical illusion; next, that his companions were playing him some phosphoric trick, and then turning round he composed himself to sleep again.

Farther on in the night he was awoke again, and then at once he saw the same figure brilliantly conspicuous on the wall. Whilst he was gazing at it, it seemed to leave the wall and advance into the middle of the apartment. He immediately jumped out of bed, rushed to it, and found—nothing. He was so impressed with the power of the delusion, that he found it impossible to seek any more sleep, and as the day was beginning to break, he dressed and made his way into the grounds, where he walked about for some time, pondering over the illusion so forcibly produced upon him. On his return to his room he wrote out an exact account of what he thought he had seen, it being then quite clear to him that it was no trick played by others, but simply a hallucination of his own brain.

At the breakfast table, however, he began to fancy that he had been cleverly imposed on by his friends, as they commenced at once bantering him on his "night's rest," "broken sleep," and so forth. Wishing to detect them if possible, he pretended unconsciousness and utter ignorance of their meaning, when, to his horror, one of them exclaimed, "Come, come, don't think we didn't see one of the women in grey follow you into your room last night!" He rushed up stairs, produced his written account, which he gave them to read, and the consternation became general.

On inquiry, of course, they found the legend of a murder done in days of yore; and the Lord Chancellor is supposed to be exceedingly vexed at an incident which has decidedly shut up one room in his house forever, if not in all probability, tabooed the mansion altogether. Thus much do the "upper ten thousand" —how truly is quite another question.

*Bedfordshire Mercury.*

———◦—◦◦◦—◦———

# 1863 – CHRISTMAS GHOSTS AND SCIENTIFIC GHOSTS.

There is for some people—happily the number is growing less every day – a horrible fascination in a ghost story. Sitting round the fire on a winter's night, the logs blazing on the ample hearth, the glowing peat giving forth its perfumed smoke, or the coal fire of ruby red relieved by black diamonds and brilliant jets of gas—the wind moaning without, the rain pattering on the window or the snowflakes falling softly on the ground – sitting round the fire is the time to tell ghost stories. There is a solemn hush as the preliminary words are spoken and the narrator begins his legend. Every syllable is heard with attention; shy glances are cast over the shoulder at the least unexpected sound; the striking of the pale-faced clock makes the listeners start; and, finally, they linger by the fire, when the time comes to separate, and there is the unpleasant journey to be made up to bed in no more cheerful society that that of a flat candlestick.

No doubt many of our readers may recall such a scene as we have described; and smiling now at their fears, remember well enough that those fears were terribly real long ago. We had in our younger days an intimacy with several ghosts – that is we had heard with a shiver, the dark stories belonging to them.

There was an old inn on the breezy common, and the back staircase was haunted by the ghost of the soldier who had committed suicide when billeted in the house. We never saw the ghost but then we never went up that staircase after dark, which might account for it; but one of the ostlers averred that he had seen him – "all whitish like, wi' a bluish bit o' light on his face, a movin' along ever so." This ostler was a firm believer in ghosts, and took kindly to spirits. Some people are said to be gifted with second sight, and after a certain period in the evening this gentleman saw double.

We remember the story of an anxious mother one stormy night in winter seeing her sailor son, who was far away at sea, come to her bedside soaked with sea water, in order to mention the circumstance that he had been drowned that very night off somewhere. Likewise of a schoolboy who had perished in a pond, making the

circuit of that pond on the anniversary of his decease, much to the terror of other scholars, who never saw him, to be sure; but that might have been because they never had nerve enough to look for him. We have heard of a ghost that always followed a person six feet behind him, and no more; of a ghost that came regularly four times a year, like quarter days, and would give no quarter to the unhappy beings disturbed, until something or other was found out; of a ghost who sat at a desk chandler's shop (it was the ghost of the late proprietor), and would not be warned off until it had revealed the fact that a penny and three farthings were owing by somebody, and not entered in the books.

It has been asked, "Why should ghosts rise merely to make our hair rise?" but here is the answer:- they keep on appearing until something is found out! Was it not so with that marvel of modern marvels, the "Cock Lane ghost?" Has it not been so with still more recent instances, within most people's experience?

Of course, we are perfectly well aware that it is a species or flat heresy to disparage ghosts at Christmas, or any other time, with certain people. There are tellers of these supernatural stories, who would as soon die as give up the ghost; they grow cheerful at the prospect of a batch of horrors, and never seem so much in spirits as, when they revel in the spirit land. How is it that some of these individuals have never scientifically done for ghosts what Cavier and Linnaeus have done for beasts and flowers? We can imagine ghosts described as follows:-

GHOSTS – This class is undoubtedly one of the most distinctly circumscribed in the whole series of being; general form of the body, human; legs, two in number but seldom visible, being covered with a light vestment; colour, usually white; body transparent, with entire absence of digestive organs; habitat, the churchyard; habits, nocturnal and migratory; divided into six orders, &c., &c.

But a description such as this would ill accord with the ghost theory or with ghostly practices – these spirits come in such "a questionable form." We have seen them on the stage, (and we heard of one in an omnibus), and their appearance on nearly all occasions was a credit to their laundress – linen spotless, except where speckled for the purpose of circumstantial evidence with red ink or currant juice; pace slow and measured (by the foot); attitude stiff, usually inelegant, as if the deceased knew no more of pose than of repose; voice ever so far down in the chest, and disproportionate to the depth of meaning. The ghost of Hamlet's father, irreverently addressed by his son as an "old mole," walks on the castle ramparts in a suit of armour; the ghost who, without any proposer or seconder, takes the chair at Macbeth's banquet, wears royal robes; the ghosts that rise up to affright King Richard wear the apparel which they may be supposed to have worn in their mortal life; the ghost, if it be a ghost, that appears in "Don Giovanni," comes as an animated statue (a thing not often seen in England); and the ghost in the "Corsican Brother" wears a clean shirt and unimpeachable pair of trousers.

But the regular ghost never condescends to wear any other attire than white, flowing drapery; never, in the face, looks anything but blue; never walks, but glides; never speaks, but solemnly intones; never comes out till night, and never goes home till the morning. Never having seen a real ghost, we are obliged to resort to the stage to ascertain its appearance. We have been given to understand, on the authority of W. Shakespeare, late of Stratford-on-Avon, that the stage holds up the mirror to nature, also, we conclude, to super nature. We were therefore distressed by the first ghost we ever saw on the stage making its appearance through a square hole in the middle of the floor; in fact, coming to business in or on, a trap. This did not look supernatural. Neither did the ghost that was shunted on, and found it quite as much as it could to keep its footing; neither did the ghost that walked on and off and that, having disappeared at the wing, we actually beheld imbibing porter with the prompter nether, above all, did the ghost that we once saw on the boards of a travelling theatre, and which in hurried obedience to the admonitions of the impresario to "cut it short," appeared before the murder was committed, and was greeted with derisive shouts.

The stage shook our faith in ghosts. They were far too corporeal. It appeared to us very material that a spiritual apparition should be immaterial, and therefore the poet had the advantage of the player. But how to raise a ghost? That, in our younger and more speculative days, was a subject which often occurred to us.

Without the aid of the necromancer, without any meddling with the black art, or any alliance with the spirit rapping community, ghosts are now being raised all over London, all over the country, all over Europe, in New York, and other American cities. Science is the spell; a simple application of philosophical principles, and shadowy ghosts are raised, and before the eyes of the spectator, assumes a solidity, until the most acute observer cannot detect the difference between the substance and the shadow placed side by side.

*Burnley Gazette.*

# 1863 – ROMAN GHOST.

Ghosts are not usually much talked of in Rome, but the *vox populi*, just now, is that the steps and corridors of St. Peter's, and the arcades on the sides of the sacristy towards Santa Marta, are haunted by a recently defunct canon of the Church, named Azocchi, who appears, with breviary in hand; "And mutters his prayer in the midnight air," to the great consternation of the Papal gendarmes and French sentries, who mount guard every night around the Vatican basilica. The *canonico* is said also have paid startling midnight visits to some of his brethren in the chapter, requesting the aid of their prayers. Parties of credulous and incredulous persons have been watching for the ghost at a respectful distance for several nights; some say they have seen him, and some not; but it is now stated that he will walk no more on earth, as the Pope, informed of his restlessness has celebrated an especial mass for the eternal rest of his soul.

*Dublin Evening Mail.*

# 1863 – THE GHOST AT HULL.

On Saturday last, a very extraordinary case in connection with the Ghost was investigated by the Hull Stipendiary Magistrate, at the Police Court, a Jew, named Marcus Bibbero, being brought up on warrant, charged with having assaulted and used threats to Mr. McGonigle, reporter of the *Eastern Counties Herald*, at Hull. The facts appear to be as follows:-

About ten days ago, the ghost illusion was announced to be performed at the Literary and Philosophical Hall, Hull, and on the night of the first representation there was a very large audience assembled. The Ghost, however, was a failure, and great dissatisfaction was expressed at the defendant, who was one of the men who brought the entertainment to Hull. The press took the matter up, and Mr. McGonigle wrote a severe criticism in the *Eastern Counties Herald* upon the exhibition, and this was followed by one in the *Hull Packet* written by Mr. T. D. Kendall, the sub-editor.

A few evenings ago both Mr. Kendall and Mr. McGonigle were at the entertainment, and the defendant having got the knowledge they were two of the gentlemen who had so severely criticised his entertainment, ordered them both out of the room, tore Mr. Kendall's coat, struck him over the eye and nose, and used some extraordinary threats to what would do for the future. On Thursday evening last, Mr. McGonigle was going into the Queen's Theatre, when he was met by the defendant and others, and the defendant struck him such a violent blow upon the face that he was covered with blood, and had to be taken home in a cab insensible. The defendant said he would make the Hull reporters so that they would never write such criticisms again.

For this the defendant was taken into custody, and the case was partly investigated at the Hull Police Court on Saturday, Mr. McGonigle and Mr. Kendall deposing that the defendant had threatened to take their lives in consequence of the adverse criticisms which they, in discharging their duty to the public, had thought fit to pass upon the defendant's entertainment. The case was remanded.

It transpired in the course of the case that when Mr. McGonigle was picked up at the theatre there were two clean cuts in his coat back, as there had been an attempt to stab him, but the knife had not penetrated farther than the coat.

*Leeds Mercury.*

# 1863 – THE LONDON GHOST CLUB.

The London correspondent of the Belfast News Letter writes:-

You have heard, of course, of the "Ghost Club." If you have not, you may perhaps desire to know something of its proceedings. I myself own up to taking great interest in the subject, as I have long been of opinion that a tete-a-tete with a ghost would be not only a great achievement to relate over wine and walnuts after dinner, but a rare intellectual treat, provided the ghost was a conversational one, that did not mind being communicative to a sympathising friend.

Some time ago, I myself suggested the originating of some eclectic body, who would take the trouble and incur the ridicule of endeavouring, in a reasonable manner, to solve the problem involved in what is commonly called "a haunted house." It is an undoubted fact that there are tenements which suffer in reputation because mysterious noises are heard in them, and that the landlords cannot get tenants to reside in them.

I myself know a case in point. An old gentleman who has arrived at an age to pooh-pooh ghosts, and spirit rapping, and everything of the sort, lately saw a house to let at De Bouvour (one of the northern suburbs of the metropolis), which he believed would suit him. He accordingly made inquiries about it, but was warned that it was "haunted." "Oh, stuff and nonsense," was his rejoinder, and he hired the house for a year. I do not intend to anticipate an interesting page in the journal of the "Ghost Club" by telling you what happened in the house in question; but this I may state, that the strong minded old gentleman who spoke so valorously and contemptuously of ghosts and their belongings was very soon compelled to abandon the dwelling, and now

deplores the expense to which he was put in moving into it and adapting his household gods to its requirements.

The club proposes to enter seriously upon the consideration of this undeveloped field of speculation. It starts with certain landmarks to guide it, which may be described as of two kinds. There is first the vague, but general, admission in the truth of the assertion of the melancholy Dane, that there is more in this world than is dreamt of in our philosophy; and next, there are not only well-authenticated accounts of apparitions, but there remains the material evidence of our immaterial presence in the lonely and deserted dwellings which exist in almost every town, city, and suburb in the kingdom.

The Ghost Club is composed of gentlemen of education, social position, and means, who are quite prepared to incur the expense, and, if need be, the ridicule which may result from their labours. I am not permitted, as a member of the supernatural exploring fraternity, to reveal the machinery by which they hope to detect fraud or to discover truth, much less am I disposed by premature revelations to defeat the object of legitimate inquiry. All, therefore, which I am at liberty at present to state is, that the club is a bona fide undertaking, and that its members are not supposed to be believers in ghosts, simply because they wish to investigate a subject which has engrossed the attention and baffled the ingenuity of the most philosophic minds in all ages of the world's history, and with respect to which certain facts and circumstances exist which are not at present susceptible of explanation. Beyond this admission the club is not prepared to go at present. It is now in negotiation with the owners of certain premises which have the reputation of being "haunted," and in the fullness of time the public will, no doubt, learn what success has attended its efforts.

*Ayrshire Express.*

# 1863 – THE MODERN GHOST.

We live in a remarkably strange and wonderfully sharp age. There was a time when English people believed most tenaciously and generally in the power and appearance of agents from "the other world" – in spirits, ghosts, bogies, and fifty other kinds of nocturnal visitors. Then every old sequestered room had its noises and bloodstains; every ancient castle its headless lady; every churchyard its uneasy sepulchral occupant, dressed in an everlasting white sheet; every dark lane its spectre; every moor its warlock. But all such illusions and mirages have passed away, along with that era of superstition which gave them birth; and now people can only come at those spectres, which were once so plentiful, by the aid of elaborate mechanism, and can only get a transient view of those curious immaterial beings, which were once common property, after much elbowing and crushing and monetary remuneration. "Ghosts" have now to be paid for, and when everything has been done we can only obtain "artificial" ones!

How the times change! And what a volume of material for reflection there is in this one solitary fact that people have to down with their money, now-a-days, if they wish to see even the shade of a ghost's shadow in the form of a scientific phantom, which they know to be a deception and an optical chimera! For a considerable period there has been a sort of "rage" in London and some of our provincial towns for artificial ghosts.

And at last we have got one of the representatives of the invisible land in Preston. Mr. Sefton, the manager of the Theatre Royal, recently entered into arrangements – how coolly and how facetiously horrible the words sound – for the production in Preston of a ghost. And this week we have had nightly, upon the boards of the establishment named, a being of that intangible genus. The dramas in which the ghost has figured have not been very good ones, so far as regards histrionic power, but the phantom, which they served to eliminate has been excellent in all its positions and developments.

Artificial phantoms and spirit "manifestations" – indeed we are very dubious as to whether there were ever any of the real sort – have long had a place in occult science. The Egyptian priesthood were capable of dodging the people with invisible agents and the managers of that goodly temple of humbug at Delphos "knew a thing or two" in the same line. In the middle ages the alchemists, the sorcerers, and those who "sold" themselves to that famous gentleman, who presides "where pepper grows," had a hand in the same thing. But all their work meant trickery and superstition. The ghostly manifestations of today are innocent illusions, calculated to pleasantly deceive us – scientific curiosities adapted for the express purpose of harmlessly gammoning us.

A brief description of the mode in which such "ghosts" as those now exhibited are "manufactured" may not be out of place. Messrs. Dircks and Pepper claim to be the inventors – but they are simply the resuscitators on a more finished scale – of the ghost. Particulars of the whole affair were given three hundred years ago, in a book called "Natural Magick," written by a quaint character, named John Baptista de Porta.

In those theatres where it is exhibited the arrangements require, in addition to the regular "boards," a second or subsidiary stage, at a lower level than that ordinarily used. It is hidden from the audience so far as direct vision is concerned. The second stage in the rear is intensely illuminated, and is capable of being rendered dark instantaneously, or by degrees, while the front stage and body of the theatre remain with either a subdued light – as is generally the case – or a full one. A massive screen of glass is placed at the rear of the ordinary stage and immediately before the second one. The audience cannot, except when very near, or on one side of the boxes, up to the stage, see anything of the screen. They simply observe the actors through it, as if no obstruction was before them. The glass serves to show them an image of the actors on the hidden stage, when illuminated; when not illuminated, nothing is visible in the quarter named. The screen is fixed in a frame, and can be easily removed. The person or object corresponding with the phantom is on one side, quite out of sight of the audience, and immediately in front of a piano-convex lens, capable of intense illumination. As soon as the light is focussed, the form of whatever it rests upon is reflected forward past a lateral transparency, behind the glass screen, and fronting the second stage The ghost scenes represented at our Theatre, this week, have been well executed in almost every particular, and have wonderfully gratified the curious, and those fond of strange appearances and weird manifestations.

The apparatus has sometimes reflected, after the fashion of ghostdom, a "murdered" lover, sometimes the victim of a dark tragic conspiracy, and, at other times, beautiful groups of departed spirits and fair friends – appearing, no one knew how, and when occasion required it, vanishing into impalpable air, and leaving nothing behind them but the bare paintings and screens. After the pieces in which the phantom scenes were introduced, burlesques, farces, &c., were given.

*Preston Chronicle.*

---

# 1864 – THE DAVENPORT SEANCES.

We will not be far wrong if we describe the audiences that will be present at the Davenport séances as being composed of persons who have more money than wit. We do not mean that they will be persons credulous enough to believe that what they will see will be "spiritual manifestations," experiments in "preternatural philosophy," or "runibulations of material things," each which the performances of the Messrs. Davenport have been described to be, and described, too, not by themselves, at any rate directly, but by learned and scientific gentlemen in London, from whom something of the logician's art, if not of common sense, might have been expected.

We do not suppose that the persons forming the Davenport audiences that will be collected together in this town, will all be in expectation of being shown something from the spiritual world. But we do think they will be paying dearly for the privilege of seeing whatever there will be to be seen. We have not ourselves been present at a Davenport séance, but we have read the reports of them that have been published; and we have not learned in them of anything which the Davenports do that does not bear all the appearance of conjuring, or juggling. The Davenports are, in fact, we believe, prestidigitators, and nothing more. They are clever, no doubt; the term is one of comparison but it does not appear that they are one whit more clever than their contemporaries.

Their séances are each composed of two parts. In the first, they submit to be bound with cords, and made fast in a cupboard, in which some musical instruments are also placed; and, in a few moments afterwards, music is heard, apparently issuing from the cupboard, articles are ejected from the door, and hands are exhibited from the top. The "manifestations" having ceased, the Brothers are seen in the cupboard, bound with cords, as at first.

Now, it has been noticed that the cabinet used in London is of a peculiar construction; it has three doors, a seat, and a small curtained opening; and it is evident that whoever designed it must have known beforehand what was to occur in it, and from this we are led to conclude that the results are due simply to clever mechanical contrivances. It has been announced, however, that the cabinet to be used at the Newcastle séances is to be provided by a gentleman who is not connected, much less in collusion, with the Davenports, and who will be present at the séances with the view of testing the reality of the "manifestations," and of ascertaining, if possible, their real nature. We will therefore say no more of the cabinet in which the operators work until we see whether the results produced in their own, can also be produced in the cabinet that will be provided for them; only let the audience see that whichever cabinet be used, it be thoroughly isolated. In asking this, they will be asking more than what the operators profess to give; because, in the opening remarks of Dr. Ferguson, who has charge of them, it is stated that the cabinet is isolated or insulated. It has been noticed, however, that only a partial isolation is made; the two extreme feet of the cabinet are placed in glass tumblers, but the central pair are not so placed.

Of the "manifestations" themselves that take place in the cabinet, we can only say that they are all very ordinary conjuration tricks, not by any means new, and of which the Davenports not even enjoy a monopoly. The rope tying is both old and vulgar. It is known and practised in various parts of the world; and a winter or two ago was publicly performed on the stage of the Newcastle Theatre. The other portions of the cabinet manifestations are likewise being performed at the present time by professional prestidigitators in London and elsewhere.

The difference between other performers and the Messrs. Davenport is that the former honestly avow that their results are produced by conjuring, deception, and humbug, while the Davenports attribute theirs to spiritual agency. We are aware that the Brothers have a written letter, in which they disavow spiritualism in connection with their acts, and declare that they do not know how the results are produced. But by others of the party, five in number, who have so considerately come all the way from America to exhibit these wonders to the Britishers, the character of "spiritual manifestations," "passive agency," and "preternatural philosophy," has been claimed for the acts of the Davenports, without the claim being repudiated by the Brothers. The acts of their colleagues, therefore, being done with a common purpose, have become the acts of the Davenports; and the operators themselves have thus, by their agents, claimed spiritual power. We are sorry for this, because if it be, as we think, that the results produced are no more than ordinary conjuring, the Brothers must know this, and yet at the same time have lent themselves to a deception upon the public.

We do not say that they ought to have disclosed the secrets of their art. They are making a very excellent thing of it. They are drawing the guineas from the pockets of John Bull in great numbers, and with true Yankee acuteness. They would cease to "draw" were they to explain the mode in which they produce the effects or they were to disavow spiritual agency. Because it is not the tricks themselves that have attracted attention. It the pretence of spiritual agency that has attracted attention to the tricks. The tricks themselves have long since become stale. They are the same over and over again; and the public has long since tired of them. But the assurance that they are done by means of "preternatural philosophy," and "spiritualism," what has obtained for the Brothers Davenport greater attention than is being received by the ordinary prestidigitators, who, either too honest to think of "spiritualism," or too "slow" to adopt it, are content to let their performances stand or fall by their intrinsic merits, and do not seek to gain guineas by means of quackery, found amongst prestidigitators, as amongst all other professionals, and by pretending to be a medium of communication between a spirit world and mortality.

We do not blame the Davenports for following their profession. It is one of the many by which men live; and we have no objection that those who like to see conjuration tricks performed should pay for the pleasure which the sight affords them. The Brothers Davenport are making their spectators—if such a term can be used in relation to people who are kept in the dark during one part of the séance and out of sight in another—pay pretty smartly and, if the people choose to be mulcted, it is their own affair. Only they are paying a very exorbitant rate for very ordinary conjuring, and can have the same gratification elsewhere at a very much less cost and, as regards the Davenports themselves, they are lending themselves to parties who are aiding in deceiving the public by pretences about spiritual agency which does not exist.

Because, obviously, there is nothing spiritual either in the results produced or in the agency by which they are produced. We all believe, of course, that there is a world of spirits. Without bringing in the Revelation of the Christian religion, we know there is a spirit world, because of many well authenticated cases of spiritual manifestations. No doubt, then, there are spirits; but will any man of sense believe that they occupy themselves in such absurd acts as showing hands and arms through a hole in a cupboard; in making disagreeable attempts to play "Dandy Jim," or the "negro melody," whichever it may be, that is always "played" upon the fiddle at the Davenport séances; in throwing off persons' coats, and investing others with them, or throwing them over the nearest chandelier; or, again, in making fiddles and tambourines, daubed with phosphorus, travel about a dark room.

There may be Pucks and Ariels amongst the spirits; but does any person of ordinary intellect believe that they do anything as absurd and mischievous as these Davenport spirits are reported to do? Or does anybody believe that, if these results are really produced by spiritual agency, and that spirits really occupy themselves absurdly as they are represented, that their occupation, or amusement, whichever it be, is of so monotonous a nature as that described, and that they never attempt any other amusement than rubbing fiddles and tambourines with phosphorus, like no other tune than "Dandy Jim," and find no other relief from weariness than in changing the outer garments of one or two mortals, who are specially favoured in being the mediums of communication between themselves and the world?

Talk about disbelieving the miracles related in the Scriptures, and about scepticism respecting a Supreme Being, such as that therein revealed to us, why, if any person believes that these ridiculous pranks of the Davenports are the results of spiritual agency, he believes things infinitely more incredulous than any related in the Scriptures, even when viewed by the light of natural philosophy only, and is credulous enough to take rank with Miss Martineau and her disciples, who believe in that extraordinary story about the cow. If these Davenport results were really produced by spiritual agency, is it not likely that the results would be different at every manifestation, and that, instead of everybody knowing what was coming, nobody would know, and everybody would be surprised at the novelty of each fresh manifestation?

We pronounce, then, against the assertion that these results are due to spiritualism or to any preternatural agency. We say they are due to conjuring, and to conjuring that is not even exceedingly clever. We say so because of the trivial nature of the results themselves, because of the monotonous sameness which also marks them, and because of the concealment employed to the mode in which the results are produced. Concealment of the operators from the sight of the audience when the results are to be exhibited from the cupboard, and darkness to hide the operators when the results in the second part of the séance are to be produced, are absolutely necessary, so far as we have yet heard, to the production of these results.

Now, if the Davenports, or those with whom they are acting, really believe that spiritual agency is engaged, let the matter be tested, by the audience being allowed to see all that is to be seen, and by being allowed to use their, eyes. Instead of darkness, let there be light; and let the audience see how the Davenports and their assistants operate to produce the results which are seen to emanate from the cabinet. Let there be no darkness, no deception, no concealment; but let everything be done openly and in the sight of the audience. In asking that these tests should be applied to the alleged spiritualism, and in asking that these means of investigation should be allowed to the audience, we do not ask anything unreasonable. The results produced are announced as "spiritual manifestations;" and if they are really what they are thus represented to be, there can be no harm to anyone, not even to Messrs. Davenport, in being allowed to see the way in which these cute young gentlemen cause the spirits to act.

If we should all see the mode in which they call spirits from the vast deep, probably not one of us would be able successfully to imitate the call. The secret, if secret there be, which makes these American youths the medium of spiritual communication would probably still be safe in the Brothers' keeping; though it is possible that humanity might be blessed with the discovery of how to have spirits at its call. If spirits really do operate in the way described, they will so operate in the light as well as in darkness. By all means, then, let us have a thorough investigation, and all the means necessary for it, of which means light, sight, and touch are the essentials; and then, the Davenports declare that they themselves know not how the results are produced, we may help them to make the discovery.

*Newcastle Journal.*

# 1864 – THE HAUNTED HALL.

"All the village said Folly Hall was haunted; therefore, as there was such an unanimity of opinion, and as so many people had been "frightened to death," but who had, nevertheless, lived to relate the tale, there could be no reasonable doubt in the village mind that it was haunted; still, I had my own, and by no means private, opinion on the subject, and as I never did, and never intend to, believe in ghosts, I treated the legend with the contempt it deserves, and expressed a readiness to pass a night within the haunted walls of Folly Hall.

Folly Hall —a queer name, by-the-bye, probably derived from some one of its unfortunate and defunct lords – was (and perhaps now is) in the county of H___shire; and as I had seen an advertisement in "Jupiter," intimating that Folly Hall with its Manor was to be sold by private contract, with all the usual conveniences and advantages – application to be made at "Welcome Inn," Tintwhistle, H___shire, I decided upon inspecting it.

Three hours ride brought me into the above-named village, and, almost frozen to an icicle, I made straight for "Welcome Inn"—where, if it belled not its enticing sign, I intended to pass the night. "Welcome Inn" was simply an inn; nothing more nor less—neither hovel nor hotel, but precisely what it pretended to be—an inn.

In a few words I stated to Boniface my wishes (I have forgotten his name, therefore the reader will pardon this threadbare cognomen). He eyed me attentively from the crown of my hat downwards, ere condescended to answer my inquiries. When at length he did speak, it was a kind of confidential half-whisper—"Don't you buy it, sir, its haunted!—ask anybody, sir! —all the village say it's haunted."

"Oh, is it? Then that very reason will induce me to purchase it," I replied, which drew a faint smile from mine host -a smile of pity, mischief, and self-satisfaction combined.

While still under the benign influence of this smile, a third party entered the little parlour, and he said the Hall was haunted! Presently the village "shepherd," a gentleman with a thin body and a thinner nose, a dirty-white neck cloth, and a brown-black suit, walked in, with a "God bless me, how cold it is – what a comfortable fire!" and he expressed his belief that the Hall was haunted! Well, it seemed as the landlord had said, that everybody in the village believed the Hall to be in possession of spirits more spiritual than his own.

After I had thawed myself by the parlour fire, and welcomed a welcome supper from the kitchen of "Welcome Inn"—during which time the company had considerably augmented—I thus addressed the superstitious representatives of a superstitious village:-

"My friends, it is my intention to pass this night in Folly Hall, which is reported to be haunted (signs of surprise and dismay)—I say reported, because I do not believe in ghosts! — (murmurs of disapprobation and doubt)—and I intend proving that fact to one and all of you; if any one present be inclined to accompany me (great shaking of heads)—he will doubtless be satisfied that I speak the truth, and although I have not heard the character of your local phantom described, I may venture to assert that before this time tomorrow, the ghost shall be laid, you undeceived, and the whole mystery explained—if mystery there is. (Decided signs of non-intervention.) Now, has anyone the courage to accompany me?" (Shepherd essays to speak, but, upon second thoughts, holds his peace.) "Has any person present," I reiterated, in a contemptuous tone of voice, "the courage to pass the night with me in Folly Hall?" (Shepherd again tries to look bold and fearless, but suddenly remembers that he has a poor sick woman to visit—exit Shepherd!) "Then, my friends, I will go alone."

Whereupon I rang the bell, and ordered a carpet bag, and the key of the Hall door. The landlord looked rather blank and incredulous, insinuating that it was past eight o'clock, and that he could accommodate me with a "well-aired bed." In a few words I explained how my challenge had been rejected, expressed my contempt for his village cronies, and informed him that I had determined on venturing alone. Seeing that I was in earnest, and would not be persuaded into a "well-aired bed," he handed me the key – a huge, rusty, Brobdingnagian specimen of a key.

Some little difficulty here arose as to who should carry my "traps" to the Hall; the "boots" was obviously reluctant, and pleaded, as an excuse, at least three days' work, to be accomplished in as many hours; but, after a little persuasion, and the more potent promise of an extravagant "tip," I overruled his fears, and prevailed upon him to shoulder my "effects."

When the company found that I was really in earnest, they expressed great admiration for my pluck, and a charitable wish that I should not come to harm, or harm come to me.

"The ghost carries a large stick, guv'nor," said a stout farmer.

"Shall I lend yer honour a blunderbuss?" inquired another.

"Better not go at all, while you can get a good bed here," suggested a little timid looking man, in red plush breeches; upon which he received a wink of approval from the host—a wink which contained a pot of beer at the very least!

I wished them all goodnight, and sallied forth on my errand of discovery.

It was a most beautiful December night, clear, cold, and frosty, while the moon shed such beams of silvery light upon all objects within the compass of her rays, that a prudent ghost would not have ventured forth from his haunt for fear of detection! All around was calm and quiet. All things seemed to be taking a rest beneath the "brooding wings of Heaven."

As we approached the vicinity of Folly Hall, "boots" began to show signs of uneasiness; which symptoms were, in my humble judgment, in nowise dispelled by his first humming some village melody, and afterwards whistling ; I made several attempts to draw him into conversation, with the view of learning something more of His Ghostship, but all I could gather was that several gentlemen, who, like myself, had been tempted to purchase the estate from its cheapness, had never slumbered a second time beneath the ancient roof, and that the "oldest inhabitant" of the village never remembered when it was habitually used as a dwelling house; and, furthermore, it was whispered that the lodge keeper had made some secret compact with the devil, which protected him from the ghost's influence so long as the Hall should remain uninhabited! And did the simple villagers believe this tale?—Of course they did—most of them!— Poor, simple, ingenuous, untutored rustics, who could believe what they had not seen, but yet would reject so many facts which were actually patent to their vision!

We now stood before the high brick wall which bounded the orchard. The "boots," after leading me to the door of the lodge, by a significant look, intimated that his mission was accomplished; therefore I "tipped" him, and he bade me adieu, and vanished, probably fearful that I should want him to carry my luggage further.

I had sent a messenger to the lodge keeper early in the evening. Informing him of my intended visit, and with a request that he would kindle a fire in the room usually occupied by the ghost.

It was now near nine o'clock; so I had three long hours to endure before I had my séance, as ghosts very rarely become visible to the vulgar gaze before the hour of midnight.

I pulled the long wooden bell handle—a sonorous sound tolled forth, like that of a church dead bell, awakening echoes for at least a mile round. After a drawing back of rusty sounding bolts, and rattling of chains, the gate shook, and strained, and creaked—and opened. A tall, lean, white visaged, bony, shabby-looking, shoeless, and-by-no-means prepossessing individual stood before me. A pair of fiery eyes stared at me for a moment. The individual at length inquired, in a strange, hollow voice, if I was the "person" who wished to see the ghost? I replied, somewhat tartly,— for one does not like to be called a "person"—that I wanted to see the Hall, and its ghost to boot, for aught I cared, and that if he would condescend to conduct me to the room frequented by the ghost, I should feel obliged.

"If you'll wait while I put on my boots. I'll show you in. Yon is the room in which I have lit a fire," he replied, pointing down an avenue of poplars which bordered the central path to a large, antique-looking window, through which I caught the faint glow of the fire within.

"Is the interior of the Hall in good repair?" I inquired.

"No; very bad," was the laconic answer.

"How long is it since it was last inhabited?"

"Don't know—not since I've been here, anyhow."

"How long might that be?"

"Well old Chiggins, the lawyer down the village, put me in ten year ago come Christmas, directly after the lawsuit ended."

"Lawsuit! Has the ownership of the property been disputed then?"

"Oh yes, years and years ago, but I believe it's all settled now."

By this time he had put on his boots, and was ready to accompany me; and though I had mentally resolved not to purchase a property whose owner was not definitely known, I determined to penetrate, if possible, the mystery of the ghost.

Certainly, a place more fitted for the haunt of a ghost could not have been found than Folly Hall. It was built in the Tudor style of architecture, and was green and crumbling with age; two or three rain-washed, battered statues adorned the corners of the building, and two weather-beaten, mane less passant lions (whose great age explained the loss of their manes) guarded a flight of stone steps, slippery and worn, leading up to the Hall door.

As soon as we had arrived at the door, my mysterious looking guide applied a huge rusty key to the keyhole (the duplicate of that which mine host of the "Welcome" had given me), and, after great exertion, succeeded in shooting the bolt. We were now in a broad corridor paved with diamonds of black and white marble. I could not repress a cold shiver as I entered this deserted habitation of the great, clammy with damp and reeking with dew, and thought of the many and various scenes those oaken panels could disclose, were they endowed with animation.

I had little time for reflection, however, it was broken by the keeper's "This way, sir," as he ushered me into a lofty room, lined with carved panels from celling to floor. In the chimney, resting on the dog-irons, a heap of damp wood was struggling to blaze, sending forth volumes of white smoke. Altogether nothing could have been more uninviting than the aspect of the chamber in which I found myself located. I turned to speak to my companion but he had vanished, and I was alone—alone in the Haunted Hall!

Over the gigantic chimney piece—which was of a very handsomely carved walnut wood—depended a large, half-length portrait of Oliver Cromwell in his armour; the frame, which had once been gilt, was now of a dark brown tint, but the likeness, itself, was a good one of His Protectorship. I could not help gazing at it; as I looked, the eyes appeared to follow my every movement; if I stood in front of the painting they stared at me; if I went on one side, they glanced at me; if I went to the other side, they still gazed earnestly at me! Now, I had heard of mysterious pictures, the heads of which were represented as possessing the eccentric power of transmogrifying themselves into animated heads, and frightening innocent people by unfolding some midnight tale of horror, or recreating themselves with pipes and punch, and then again hanging themselves up on the wall. I say I had heard, or read, of such pictures, and only smiled to myself when I thought what a very suitable picture was this one of Cromwell, with its peculiar eyes, to endow with some such (to the superstitious) unpleasing faculty! Casting my eyes round the room, I saw nothing else at all likely to cause nightmare; so, after poking up the logs and trimming up the oil lamp which had been left me, I threw on an additional log, and, placing my dram-bottle on the table, arranged myself as comfortably as possible in a great leathern armchair which stood by the fire place.

It was a bitterly cold night – I could scarcely keep myself warm, even though a fire was blazing not two feet from my chair, and a thick woollen rug was wrapped around my shoulders.

I took a long pull at the "needful," and fell to picturing hotly-contested battles in the glowing embers before me.

Two hours had I sat thus, when I began to doze, and the fire to burn low, until only one small flickering flame occasionally darted up, and, to add to the impending darkness my lamp had turned obstinate, and would scarcely burn – to the fire I could not add, because the lazy keeper had left no "store" for the night, and the light I could not trim, on account of the same "unworthy" having left the cotton short, and half-filled the lamp with water. Need we wonder then, that at length, both fire light and lamp expired, and I was left in almost complete darkness!

This aroused my slumbering senses, so that I gazed for some time at glowing, though not blazing, embers. But sleep shortly overcame me, and I was lost in dreams – weird and horrid dreams which aroused me again.

Once more I began to doze, when I was awoke by the jarring of the Hall door, as if somebody had closed it; next, a most deafening sound greeted my ears – a sound as though a dozen chain cables were being drawn vigorously down the stairs! My first impulse was to spring to the door, dash out into the hall, and discover the impostors—(for even at that awful moment I scorned the idea of supernatural influence) but upon a moment's consideration, I deemed it more prudent to remain quiet, and patiently watch the course of events.

I do not for a moment deny that I was startled, but as to imputing the sound to any superhuman cause, nothing was further from my mind.

I had not sat quiet for more than five minutes before I heard a noise as if some person were carefully and slowly approaching my door. This put me upon the alert. I heard the door handle turn -somebody was with me in the room but I could see nothing; I strained my eyes to pierce the darkness, but to no purpose. Next, the intruder drew to the fire place. For a moment all was again as death; I scarcely breathed—my brain seemed on fire with prolonged suspense—the minutes seemed hours to me. Knowing, as I did, that some creature was within three or four feet of me, and in the dark, who would not to say the least, have felt awkward?

My eyes glanced above the mantelpiece where the picture of Cromwell hung. To my utter astonishment two small circles of blue undulating flame, about the size of sixpences, darted out from the wall, brilliantly for some minutes, and then gradually died away. Well, this was strange! I remembered the peculiarity of the Protector's eyes, but had observed nothing luminous in them. Moreover, a pair of hands, similarly illuminated, had come at the same instant down from the eyes, and travelled to the handle of the room door, opened it, and disappeared!

Once more stories of haunted rooms and pictures returned vividly to memory, but were instantly banished, for it struck me that I was the victim of some trickery. Yes, that was it!—some miserable attempt to delude my ideas, and bar me from purchasing the estate. With these thoughts I felt as easy and comfortable (with the exception that I was very cold) as though I were seated in my own cosy study at Liverpool.

After this singular ocular demonstration on the part of His Protectorship, the "cause" of the "effect" beat a hasty but stealthy retreat through the Hall door. I flew to the window, gently pulled down the shutter, and there, in the pale bright moonlight, was revealed the ghost!—a flesh, bone, and blood ghost! – quietly making off with my carpet bag which he placed under his arm, and without so much as casting a parting glance at the Hall, strolled down the avenue of poplars—the Lodge keeper.

Once more I had triumphed over superstition!

A very few minutes sufficed to gather my rug around me, and follow in the ghostly footsteps of my late visitor, and the track of my departed bag! I reached the lodge, the door of which was ajar, and saw the solitary inmate in the act of washing from his hands the phosphorus which had so lately been employed in brightening Cromwell's eyes! The mystery of the picture and the illuminated hands was explained! The man turned his head, and beheld me on the threshold of the door, —his eyes gleamed like meteors—the expression of his face was most horrible. One only conviction thrust itself upon my mind – the man was a rogue!

His countenance changed, he dropped on his knees before me, and said imploringly, "For God sake sir, don't expose me. I've lived here ten year, and the ghost of the picture at the Hall I like better than the ghosts of paupers in the House. (He meant the workhouse, whence he came to take care of the Hall.) Here is your bag, sir; take it, take it, but have mercy on me."

My good nature, I am sorry to say, overcame my honesty. I did not expose him. I did not intend to purchase the Hall. So I left him in quiet possession, as I believe he remains to this day.

The early train conveyed me back to Liverpool; and the theory of ghosts, spirit rapping, and the whole catalogue of supernatural phenomena was forever banished from my creed.

At the conclusion of the paper, I looked up, expecting a stray compliment for my pains. Gentle reader, what think you I beheld? Why, daylight faintly struggling through the chinks of the shutters, and all guests (save the young fellow who could edit) fast asleep! I felt nettled, a sort of rising indignation was in my breast, but the hushed voice of my literary friend sounded, in accents of earnest entreaty, in my ear, begging of me to present the MS. to him—he fondly hoping someday to make it the substance of a work, which he would "edit." Poor youth, he died before another Christmas came round, and his last words expressed a hope that I would publish the MS. I promised to do so; how far I have fulfilled that promise, the patient reader already knows. And now, my pleasant task being accomplished, I have but one more sentence to add, which is to heartily wish a Happy New Year to the reader.

*The Enniscorthy News and County of Wexford Advertiser.*

———◦◉◦———

# 1864 – TWO SPIRIT MEDIUMS IN LONDON.

A correspondent of the Glasgow Herald, who is vouched for by the editor as "a gentleman holding a prominent station in Glasgow," gives an account of two visits he paid to certain so-called spirit mediums in London, and the result.

My friends directed me to a Mr. Conklin, 25, Cecil Street, Strand, who had recently arrived from America, and who was stated to have made many spiritual revelations to Mr. Lincoln, President of the Federal States. I accordingly waited upon that gentleman, and arranged for a séance at my friend's house that same evening at seven o'clock. He kept his appointment precisely, and

immediately on entering the drawing room, without exchanging salutations with anyone, laid his hands upon the table, and invoked the appearance of the spirits. I feel that it would be trifling to detail at length the silly and contemptible attempts, made by Mr. Conklin to guess the names which my friend and myself had written down, and the equally futile attempts to give true and correct answers to our questions. The only manifestation he professed to have made that evening was to move the table—a drawing room one, of the ordinary size. Certainly he did this in a very clever way by the aid of his fingers and toes, but when one of our party was appointed specially to watch his movements under the table, I assure you that it suddenly became a very quiet, well-behaved table, and did not move a single inch.

I may dismiss Mr. Conklin stating that he is what is called a writing medium, and his only ingenuity appeared to consist in being able to write backwards. This may be a difficult accomplishment, but the possession of it is certainly no evidence that his hand is moved by spirits, as he alleges. While the company are writing out the names of the spirits they wish to converse with and the questions they wish answered, Mr. Conklin affects to keep his face covered with his hands; and if parties are silly enough to give him a glance at what they are writing, of course he will occasionally stumble upon a good guess.

Being anxious to exhaust the alleged evidence of these absurdities, I availed myself of the suggestion of some friends to wait upon Mrs. Marshall, of Upper King Street, who has the reputation of being one of the most powerful mediums. I found this lady at home, but as her dimensions are somewhat of the Daniel Lambert style, and rendered her transit a little difficult, I accepted her invitation, along with my friend, to have a séance in her own room. We accordingly sat down once, along with her niece—making a party of four, around a small, three-legged table.

At first everything looked suspicious; slight pulsations were felt in our hands as we placed them flat on the table, and then gradually increased to loud knocks. The table then commenced to move from side to side in a somewhat violent manner, and at length, in reply to Mrs. Marshall's question, three loud knocks were given upon the table, said to proceed from the spirits, to express their ability and willingness to answer all questions put to them. I was then confidently invited to write on a slip of paper the name of the spirit I wished to converse with. I retired to another table, and, taking care that no eye but my own should see a single letter, I wrote the name "King Radama," and, returning to the party, said, "Now, Mrs. Marshall, you appear very confident of your spiritual powers, and to show you my conviction of the absurdity of your profession, I will give you £20 if you simply inform this company the name which I have written upon this slip of paper which I hold in my hand."

Mrs. Marshall being what is called a "spelling medium," a sheet of paper with the letters of the alphabet was then placed upon the table, and I was requested to put my finger upon each letter, beginning at A and the spirit would spell the name by giving three raps or knocks at each letter. I at once saw that the lady calculated upon the chance of my showing some little hesitation as I touched each letter of the name, and I confess I was ungallant enough to deceive the lady by showing just a shade of trepidation in touching the letters M A R Y. Mrs. Marshall accordingly guessed "Mary." I tried a similar feat with the name Jessie, and I need not add that King Radama did not make his appearance, as the "mediums" did not even know his name to call him.

In Mrs. Marshall's séance, as in Mr. Conklin's, the only manifestation alleged to have been made was the table rapping and turning, and, of course, there will always be a number of people silly and credulous enough to believe the grossest absurdities upon such unsatisfactory evidence. For my own part, I told the lady mediums plainly that so long as they sat close to the table, half encircling it with their dresses, I would not attach the slightest importance either to the rapping or motion of the table. As an evidence of how guarded we must be in testing evidence of this description, I may mention that while in the middle of our séance with Mrs. Marshall, a gentleman of most respectable appearance and manners called, and, professing to be simply desirous like ourselves to elicit the truth, begged to be allowed to join my friend and myself at the table. I politely told him I could allow no stranger to take part in our investigations; and without coming to the certain conclusion that he designed to act as a confederate with the mediums, it will be at once apparent how easily some people might be imposed upon by such a combination.

From the experience above narrated, I have come to two conclusions: 1st:- That public professional mediums are deceivers. 2nd:- That believers in them are credulous fools.

To show that I do not make these statements unadvisedly, I hereby offer: 1st. to pay the sum of £100 to any medium in the world who will show me table rising in the air without material aid. 2. To pay the sum of £100 to any medium who will truly and correctly answer a question which I will ask; or simply state the question itself which I will write on a slip of paper and seal up in an envelope.

*Lancashire General Advertiser.*

———— ·◉· ————

# 1867 – A GHOST IN WOBURN SQUARE.

It has been said that the ghosts as well as the fairies of olden time have ceased to "walk" this lower earth in consequence of the "schoolmaster being abroad." It is doubtful whether a schoolboy, in passing through a lone churchyard at midnight, would now, despite the statement of the poet, whistle a single bar "to keep his courage up." Indeed, so incredulous have even the vulgar classes become that the rumour of the ghost of a "woman in white" haunting nightly the stunted groves of Woburn Square, instead of causing them to be shunned by terror-stricken passers-by, induced crowds of persons to go thither nightly last week to see the phenomenon. The *Lancet* gives a simple explanation of the cause of the excitement. The patch of light which the credulous have magnified into a phantom woman in white is produced by the reflection of a gas lamp passing through a gap in the bushes. Our medical contemporary suggests that if the lamp were temporarily extinguished the ghost would disappear.

*Illustrated Times.*

———— ·◉· ————

# 1867 – FAMILY GHOSTS.

What is the reason why ghost stories have a peculiar charm at this period of the year? Is it that the long nights naturally recall our thoughts to the shadowy beings of whom night is the peculiar time? Or is it that we want to increase the relish of the Christmas fireside by tinging our comfort with a little imaginative fear to make it more piquant? For if there was no fear —or suggestion of fear, at all events—even to minds thoroughly incredulous about ghost stories, there would be no pleasure in them. The lurking sentiment of awe is as much necessary to their enjoyment as the lurking sentiment of pain to the enjoyment of tragedy. You know that the tragedy is only a play, and you know that the ghost story is only a yarn. Nevertheless, the half-conscious coming and going of pain and fear, in both cases, is an indispensable element of the admiration and the joy.

I am going to deal on this occasion with a special class of ghost, and a class, let me tell you at once, of the highest respectability. There are ghosts and ghosts. We are not to deal just now with our plebeian apparition —your murdered misers, haunting old tumbledown places, and that kind of thing—but with spirits boasting the entree into the best houses in the kingdom. There are parvenus among them to be sure, but they are parvenus whom the highest people are obliged to receive—to receive, ay, and to treat with great respect into the bargain. They make themselves quite at home, indeed, and find their way to rooms in the highest mansions, where none but members of the family are in the habit of dwelling.

Family ghosts, I say, are a special class of ghost. Let me add that they are a modern class of ghost. I find no trace of the family proper among the ancients. Like family ghosts are essentially feudal —not classical. They belong to a life of castles in the country—to races living for generations surrounded by the same woods, dying in the same bedrooms, being buried in the same church vaults; in a kind of isolation throughout, which made the consciousness of common blood or kinmanship all the stronger. It is to this concentrated sort of existence, with all that it implies, that we must look for the germ of the particular belief under review. The family ghost belongs to the family as a family, though it is not necessarily seen only in certain places. Nevertheless, as the old families of Europe have generally lived most of their time at their principal seats, these seats have in most cases come to be considered the peculiar haunts of the family ghost.

The White Lady of the Hohenzollerns, for instance, has usually been talked of as loving to appear in Berlin. Her reputation had reached England as early at least as Charles the Second's time, for she is mentioned by Aubrey in his Miscellanies. "Also at Berlin," says that quaint old gossip, "when one shall die of the electoral house of Brandenberg, a woman dressed in white linen appears always to several, without speaking, or doing any harm, for several weeks before." The father of Frederick the Great fancied that he had seen this supernatural lady-in-waiting on one occasion; and her appearance was gossiped about in the newspapers during the revolution of 1848; but she has not, I believe, been heard of lately.

As the White Lady is associated with Berlin, so the little Red Man belongs to the Tuileries. The little Red Man—a fearful hunchback, with a squint, dressed in scarlet, and having a serpent for a cravat—is said by the tradition to show himself in the Tuileries before any calamity which may befall its masters. This legend is sure to live, for Beranger has based on it one of his best songs, "Le Petit Homme Rouge." With admirable philosophical humour, Beranger makes him appear in 1792, in sabots, singing the "Marseillaise;" and again during Charles the Tenth's reign in a big Jesuit's hat. There was an attempt to set going a story that Bonaparte had seen the malignant little hobgoblin in Egypt; but this never took root. The Little Red Man belongs to the Tuileries and the Bourbons.

In these two conspicuous instances, the apparitions portend disaster. And this is true of the vast majority of the apparitions which such legends record. Very commonly the family ghost has injuries done in a long past age to avenge; and he comes to predict calamity, because he loves the office. Thus, the Monk of the Byrons, as their descendant the poet tells, was wont to visit Newstead, for no good. He had been expelled by the Byrons at the Reformation from the abbey, and his spirit came to vex those who had succeeded his order. The wrongs of the Drummer of the Ogilvies, Earls of Airlie, in Scotland, are more strictly personal. Many generations ago he was murdered and flung out of the windows of their castle, with his head sticking in his drum; having been found, it is said, aspiring to the love of a daughter of the house. Ever since that time, his drum has been heard beating when misfortune has been impending over the race; and it is said that a lady visiting the family during the present generation, and ignorant of the tradition, heard him beating his tattoo while she was dressing for dinner, and startled her host at table by asking who his drummer was? A premature death in the family circle—so runs the story —followed this incident.

*Frome Times.*

---

# 1868 – A GHOST MYSTERY SOLVED.

A ghost mystery has been solved at Weston-Super-Mare. In a house in Alfred Street in that town strange noises had been heard, furniture displaced, and others of the vagaries practised in which disembodied persons are supposed to delight. A gentleman who had a desire to ascertain for himself what ghosts were really like, asked, and obtained permission to enter, and remained in the haunted chamber. As he was ascending the stairs a large tin pot was hurled at him by some invisible hand, and afterwards on entering the room he was assailed by hideous noises, followed by the falling through the skylight of a stone of considerable size. Starting from the room the would-be ghost-layer came upon and seized a youth, who, after some hesitation, admitted that he had been employed to throw the missiles, and that the other spiritual phenomena were produced by beating an old mop stick against the under part the staircase.

*Bridlington Free Press.*

## 1868 – HAUNTED HOUSE IN SOMERSETSHIRE.

The haunted house at Muchelney is one of those extraordinary cases which puzzle the scientific, furnish food to the superstitious, and excite the sneers of the supercilious and would-be-knowing. The farmhouse, an old substantial one, stands alone at the entrance to the village of Muchelney, about three miles from Langport. Its only occupants are Mr. Traves, his housekeeper, and a young servant girl. Soon after Christmas last a slight shock of an earthquake, as supposed, was felt in the neighbourhood, and since then the farmhouse has been the scene from time to time of noises and "manifestations."

The most common form is noise resembling at first the running of fingers over a hollow partition, or as if passing rapidly upstairs, and always ending abruptly with a kind of discharge, as loud as that of a rifle, but with no reverberation whatever – merely a dead thud – often followed successively kept at intervals for days together, and then becoming silent for weeks.

For some time the tin cover of a copper in the kitchen was wont to be thrown violently off upon the floor, and the bells about the house to be set ringing. But these are at present quiet, and the newest manifestation is in one of the passages, where a clock stands, with a table near, against the wall, and over it some bridle bits hung upon nails. About a fortnight since, during Mr. Traves's absence in the hayfield, the housekeeper and servants were terribly alarmed by the table being suddenly turned violently upside down, and the bits thrown off the nails upon which they were hung. The females immediately summoned Mr Traves, who came in, and expressing his determination to judge for himself, took a seat near the table and watched. He had not been seated five minutes ere the table was again suddenly dragged, as it were, along the floor, and dashed down.

We plainly saw the breakage which resulted, and heard the story from Mr. Traves's own mouth. It was only one of several stories of an equally startling nature. The mysterious part is that the walls are entirely unshaken and the floors undisturbed.

*Pulman's Weekly News.*

---

## 1868 – THE CHELSEA GHOST.

We have had Cock Lane Ghosts, Brompton Ghosts and Ghosts of every degree of character from which Chelsea hitherto has enjoyed immunity, but now we have a veritable Chelsea Ghost, at least so say the churchyard loungers of St. Luke's Chelsea, who declare that not his sable majesty but his spectral majesty doth walk in the witching hour.

We thought the last of the departed spirits had gone Home lately in the Chancery Court, but, no, it appears that to Chelsea was left the honour of the final parting, and so for some evenings past the neighbourhood of the above church have been quite in a consternation to see the "moving spirit clothed in white." It seems it was a very impatient ghost, who didn't choose to wait until "churchyard yawns and graves yield up their dead," for it travelled before its time, and at early eve, to the dismay and wonderment of scores of youths scarcely in their teens.

At length, after to a certain extent disturbing the neighbours from their propriety, his ghostship fell into the hands of Policeman, Y. Z., who, discovering it did not dissolve into thin air, straightway took the rambling phantom, not to the charnel house but to the Police Station. It was found, however, that the subtle spirit of this ambitious ghost was alcohol, but having been sufficiently careful in his nocturnal wanderings to keep without the meshes of the law he was set at liberty. The neighbourhood, however, is—or up to last evening—still "haunted" by the idle gossipers, all giving free scope to fertile imaginations, getting the Blues for their pains in the endeavour of those functionaries of peace moving them along.

Thus this ghost story, like all others of a similar character, the origin of which being a mysterious mystery, amounts to nothing.

*Chelsea News and General Advertiser.*

---

## 1868 – THE SOLUTION OF A GHOST ALARM.

A gentleman residing at Peckham Rye was recently troubled with a "ghost visitation" similar in character to that which startled an aged lady and her household in Kensington. No clue could be obtained to the mysterious rappings for some time, and as each night drew near the female inmates of the "haunted house" gave themselves up to terror. At last the gentlemen discovered the "ghost," which proved to be a bat. The creature had taken refuge just above the door, and, in endeavouring to flee away as darkness came on, caused the mysterious rappings with its wings. The bat destroyed, the knocking ceased.

*South London Press.*

---

# 1869 – A GHOST CAUGHT.

The *Teviotdale Record* says:— The capers of ghosts in that district have hitherto been confined to sundry wonderful leaps over hedges, and the molestation of people at night by the roadsides, and so often have these been occurring that the "men in blue" had to be called in to put down the "ghosts in white." On Wednesday evening, the latter were patrolling the Bongate road, the neighbourhood of the favourite haunt of their ghostships, and from this mystic language heard, the police lay down behind the hedge to await the issue of the conference. They had not waited long until a tall figure emerged from a gloomy portion of the field, and attacked a party on the road, but, on the police coming in sight, the ghost split in two, and would have dissolved but for the bluecoats who gave chase, and captured two young men. In order to make up a proper ghost, one of them had been mounted on the other's shoulders, and with something white thrown over, the seven-footer was no joke to meet on a dark road.

*Paisley Herald & Renfrewshire Advertiser.*

───◄(●)►───

# 1869 – MRS. BROWN'S GHOST STORY.

If anyone was to say to me, "Mrs. Brown, do you believe in ghosts mum?" I should say, "That depends on circumstances;" for I'm sure, if ever there was a woman I'd take the word on, it's Mrs. Padwick, as is a blood relation by the mother's side; and I'm sure to 'ear 'er tell about the ghost as 'er and Padwick saw when their weddin' tower, as they took quite genteel, thro' 'im bein' well-to-do, by the St. Alban's coach, as took 'em up at the Peacock at Islington, as is close agin the Angel, where the mail coaches did used to start from, a-blowin' their horns, in bran' new liveries on the king's birthday, as shows the flight of time, thro' 'im a-dyin' in '30, as was well on in years, and railroads 'avin' run the mail coaches off the road.

Not as ever Mrs. Padwick was one to talk about it, and wouldn't preaps never 'ave mentioned it agin only thro' me a-settin up late with her one night, three winters ago, with a 'eavy cold on 'er chest, as I thought would 'ave turned to jaunders, for 'er eyes was yokes of eggs for yallerness, with a pain between the blade bones like a carvin knife drove thro' you unawares.

Well, we was a-avin' of a chat together over all manner; leastways, she was in bed a-settin' up, with a shawl round 'er shoulders thro' 'avin 'ad for supper arrer root made with water and a little brandy in it, with a bit of thin dry toast, as wouldn't lay 'eavy on the constitution.

I'd took my nipper on a little table near the fire, as was a bit of cold griskin, and a little somethink 'ot, thro' the beer a-strikin' chilly, tho' only 'arf a pint, as is my allowance at night.

She says to me all of a sudden, "Why, Martha, it's over forty years since I was married, as my weddin' day were the day before yesterday; and if this aint the werry night u me and Padwick see the ghost as 'aunted the 'ouse where we was a-stoppin', thro bein' snowed up"

I says, "Go along with your rubbish, as is all imposi-tions, the same as the Cock Lane ghost, as my dear mother remembered well, tho' I must say as in course such things might be, thro' it bein' well-known as Lady Marley's ghost was seen to walk every night thro' Cockerton churchyard, and strangled the beadle in 'is cock-'at, as were a-watchin' for 'er in the porch, thro' not a likin' to be pryed into, as no lady wouldn't in 'er grave clothes."

Says Mrs. Padwick, "Don't jeer nor jest, Martha Brown, at ghosts as is disembowelled sperrits, and may be judgments on us, for what we knows."

I says, "Mary Lou Padwick, I aint one to do it, thro' is a believin' in sperrits."

She says, "I'm glad to 'ear it, for I've see a ghost with my own eyes as white as your nightcap border."

I says, "You don't say!"

She says, "I do, and so did Padwick, as wasn't no religion, tho' brought up a Quaker, as he never stuck to; but must say nothink could not 'ave been more aperient to the naked eye than that ghost as come into our room at the old 'ouse belonging to Padwick's uncle on the Luton road, as 'ad been millers, father and son, time out of mind.

We'd only been man and wife three days when we see it, and was a stoppin' at the old 'ouse, as were a ramshackle sort of place, and smelt damp and mouldy, and of all the dismal 'oles it was that bedroom, as even a fire didn't seem to cheer up.

We'd been a-bed ever so long, when I started up sudden thro' earin' a noise; and if there wasn't a man a-settin by the fire, as I can see 'is face now! for it was partly turned towards me; and as I'm a sinful woman, if 'is throat wasn't cut from ear to ear!

I give such a yell as woke up Padwick, and he see 'im too tho' vanished in an instant like smoke, as in course they will do thro' not a-likin' daylight to break on 'em. I was up in an instant, tho' pitch dark, and couldn't rest in that 'ouse, and set off by eight o'clock, tho' the snow were on the ground, and drove back to town in a tilt-cart, and never knowed till years arter as that room were reg'lar 'aunted, thro' the old miller, as were Padwick's father's uncle by the father's side, and did used to live in that 'ouse, 'avin' of 'is throat cut in that werry room in the dead of the night, and his own sons always thought to 'ave a 'and in it, and never 'eard on no more; but brought in suicide by the inquest as set upon him, and buried in a cross road, as is the reason be can't rest in 'is grave, tho' a stake thro' the body to keep him down; and that's 'ow the property come to Padwick's uncle."

Not as any ghost need 'ave come a-troublin' 'er nor Padwick, for I'm sure they never got a farthing of the money; and as to the night's lodgin', one wouldn't think as no ghost would be that mean to begrudge it to anybody; as is reg'lar dog in the manger, as the sayin' is; but certainly werry awful not to be buried decent, as is what a crossroad and a stake cannot be called; though I must say I do not 'old with them symetries, as aint like a regular churchyard, with a tombstone and railin's, or even a grave turfed up decent, as is a thing we all looks forward to natural; and I'm sure poor Mrs. Whelan slaved her life out to pay up 'er burial club; and then to be swindled out on it by that old waggerbone Macorliff, as bolted with the deposits and left 'em all to die unburied; or the parish, as is never decent; dead or alive.

I says, "Lor, you don't say so."

Jest then she give a snore, and I see as she were a-droppin' off, and felt that uncommon chilly thro' 'earin' of that ghost, I thought as I'd 'ave a little drop more of somethink as 'ot as I could drink it, and looks round at the fire; and if it wasn't werry near dead out, and not a bit of wood in the room, thro' that gal 'avin' forgot to put it in the scuttle that last thing, as I told 'er to.

It was 'owlin' wind and bitter cold, and I knowed as the coal cellar was kep in the back yard; but felt as I must go and get a bit; and jest then Mrs. Padwick wakes up and says as she'd got a chill, and spoke quite sharp about me a lettin' out the fire, as she must 'ave a fire.

So down I goes, with my work (as were a flannin petticoat as I'd been a 'errin-bonin') over my 'ead, for to get the wood, so I didn't 'arf like the job, partikler arter talkin' about them ghosts as made cold water run down my back; for I'd 'eard say as old Chandlers, as did used to live in that werry 'ouse 'ad 'ung 'isself behind the back kitchen door to the jack-towel roller, as is a awful end for any one.

I'd jest got the back door open, and when I remembered as I'd forgot the coalscuttle as was werry low, so goes up to get it; and as I come down agin the backdoor flowed open wide without me a-touchin' it, and if somethink white didn't fly slap in my face as struck as cold as death, and knocked me back'ards.

I give a scream, and down I fell, droppin' the candle and coalscuttle and all; and then I rushes like mad up to Mrs. Padwick's room, as come a rushin' out and give me a shove back'ards all down the stairs agin, and double locked the door in my face, a-thinkin' I was thieves, as woke up the gal, and down she come a-hollerin' , and tumbled over me in the dark, a-layin'

on the stairs, as she pretty nigh stomped to death, as 'ave a heavy tread.

I says, "Susan, it's me as 'ave see a ghost."

Them words set 'er off a-yellin' frightful.

I says, "Be quiet, or you'll be your missus's death," as I did not wish no 'arm to, tho' it was a unfeelin° act for to lock the door, let alone knocking me back'ard as she didn't go to do.

It was as much as ever I could do to quiet that gal, when I 'eard a step a-comin upstairs stealthy-like. I thought it was all over with us both, but 'ushed that gal as was crouched up with me on the landin'; and 'eard the footsteps a-comin', and a-comin', and all of a sudden there was a flash of light in both our eyes.

I 'ad hardly no breath in me, but the presence of mind for to say, "Who's there?" as answered, "What's the doors open for?" and proved to be a perliceman as 'ad found the back door open; and glad I was to see 'im as went and got the wood and coals for us, and thro' givin' 'im a glass of sperrits. When Mrs. Padwick unlocked the door, as I 'ad to beg and pray on 'er to thro the key 'ole ever so long, and do believe as she'd 'ave 'ad an illness as would 'ave took us both off, only I made 'er some more arrer root, and give even that gal a drop of somethink 'ot as was all shivers; and 'ours afor I got to sleep, and must say as I do think as it must 'ave been somethink out of nature as come slap in my face, tho' the perliceman said it must 'ave been the gal's stockin's as she left 'angin' out, and the wind blowed in my face; not as I were a-goin' to argue with a ignorant young man like that as said he didn't think as I should see anythink much wuss than myself if I was to go a long way, as was werry insultin', tho', preaps, without my 'air I may look strange in my nightcap, as makes a deal of difference to the 'uman 'ead; but do believe as that perliceman 'ad 'ad somethink afore I give 'im that drop, for if he didn't put 'is back agin the wall and larf like foolish when I was a-tellin' 'im about that ghost, as shows as he 'adn't no manners nor yet feelin's; for when I said that gal 'ad trod wiolent on my nose a-rushin' downstairs with 'er bare 'oofs, he larfed wuss than ever; and as to Mrs. Padwick, whether it was that ghost or what it was, I don't know, but she was dreadful bad in the mornin'; and as to my 'ead, I thought bust it would; and what I thought bad in that perliceman was 'is a drainin' that brandy bottle as he must 'ave done when we wasn't a-lookin', for there wasn't a drop in it next mornin', and I only drawed with my own 'ands, and broke the neck off with givin' of it a twist.

But I must say, as in course no one as aint a 'ebrew Jew nor yet a 'eathen Turk couldn't bus believe in 'em; and as to Jews, I'm sure poor Mrs. Israel's aunt, as good a soul as ever broke bread, put her 'ip out in Bonner's Fields, 'Ackney, thro' some boys a frightenin' 'er with a lantern and a sheet, a-comin' 'ome with a 'eavy load, as shows she believed in ghosts, and 'ad cause to, with a limp to 'er dyin' day, as was a drawback to a purchasin' gentlefolks' wardrobes, as she were not above bein' seen a carryin', nor yet cut-glass jugs as was blowed like crystal, and lovely fruit done in wax as looked that temptin' as made your mouth water, as the sayin' is.

But if I was to set up forever with Mrs. Padwick you wouldn't never ketch me a listenin' to none of 'er ghost, as is a solemn subject, and did ought to be laid with 'oly water reg'lar, as I've 'eard tell in the Dead Sea, as is the place for 'em to be at rest in, and not bother parties as never did 'em no harm, livin' nor dead, and not like the resurrection men used to be about when I was a gal, and known for to rob the departed, tho' quite as well for that lady as they'd been and buried alive in 'er rings, and was brought to life thro' the feller as 'ad broke into 'er coffin a-sawin at 'er finger, as brought the life back into 'er thro' that ring bein' swelled, leastaways the finger, and grasped 'im tight, and 'eld 'im tiller cries brought 'elp, as lived to be a great-grandmother; all the waggerbones 'ung, as served 'em right, for a-disturbin' the dead, as did ought to be let alone in their silent tombs; but for all that, will sometimes take to walkin', and often apparitions to them as is born at midnight, as Mrs. Preedy's twins was, and a mercy they was took, for dreadful objects! they might 'ave been 'aunted to their dyin' day, as would 'ave been werry unpleasant to their mother's sister as 'ad the care on them for the month, and died within a week when not nine days old, so aint likely to be troubled with no ghosts in this world, and never shall 'ear twelve o'clock strike, and not think of them, and ghosts into the bargain."

*The Tewkesbury Register and Agricultural Gazette.*

———◦《◉》◦———

# 1869 – THE TOWER GHOST.

You want a ghost story? A real ghost story, of course. It is only the genuine article that has any claim on the sympathies or is worth the telling round the Christmas hearth. An invented ghost story is the most detestable thing in shams. It is an insult to the listener, who has a fair right to complain of having his hair set on end, his eyes distended, and his flesh set creeping under false pretences.

The story I am about to tell is true. It is one of the best authenticated ghost stories in the world. Moreover, it happens to be associated with one the best known buildings in the world, which saves me the trouble of describing the scene of the adventure, and endeavouring to realize it to your minds by elaborate word-painting.

The scene was none other than the Tower of London. The time winter, well toward Christmas, and the

circumstances, so far as memory serves me, were as follows:-

The keeper of the Crown jewels—Graves by name, to the best of my recollection —had apartments close to the room in which those priceless gems are deposited. He was a family man, and his wife and daughters, and no doubt the swains on whom they looked with favour, were all assembled late one night in these comfortable Tower rooms. For it must not be supposed that because the Tower is grim and stony, with histories of bloodshed and treachery, and every kind of wickedness clinging to it like the lichens about its walls, that it has no snugness or comfort about it. Prisoners sent thither, and cooped up in stone tanks, with a sorry outlook toward Tower Hill, where the headsman awaited them in the chill early morning, used to find anything but snug lying in the Tower. But those days have passed away, and it is now possible to live in the grim fortalice as pleasantly as in a Belgravian mansion, always supposing that you are not afraid of ghosts, and do not suffer the haunting memories of the place to overcome you.

For that the Tower is haunted there cannot he a doubt, as this story shows. The family of the jewel keeper were, as I have said, enjoying themselves in a harmlessly social way. Mrs. Graves sat next to the fire place; her husband on the opposite side of the table—not on the other side of the fire, but in front of it, with the table between. The others were ranged about the room indifferently.

Suddenly Mrs. Graves, looking up, turned her face toward her husband, and uttered a cry of alarm. "Good gracious!" she exclaimed. Her husband looked at her, saw that she was white with terror, and all of a tremor. "What's the matter?" he demanded. "Oh, look, look! See! Behind you," was her piteous exclamation; and with that she fainted away.

Graves did not look behind him, for rising in alarm happened to glance at the looking-glass over the mantel-piece just before him. In that glance he saw something which riveted his attention. He saw what he described as a rising smoke, or vapour, which came from behind his chair, floated upward somewhat in the form of a human body, but with trailing lambs that lost their form and dwindled off into nothingness, and which almost immediately faded wholly from sight. Terrified beyond measure, he knew not what to think, and was about to move to his wife's assistance when a loud shriek from the ramparts without broke the solemn stillness of the night.

That shriek was twice repeated.

Reflect here for a moment that two persons out of those present in the room had distinctly seen that which presented itself to their view as a spectral apparition. The wife had seen it—for, as it afterwards transpired, it was the rising vapour in human form which had caused her to shriek out and subsequently to swoon away; and the husband had seen the same appearance reflected in the glass, neither of them having time or opportunity to compare their separate or distinct impressions. Two persons, let us say, in brief, had seen the ghost.

And immediately on its recognition by the second of these persons a shrill scream was heard on the rampart outside the window of the room. As that scream was repeated, Graves, alarmed for the safety of the property in the jewel room, and fearing some trick, at once rushed out, accompanied by some members of the family, to see what had happened.

This had happened.

The guard going their rounds had found the sentinel at the door of the jewel room asleep at his post They found him lying on the ground insensible, and it was when they raised him and tried to awaken him that he uttered these screams of terror, and instantly relapsed into unconsciousness—yes, unconsciousness, not sleep; for, as they soon found, what they had mistaken for doze was, in reality, a swoon. The man had fallen down in a fit, and his rifle with the bayonet fixed lay under him.

This was a remarkable coincidence. Beyond that it was not possible for the moment to carry it. It was certainly strange that the instant when the apparition appeared to Graves and his wife, there should be a sentinel outside the door falling down in a swoon, out of which he only recovered to relapse into shrieks of terror.

For some hours this unfortunate man—he was a young Scotchman, if I remember rightly—lay in the guardroom as a rigid corpse, and with only occasional convulsions; but at length, as the night wore on, he showed signs of recovery. Medical assistance was obtained, and though he was never quite himself, he was able to convey in a few words an account of what had befallen him.

This was his narrative:-

He said that he was pacing to and fro outside the jewel room, when, on coming to the door, he was startled by a peculiar appearance. It was at first only like vapour stealing out from under the door, and rising as it emerged; indeed, his impression was that the room was on fire, and he was about to give an alarm when the smoke —the vapour —call it what you will, began to assume form, half human, half animal, with distinctly tangible limbs and head, that had something of the bear in its outline, as he thought, though there was a human look in the eyes that utterly overcame him.

Desperate with terror at this sight, he yet had some latent suspicion that it might be designed to take advantage of him, and he instantly lowered his rifle and made a charge at the door with his bayonet through the figure. As he did that the apparition faded away; and convinced that he had seen a ghost, he felt himself utterly overcome, and, losing all consciousness, supposed that he dropped to the ground and lay there until the guard came round.

It is not unusual for soldiers to invent stories to account for neglect of duty, especially such serious neglect of duty as sleeping at their posts. It was, therefore, with some incredulity, that the captain of the guard listened to this statement, and was only deterred from sending the man to a prison cell by the presence of Graves and the remarkable manner in which this seemed to dovetail with his experience. The wife had seen the ghost. He had seen the ghost. What more likely than that it should also have appeared to the sentinel on duty?

But were there any means of arriving at the truth of his story? Did anything seem to corroborate or to contradict it? These are natural questions, and the reply is—Yes; the statement was corroborated in two distinct forms.

The sentinel had declared that in the excess of his terror he yet had presence of mind to charge the door with his bayonet. The door was examined, and there was found an indentation newly made by the bayonet's point.

Here was corroboration the first.

Corroboration the second assumed a more serious and impressive form. So far, the man might have been shamming, though it would have been a strange coincidence if he had, in order to screen himself from the consequences of his neglect duty hit upon an excuse, which so completely dovetailed with what had happened in the rooms occupied by Mr. Graves. But here is pretty conclusive proof that the man was not shamming. He died before morning from the effects of fright.

To the truth of this story, therefore, he bore witness with his life.

Thus, then, we have a recent and clearly established fact that a ghost did appear to three separate individuals, within a few yards of each other, on one and the same night. Between these persons there have been no collusion. Each saw what he or she saw, without knowing what the others had seen; the effects of the apparition were alone visible to them and the third parties, and looking at this and at the wonderful manner in which the whole thing hangs together, I think I am justified in calling this a true ghost story, and in asserting that it is one of the most authenticated ghost stories in the world.

*South London Press.*

⦿

# 1870 – A SHILLING SEANCE.

It is not everybody (says a correspondent to a contemporary) who can afford a crown to see a séance, even for the privilege of communicating with Benjamin Franklin or Socrates. If we have shilling dinners and shilling pits at theatres, why not shilling séances? No sooner said than done. We have them. The shilling séance is henceforth an institution. It is true that you cannot, as at the higher priced entertainment, summon your great grandmother, or any other spirit, at will. You most "take them as they come."

The spiritualistic salon consisted of two small drawing rooms connected by folding doors, and soon after eight proceedings commenced by the proprietor of the "Progressive" Library. He took his seat at the table in the front drawing room, arrayed somewhat incongruously, as it struck me, in a drab overcoat, like the driver of an omnibus. Opposite him sat the medium, a young man, habited in, I presume, his "customary suit of solemn black," with a large jet watch chain and cross, looking more like a very respectable undertaker's assistant than anything else. This was, of course, quite in keeping; and his name, "Mr. Morse," had, to classical ears, a nice, softened, deathly sound about it.

Had I been altogether unused to the manners and customs of trance mediums, I should have thought the poor young man was taken suddenly ill, for he turned up his eyes and wriggled about in his chair opposite our progressive president, in the most alarming manner. This, I was informed, was the signal of a spirit taking possession of his body, which he himself had vacated *pro tem*; his mental alienation being produced by spirit mesmerism. Possession being gained, the disagreeable symptoms subsided, and the "intelligence," in a soft and simpering voice, described itself as that of a publican, "passed away" some seven years, and now full of regretful remembrances of the "poison" vended at the public in question. This I found did not refer to adulteration, or cast any aspersions on the quality of the refreshment supplied; but the repentance was occasioned by the spirit's having taken up teetotal principles.

It may be mentioned *en passant* that the president of the evening was great on the subject of abstinence. When the "spirit" added its name and previous address the simpering voice was explained. It belonged to a female, Maria Crook, late of the "Crown and Can," Clerkenwell, and now of Highgate Cemetery. I notice that, in the "Postal Directory," there in such an establishment as this in the locality specified, kept by a person of the male sex, with surname answering to that above. How far the medium profited by this source of information previously, is, of course, only known to himself.

After "coming to" for a short time, the young man "went off," but this time the voice was rough, and the dialect an imperfect imitation of the rustic. It purported to proceed from the spirit of a "navvy" —name and address declined—who had worked on the South London main drainage works (the great "shore," as he termed it), under "a feller we used to call old Bags-o'-tea, cos we never could make out 'is name," this being presumably Mr. Bazelgette. We had a graphic account of this gentleman's *rencontre* with his grandpapa after his decease, and of his being taught by the old gentleman how to influence "them shivery shaky kind o' people called mediums." He had never advanced beyond the earth sphere, and most of the spirits who influence tables, &c., are, he informed us, of his status in society. We can quite think so. In order to pay a visit to America he attached himself to a medium who was going thither. Being asked whether he could not get on alone, he said, "Not more than 100 miles at a stretch, and then I finds it easiest to go slantindicular, fifty miles up and fifty miles down, instead of straight to the place." It was now half past nine, and the proceedings closed, and so we departed accordingly.

*The Tewkesbury Register & Agricultural Gazette.*

---

# 1870 – A STILL NIGHT.

At about midnight of the 23rd of last month, two grave and elderly gentlemen were returning from the village of Chelvey to Brockley (in Somerset). They had spent the evening together at the former place, engaged, with their host, in quiet conversation upon the ordinary topics of the day; and they set out together on their way home in a vehicle drawn by the doctor's horse—a well-broken, steady, and experienced roadster. The Doctor drove. The Rector sat by his side, both silent, staid, and contemplative. The road was narrow but open, and the night was still, fine, and clear; there was no moon, and the travellers had no lamps. They had proceeded but a short distance when the horse evinced a nervousness very uncommon to the animal, and more than once showed a disposition —now to halt, now to turn, and anon to hurry forward on the extreme roadside. The Doctor, roused to unwonted attention by the timidity of his favourite and reliable horse, cast his eyes forward along the road, directly in the centre of which, a sight met them that gave a strange shock to his own strong nerves. Hurrying on, with no appearance of muscular effort —turning neither to the right nor the left, a tall figure, draped in a long cloak, reaching nearly to the ground, floated, rather than walked, before them.

The Doctor, without speaking to his companion, looked long enough upon the weird figure to note these startling particulars, and to arrive at the conclusion in his own mind that he was the subject of a special and peculiar illusion. Looking upon the spectre with the feeling of a mere man of science, and quieted rather than alarmed by the nature of the appearance which he had now no doubt was visible only to his own disordered sense sight, he occupied himself in a hurried examination of his own physical condition, in which, however, he detected none of the expected symptoms. He was strong, calm, sound in health, collected and clear—physically and mentally. "Nevertheless," murmured the doctor to himself, "this is a marked and decided case of optical illusion for which I may yet find some cause."

"Did you speak?" said the Rector, in subdued tones.

"I did—involuntarily;" replied the Doctor, speaking also scarcely above a whisper.

"In speaking, involuntarily, were your thoughts and speech addressed to the "thing" before us, my friend?" asked the Rector.

"Good God, yes. Do you, too, see what I have for the last few minutes been observing?"

"I have seen and am seeing with you," quietly responded the Rector. "Look more carefully to your horse, speak to it cheeringly and soothingly, and let us go on."

The Doctor obeyed, but even his well-known voice failed to quiet the now trembling animal, the management of which was becoming every moment more difficult.

"This can't go on; we had better alight, or wait, or turn back," observed the Doctor, striving in vain to guide the now unmanageable horse.

They had by this time reached a wider part of the road across which led a still broader. Lying in the centre of this crossing was a triangular bit of turf, bare and treeless. Upon this spot the figure vanished; and the horse stopped, refusing to pass beyond it.

"Doctor," whispered the rector, "We are alone. Were you watching?"

"Not carefully," said the Doctor, half out of breath with his exertions in repressing the frightened horse, "not carefully, but I think it went to the right."

"Nay," replied the Rector, "Neither to the left nor to the right; neither upwards nor downwards. I marked it accurately to the last; it faded, died out, disappeared—not suddenly, but slowly—as sure as you and I are together here."

No small amount of time and care were necessary to get the horse home; and for an animal famous for its steady strength of nerve, courage, and docility, it has become within the few days that have transpired, as nervous and timid as a fawn.

This is all. While I sit here in the Doctor's sanctum, transcribing the notes of his journey from Chelvey to Brockley, the Doctor is collecting and comparing cases from the dry and uninviting volumes littered upon the table and the floor, turning only occasionally from these to the latest reports of the learned societies upon optics, to the splendid but to me, unintelligible, theorems of Brewster. The Rector —an old tutor of his college—is here, too, tracing innumerable diagrams with the view of reducing this appearance and disappearance to some law of physics. Nothing, reader, will come of their labours. You and I know that. Professor Schoff was here, but he has gone away up the Coombe, sneeringly. Professor Schoff and my old friends have had a difference, and have been hard upon each other. Professor Schoff insists that the two learned noodles saw a reflection of their horse and themselves, built up, pyramid fashion, and cast feebly upon the white road by the light of the old moon, which being in its last quarter, would be on the south-eastern horizon at that hour; and being there would cast distorted, faint, and elongated images of just sufficient distinctness to frighten horses or other animals. Thus of the appearance.

As to the disappearance, Professor Schoff says that the shadow, being faint and thin, would disappear upon the darker ground of the grass plot, for want of that contrast in field and shadow afforded by the whiter road. Professor Schoff banged the study door as he went out, and the effect of the loud report upon my nerves, proves to me that I, for one, must side with the Doctor and the Rector, who have thrown aside their books, papers, and instruments, and now believe that they saw a "thing" of which they cannot, and ought not to attempt a further description or elucidation. Hah! Professor Schoff has gone; but old Betsy Prodgen, who was born in the parish of Brockley well-nigh seventy years ago, is in the kitchen, and this, in substance, is what I overhear her saying:—

"Mrs. Hucker (she is addressing the rectory cook) the greatest of fools are the wise fools. I am angered to hear what you say of the discussion in the study by the Rector, Doctor and Professor. Rays of incidence—reflection—refraction —convergence —divergence—angles—foci and rubbish! What has those blasphemous terms or the blasphemous science to which they refer, to do with what they have seen? Shame upon their unbelief! Listen ma'am. Just 94 years ago the Rector of this parish was the Reverend Mr. Hubertson, a hungry, reckless spendthrift. The miser is hungry and reckless; the spendthrift, Mrs. Hucker, would draw bills upon his wife's reputation, or his children's bread, to raise coin to squander upon the gratification of his depraved tastes or idiotic cravings. No wonder, then, that this should happen—Parson Hubertson cooked a will! It was done in this wise.

In the early barking season of 1776, James Stevens, the then woodward of the Brockley Manor, was mortally injured by the fall of a tree in the Park, and was carried crushed and mangled into the kitchen of the Rectory. The parson, and an old and wicked college friend of his, who was staying with him as a guest at the time, provided a means for the removal of the dying man to Chelvey, where he lived, and accompanied him home. James Stevens' wife and children received the mournful procession, and saw in their agony that the sufferer's very hours were numbered. James Stevens had been a striving and a successful man; and it was pretty generally known that he had a large sum lying in one of the Bristol banks to his credit —five hundred pounds and more as it proved to be. Parson Hubertson, and his college friend, and a man-servant of the latter, sat up through the night; and before the morning that succeeded it, James Stevens died, having previously signed a will drawn up by his friendly watchers, wholly, the dying man believed, in favour of his wife and children; but wholly, it turned out to be, in favour not of them or either of them, but Parson Hubertson! Widow Stevens died twenty years later in the workhouse; and her children went forth into the world penniless. Parson Hubertson died later, at the Rectory; and his end was hard and frightful. Parson Hubertson's body was buried but his spirit was never laid; and at barking time in every year, and to this day, that spirit appearing in the hard outline of the tall form it occupied in the body, makes a journey to and fro at midnight between Chelvey and Brockley; and the draped figure seen by the Rector and Doctor was Parson Hubertson's Ghost."

*Berkshire Chronicle.*

# 1871 – A TALE OF MYSTERY.

(The papers of the Pas de Calais, the French department just opposite to the English coast, have been publishing a most mysterious story, which we find enlarged in a contemporary, as if sent by one of the chief actors in the strange story. The writer, at the end, pledges her word of faith for the trust of her fearful experiences.)

"I was just eighteen, and had only been married a few months, when, having nothing particular to detain us at home, my husband decided to take me for a pleasure trip through Normandy. At Avranches we rented a house from a furniture dealer which the old lady informed us had been rented to two English gentlemen, who kept a great many dogs. They paid their rent regularly, to be sure, but still she had a suspicion there was something wrong about them.

On the ground floor were two large rooms, and a kitchen at the back, which looked into a good sized garden full of weeds and overgrown shrubs, with two or three broken stone figures almost covered with green moss, and looking very desolate. The rooms were perfectly crammed with furniture of all descriptions, which the old woman accounted for by saying that she had bought some from people who were leaving the town, and not having room for it in her store, she had placed it in the vacant house.

The rooms we were going to live in, like the rest of the house, were in a very untidy state, and I felt myself bound to set to work to put them in order, therefore, having obtained a broom and a dustpan I rolled up my sleeves and commenced. In a little cabinet I found the floor under the sawdust covered all over with large blotches, which looked like, and certainly were, blood. I slowly got up and began to peer at the walls for further traces of a crime, which, by some strange fancy, I felt sure had been committed. No detective could have examined more closely than I did every article in that room, and my search was rewarded by finding spots over the paper and on the inside of the door, and on the frame of the window what appeared like the marks of bloody fingers.

And now the feeling for which I am unable to account took possession of me; a desire to get rid of these signs of, as I really believe, a murder, and to do it before anyone could come and find out my occupation. I did not wish even my husband to know of it. I had just finished my work when my husband returned; but not one word passed my lips as to what I had seen. Being very tired we went to bed early, leaving as was our custom, a light burning in the room.

We had not been asleep very long when we were rather rudely awakened by the loud ringing of a bell in the hall. It was the bell belonging to the front door, and was almost as large as those used on steamers, which ring to intimate to the passengers that they are desired to step to the captain's office to pay their fare. My husband got up, put on a dressing gown, and going into the front room opened one of the windows and looked out. I quickly followed. Standing by the door were two men wrapped in cloaks, and so muffled up that we could only see the upper part of their faces. They stood perfectly still and did not speak. Tom spoke to them in French, asking their business, but received no reply, only the bell rang again with increased violence. We spoke to them in English, with no better success, and the bell continued ringing. My husband was on the point of going down stairs, but I begged of him not to do so because he had neither pistols nor any other weapon with which he could defend himself if he should be attacked.

While we were consulting as to what was best to be done, the bell, which had ceased for a few moments, rang out another peal, but on again looking out, there was no one to be seen, and the street, which was dimly illuminated by a moon only a few days old, and in the distance by one dismal lamp, contained no living creature. We did not attach any particular importance to this occurrence, thinking that, as we were strangers, someone had, perhaps, desired to play us a trick; and we returned to bed, and were soon asleep again. It seemed, however, that our troubles were only beginning. We had not been asleep an hour before we were again annoyed by the peals of that abominable bell. We looked out as before, and there were the two men. "This is too much of a joke," said my husband; "I shall try what effect a pitcher of water will have on these gentlemen," at the same time turning to go to the bedroom to fetch one. I remained at the window watching the men, who turned round and walked off down the street. They stood for a moment under the lamp, and I heard a laugh; it seemed to come from them, yet it pervaded the whole house, and echoed from room to room.

There was something so utterly fiendish in the sound that Tom and I looked at each other, but could say nothing; we rubbed our eyes and wondered if we had been dreaming. In all this, strange to say, the discovery I had made in the afternoon never recurred to me.

Again we went to bed. By this time it was nearly twelve o'clock. Sleep, however, had departed from our eyes, and we amused ourselves with all sorts of conjectures about the men who had so wantonly disturbed our slumbers. About half past twelve o'clock there came through the whole house a shock which, if it had been in San Francisco, I should at once have said was an earthquake. The door, which had been partly closed, flew wide open; the windows rattled; and we sat up in bed, staring around us, and wondering what would come next.

"Little woman," said Tom to me, "I am beginning to think this house is bewitched, and that we are not to get any sleep tonight." He had scarcely done speaking when a noise commenced in the room over our heads, which sounded like people quarrelling or rather fighting. We could hear no voices, but furniture seemed to be dragged about, and tumbled down; and after a while, something fell on the floor with a dull thud, like a heavy body, and then all was silent.

After a few minutes, we heard a sound as of someone coming down stairs stealthily; whatever it was it passed the door of our apartments, and went into one of the rooms below. Then there was a noise as of somebody falling over the furniture in the dark; then perfect silence.

Tom looked at me and said he believed the noise was made by rats. I felt sure that he did not think so, but was ashamed to say I was afraid; therefore I assented that rats did sometimes make very strange noises and, after a while, as we had no more disturbances, we fell asleep, having decided that we would get the key on Monday from the old woman, and have a look at the rooms upstairs.

I confess I was disappointed at the appearance of these rooms. There was nothing dreadful to be seen, they were only very dirty and untidy. In the room from which had come the noise, there were seven or eight very heavy cane seated chairs scattered about, standing up, some tumbled down, and in the centre a card table;

no other furniture. There was no carpet on the floor; and the windows, of which there were two, had outside shutters, which were fastened on the inside with strong bolts. There was evidently no chance for anyone to get in by the windows.

In the room adjoining was a bed which had been left unmade, a wash basin, half full of water, two or three chairs, and two small tables, with a variety of other litter which I cannot remember, but which made the room look very untidy and dirty. On one of the tables, which stood in the corner of the room was a small looking glass, with a common wooden back to it. I took up the glass hardly thinking of what I was doing and began to examine it. Tom and the old lady were talking by one of the windows, and did not observe me. On the back of the glass were the marks of four fingers, in the same red stains as those I had discovered down stairs, and a thumb mark on the outside of the frame, which, however, being of coloured wood, was not noticeable, except on close examination. It was as if someone had taken hold of it with a bloody hand.

The moment I had discovered this I had again the same insane desire of concealment, and actual fear that other people should find out what I was impelled to hide. I put down the glass, covering it with a towel which lay near, and joined my husband and the old woman at the other end of the room.

The two other rooms had nothing in them but broken furniture, and all the windows were strongly fastened inside. We prepared to go down stairs again. Before we went, however, I picked up all the fallen chairs in the large room, and placed them by the wall at considerable distances from one another, and the rooms were again locked up, the old lady departing with the key. That night was very cold, and not wishing to have a fire in our bedroom, we closed both the doors, which, as I said before, had only latches. At half past eleven o'clock, we were awoke by the sort of earthquake shock before mentioned; and the doors both flew wide open, with a loud clicking of the latches.

Tom jumped out of bed, and, I am afraid used blasphemous language. We looked into both rooms and into the hall; there was nothing to be seen. Then the noise began overhead, just as before; the furniture was tumbled about, and the fall of some heavy body on the floor was heard very distinctly, and this was repeated at intervals until half past three, when all was silent; then the stealing down stairs, and the apparent stumbling over furniture in the room below, which always ended the disturbances. We searched upstairs and down, in every room we could get into, but could find nothing.

The next day I determined to investigate thoroughly the two large rooms down stairs, which, as I told you, were filled with furniture. I took an opportunity to do this while Tom was away from the house. A set of blue and white, and gold furniture attracted my attention more than anything else. It was in what, I think, they called the Louise Quatorze style, and had been very splendid in its day. On the back of one of these chairs I saw the same marks of the bloody fingers I had seen on the looking glass. This particular chair was upset on the floor, and I raised it up, putting it carefully away in a dark corner where nobody would be likely to notice it.

These disturbances did not occur every night, but quite often enough to puzzle and annoy Tom, who, however, always thought "the next time he would certainly find out what caused them." The strange influence I have before mentioned grew stronger day by day. I wandered about the house whenever I had an opportunity, with a dread upon me that I had something terrible to conceal.

I tried in vain to tell my husband; I could not force the words from my lips. At length the month was over, and I summoned courage enough to ask Tom to take me away from the town; everything in and about it had grown hateful to me, and I pined for my English home and friends. I told him I should die if I remained at Avranches. He called me a foolish little woman, and asked me why I had not told him this before, but I had no reply to give. We went home, but it was a long time before I got rid of my nervous fear; and I have never been able to account for the terrible feeling which took possession of me in what I cannot help calling the" haunted house."

*Illustrated Police News.*

———◦◉◦———

# 1871 – GHOSTS AND GHOST SEERS.

The above was the subject of a lecture delivered it Hyde Lane Schoolroom, Hyde, on Tuesday evening, by the Rev. Henry Griffith., of Bowden, to a numerous audience. The Rev. F. Robinson opened the meeting with prayer, after which he briefly introduced Mr. Griffiths to the assembly.

The lecturer said he did not know how much belief was paid in this locality to ghosts and goblins, but even the better educated towns were not wholly free from its influences, and there were thousands of living witnesses to its power, still he was glad to say public opinion was turning against the belief in such things, and against spirit rapping, for every fresh discovery in science made its existence more desperate.

There was a time when it was capital punishment to believe in such a thing, but now neither priests nor magistrats could interfere; people could think

for themselves. He believed his audience consisted of people of three classes, the advanced sceptic, who laughed at everything of the sort, as he believed it was physically impossible; sitting by him was his counter, whose imagination was always on the stretch for something wonderful; then there was he who was a hero in company, and who would meet any ghost at twelve o'clock at noon, but who would rather part with his finger than go to a churchyard at midnight and pick up the head of a skeleton.

He (the lecturer) would begin his subject with a touch of physiology. There were five senses, taste, hearing, sight, smell, and touch; these formed the connecting link between the spirit and the external world. Each organ had its special function, the gustatory nerve produced taste, the olfactory nerve smell, the auditory nerve hearing, &c., and as their use were always the same, people knew what was passing around them, but sometimes things might be brought about by entirely different means, so that people ought to be very careful in judging of them, as they might come to false conclusion. For instance, a fire would make a person feel hot, so would a fever, although others around him might be shivering with cold. A marquis, now dead, felt the gout in his toe 30 years after he lost it at Waterloo; and a gentleman whom he knew had been obliged to change his residence for one which was warmer, as he could not keep his fingers warm, though they had been torn off by an engine 20 years before.

Taking the sense of taste, children were generally fond of jam, but it was possible to make them shudder at the very name of it. He related several stories bearing upon the point, one in which an old gentleman in Scotland, who was very averse to garlic, was made miserable from having it mixed, so he thought, by his cook in every meal he had. He believed it was done intentionally, and he discharged cook after cook to remedy the evil, but all to no purpose. A physician was called in, and it was then found that the roof of his mouth was diseased, and that the garlic existed in himself, and not in the food he ate. Improbable as some persons might think it, there was scarcely anything more offensive to him (the lecturer) than mignonette.

There was also an instance of a gentlemen standing high in the political world who once fell off his horse and broke the bridge of his nose and since that event everything smelled like a turnip field. (Laughter.) Disease of the auditory nerve would sometimes cause people to hear buzzing and whistling sounds in the ear. He knew an old lady who, during her earlier years, had been a nurse, and who would sometimes declare that she heard the shrieks of children. Boxes, cellars, and even the pockets of the persons in the house had to be searched to pacify her, but to no avail, and she had since died appealing to heaven for the protection of infants.

Sir Isaac Newton also saw a spectrum in his room at night whilst in bed. The lecturer related many other stories of objects, human beings, &c., seen by persons; some were very amusing, whilst others were of a more touching nature; persons suffering under some bodily infirmity had frequently seen apparitions in almost every conceivable form, daily, nightly, or on special occasions; in a few cases they had disappeared as their health had been restored, but there were other victims, who although they knew the visions they had seen were not real, were still subjected to considerable annoyance from the horrible sights they beheld, and they preyed so heavily upon their minds that death had been the consequence.

He also stated that Capt. Clifford, a naval officer and a Catholic, one night saw a figure resembling his confessor in his bedroom. He spoke to him, and on receiving no answer went towards him, but the apparition retreated. It subsequently sat in a chair, and he went to the same chair and seated himself thereon. After this it sprang into bed, and he then blew out the candle and got in bed to it.—(laughter.) That was something which many would not dare to do.

At Plymouth, many years ago, a ghost was seen by a number of persons. There was a club connected with science and literature, which held its meetings in a certain tavern, but some having an objection to assembling there they made arrangements for carrying on their meetings in a greenhouse in the garden belonging to the house, and entered by a side gate. One of the rules was that the members should take the chair in turns, and one night information was received that the president for the night was exceedingly ill, in fact was dying. The chair was left vacant out of respect to him, and the subject turned on to the loss they would sustain by his death. While so engaged a figure enveloped in a sheet, and possessing the death like features of their sick brother, stalked into the room, took his seat in the empty chair, got hold of a glass on the table, replaced it, and then marched out of the room again. This was seen by the whole company, numbering over 60 persons. After talking the matter over for a short time, a deputation of two members was appointed to go and see how the man was going on at home, and they learned that he had just died. The members of the society resolved to keep it quiet, a very foolish thing to do, as the truth ought to be made known.

Some six or seven years passed away, and an old woman, who had had charge of the deceased man, fell ill. She then informed her physician that she had been directed to keep a close watch over the member of the club before mentioned, but while under her care she began to feel drowsy, and went to sleep for a short time. On awaking she discovered that her patient had vanished, but on going to look for him she found him returning to the home. She put him to bed again, and he shortly afterwards died.

The audience had heard of the ghost of a man who disliked garlic, that of the turnips, and the ghost at the greenhouse, which was no ghost at all but the man himself, and others he had mentioned. There were national ghosts, family ghosts, personal ghosts, and many others, but they had their existence only in diseased persons' minds. He had seen several himself, and his teacher at college was so troubled with them that he could not realise with certainty what was real and what was not, and when teaching his class would often poke his scholars with a stick to test whether they were mere phantoms or human beings. At first they did not like it, but in time the annoyance wore away. He condemned in no slight degree the conduct of nurses frightening children by telling them of ghosts and goblins, and said that had he one ever so perfect in other respects he would at once dismiss her for such an offence, as she might do such injury in a day that 50 years of schooling could not eradicate. Was there a mother present who would like to see her bright-eyed boy or girl grow up afraid even of their own shadow? If they valued their children's welfare they would save them from that, for pitiable was the life of those who began their existence in the fear of ghosts and such like things.

Should any of those present behold anything of the sort he would advise them, if they were not teetotal, to sign the pledge at once; but if they were sure that it had not sprung from drink, let them ask their companions, if there were any with them at the time, whether they had seen the same phenomena, if not, then call in a physician, and get their health regulated. He advised all people to endeavour to disbelieve in ghosts, though they might make allowances for those who stated that they had seen things supernatural, as they might feel convinced in their own minds that the figures were real. He could pity believers in ghosts, but he asked his hearers to laugh at those imported from America, the table rappers. They had nothing to fear but sin; they must keep a good heart and look upwards.

A vote of thanks was proposed by Mr. Pickstone, seconded by Mr. Pennington, and carried, for the lecturer's kindness in coming to Hyde, and delivering the lecture.

Mr. Griffiths suitably acknowledged the compliment, and wished

"To each and all a fair good night.
With rosy dreams and slumbers bright."

The meeting separated shortly after half past nine.
*Hyde & Glossop Weekly News.*

# 1872 – HERR DOBLER'S "DARK SEANCE."

On the afternoon of Monday, the 8th inst., Herr Dobler gave a private "Dark Séance," at the Star Hotel, to a few gentlemen of this city. Amongst the visitors present we noticed Colonel Norbury, Messrs. Southall, Holland, Beale, R. P. Hill, Canning Hill, F. Bentley, P. C. Cleasby, Captain Prescott Decie, A. Joscland, E. J. Spark, and many others.

The séance was given in a room from which all daylight was effectually excluded, and which there was not any furniture save about a dozen chairs and a small table. The first part of the séance was the now celebrated rope tying trick, which was first introduced to the notice of the public some years ago by the Davenport Brothers.

The company being seated, the lights were extinguished, and in the course of two minutes, on the gas being re-lit, Herr Dobler was found to be most effectually tied to the chair on which he was sitting. His hands were fastened behind him so securely that, to all appearances, it was impossible for he himself to have tied them, and his legs were also firmly tied to the legs of the chair with the rope brought down from his hands. The fastening of the rope, around the wrists especially, was very critically examined by the company present, and a part of the rope was then sealed with wax, so that it might be ascertained, in what was about to follow, whether or not the performer extricated his hands from the rope.

On the company being re-seated and the gas again extinguished, the floating instrument "manifestation" was given. A tambourine, which lay on the table (and which had been touched with phosphorus, so that it might be seen in the dark) and also a bell were at once raised from the table, and floated in the atmosphere, first in one part of the room and then another, over the heads of the company. Occasionally the clink of the bell in the tambourine was heard. This lasted some three or four minutes, and, on the light being forthcoming, the tambourine was discovered on the head of a gentleman present, who had, during the manifestation, held the feet and knees of Herr Dobler, with a view of ascertaining if there were any muscular movements on his part. This gentleman declared that he felt no moving whatever by the performer, but that previous to the tambourine alighting, he felt a sensation on his head as if three or four hands were touching it.

The remarkable coat trick was next given. The coat of a gentleman present having been handed to Herr Dobler (who, be it remembered, was all the time securely fastened by the ropes to the chair), the light was extinguished, and in a few seconds afterwards it was found that the coat was actually fitted on the performer's body,

his arms being through the sleeves, although his hands and feet were tied as firmly as ever, and the seal on the rope at the wrist unbroken; and again, shortly afterwards the coat was taken off and conveyed through the air to the owner in less time than would be occupied by a person pulling off a coat.

On each of these last occasions—as before—a gentleman present held Herr Dobler by the legs and feet, to assure himself that there was no muscular movement by him, and ultimately a lady's muff was instantaneously transferred from the table encircling the performer's arms, and likewise transmitted into the hands of one the visitors, notwithstanding that both arms were at the same time very securely tied and sealed at his back.

The séance lasted about half an hour, and it certainly is a marvellously strange and clever entertainment. So far as can be observed, and the closest investigation is sought—it would seem to be impossible to perform the feats; but Herr Dobler accomplishes them in a most easy manner with great rapidity. The "manifestations" are beyond doubt, astonishing, and cannot fail to interest all who witness them. Herr Dobler, as will be seen by advertisement, gives his varied entertainment in this city next week, and his first programme will take place in the Music Hall, on Monday next.

*Worcestershire Chronicle.*

———•◦•———

# 1872 – THE APPEARANCE OF ANOTHER GHOST.

Those who delight in reading about and discoursing about ghosts and apparitions have had of late a plentiful stock of material, albeit in every instance the supposed spectre has turned out to be real flesh and blood. The Peckham ghost is fresh in the recollection of most persons. The exploits of Spring-heeled Jack are still remembered as having frightened London half out of its wits. The miscreant made night hideous by his tricks, leaping over hedges to the terror of lonely pedestrians, waylaying females, scaring children, and even rendering the drivers in charge of the mails helpless with terror.

The suburbs of London were in a far different state forty years ago, when all this happened, to what they are now, and it can easily be imagined how great was the consternation this occasioned among those residing in them. People were afraid to venture out after nightfall. Stories of the wildest and most extravagant nature got into the newspapers, and formed the staple of conversation. By many, Spring-heeled Jack was believed to be a veritable demon; others declared him to be a nobleman in disguise who took delight in his cruel sport; while the majority were in favour of his being a vulgar footpad who first terrified those whom he subsequently plundered. Thus, while some credited him with horns and eyes of flame, an opposite set of eyewitnesses were in favour of a mask and a whitened face; and society was divided between believers in hoofs and those who asserted, with hardly less folly, that the extraordinary leaps in which he indulged were effected by means of springs in his boots, powerful enough, some said, to carry him over houses!

Seeing the altered state of things in these days, it might have been thought that any successful revival of such a piece of folly or wickedness was impossible. Our suburbs are not only lit, but watched, and in place of fields and lanes consist for the most part, of broad thoroughfares with dwellings in all directions.

In spite of this, South London was a short time since in a state of commotion owing to what is known as the Peckham ghost. Not the stone throwing "ghost" which a few months since destroyed scores of panes of glass in certain streets; but a mysterious figure, quite as

alarming in manners and appearance as that which terrified a past generation. As in all such cases, much has to be set down to popular exaggeration, and the tendency of stories of the wild and wonderful to grow in the telling. This we can hardly be expected to credit that the figure in question is eight feet in height, springs over stone walls and lofty hedges, and on nearing a victim changes from grim blackness to white.

One Sunday evening, a few weeks ago, two of the daughters of Dr. Carver, the headmaster of Dulwich College – young girls of from fourteen to sixteen years of age – were with their governess, setting out for church. The younger of the two happened to be in advance and had just passed through the open doorway on to the step, when she saw moving rapidly towards her, across the carriage drive, at about eight or ten yards distance, a figure enveloped in white and with arms extended. Startled and alarmed, the young lady screamed out, and sprang hastily back into the porch, communicating her fright to her companions. They, meanwhile had caught sight of the miscreant; but in the alarm and confusion which ensued – the door being only partly open – they

THE APPEARANCE OF ANOTHER GHOST

were unable to observe in which direction he made his escape.

On the following morning, distinct traces were discovered in the crushed and down-trodden grass, of someone having stationed himself behind a small shrubbery on the front lawn, from which he would command a full view of the doorway without being seen. The effects of the apparition were at the time, as may be supposed, somewhat distressing; but it was attended by no serious consequences. This was not the fault of the miserable perpetrator of what he no doubt regards as a capital joke. What satisfaction such a joke could afford over a morbid mind it is difficult to conceive.

Shortly after this, indeed it might be said to be nearly at the same time, a ghost made its appearance at Camberwell.

On Saturday night last another spectre made its appearance this time not in the suburbs of London, but in a lane within a short distance of the town of Bury. For the following report of the affair we are indebted to the *Welbourne Advertiser*:- "On Saturday night last, James Sanson was driving a carrier's cart with a pair of horses down Deadman's Lane. When within about two miles of the town he was suddenly surprised and alarmed at beholding a white object behind the foliage. His horses appeared to be more alarmed than himself, and started off at a gallop. Sanson was moved to an extremity of fear upon beholding an unearthly figure all in white present itself within a few paces of him. The figure (which he positively asserts to have been a ghost) twisted itself about and performed a number of antics fearful to witness; it shrieked and gibbered at once discordant and appalling, and, notwithstanding the terrific speed he had urged his horses to, the spectre kept by his side for the space of several minutes and then, with one wild shriek, disappeared as suddenly as it had presented itself."

*Illustrated Police News.*

———◦◉◦———

# 1872 – THE SO–CALLED GHOST.

Sir,

Such a considerable amount of "Ghost" literature has found its way into one of your contemporaries, and so little has been done towards unravelling and exposing the mystery that I think it high time something definite were done towards accomplishing this object. Residents in Peckham, Camberwell, and other parts of South London have printed letters with their names attached, professedly giving accounts of midnight meetings with the "Ghost;" navvies, who pretend to have been

frightened, discuss the matter over their pots of beer; a chorister speaks of having been either touched or spoken to by it; while others relate their various adventures; and yet, against all these, I discover, on making inquiries of policemen in the different districts alluded to, that not a single constable I have met believes in the story.

Only this very evening (Thursday) when the news of the arrest of a drunken white-jacketed bricklayer (whom the little—and big—boys of Peckham had at once magnified and transformed into the "Ghost") was the cause of the greatest excitement in the neighbourhood of the High Street Police station. I questioned a constable on the matter. He laughed at the very idea; and the practical view that he took of the affair contained an immense amount of common sense—said he: "There ain't no ghost, sir; it's all a got-up affair. You take my tip. Somebody in a white Macintosh was the first one to set it going. One person mentioned that he had seen this man with the waterproof; and that it seemed, at first sight, more like a ghost than anything; and then this remark got added to and improved upon until at last people got to talk about, and magnify the tale that they could not rid themselves of the idea that someone was about. So, when they see a tall man walking about during the evening in a white or light coat, they become scared and run off, swearing they've seen and been touched by the Ghost! Why just look at this very evening; a tall bricklayer who has had a drop too much gets fighting outside a public house in Peckham, and by some means or other either touches or falls against a woman. The female, seeing he has on a white coat, at once concludes he's the ghost; makes a great hue and cry about the matter; and two of our men have to march him through Peckham, followed by a crowd numbering scores, who fully believe that he is as the woman reported. The idea of talking about spring-heels, and of jumping six-feet walls," concluded my informant, in the most intense tone of disgust, "why," said he, "how is it we've got no orders about the thing. Don't you make any mistake, sir, if there were a ghost or anything in the shape of one, we should soon hear of it, I can assure you."

Now this policeman's remarks, which bear out in substance precisely the opinions of other constables in different districts, seem to be very sensible, and their truthfulness most probable; and I hope that by placing them before the inhabitants of South London through this Journal they may be enabled to satisfy themselves that there is really no danger nor fear of encountering this so called "Ghost."

Yours obediently,

F. E.

*South London Chronicle.*

———◦◉◦———

## 1873 – GHOSTLY MUSICIANS.

A family of Eddys—Horatio. William, and two sisters —in Chittenden, are startling the neighbourhood for miles around by their wonderful spirit manifestations. Mr J. C. Williams of Danby, recently visited the family, and, with others, made a circle of sixteen around a table on which were a violin, guitar, tambourine, bells, and other musical instruments, The house had previously been thoroughly searched to ascertain whether there were any secret passages or trapdoors, but nothing was discovered to show the practice of deception or fraud. The doors leading into the circle room were sealed, Horatio Eddy, who sat for the circle, was thoroughly tied and seated beside the table. The light was then extinguished, and immediately the musical instruments began to play, sometimes five or six of them at once. On lighting the lamp the medium was still firmly tied. The light was again extinguished, and in less time than it takes to tell, the medium's coat was taken off, and when the lamp was re-lighted the garment was found thrown over the head of one of the visitors.

At another time a pan of water was placed on the table, and, while the instruments were being played by unseen hands, was found turned bottom upward and not a drop of water spilled. A gentleman in tuning it back spilled half the water. Afterward a duel was fought between two spirits claiming to be those of George Dix and Robert Kidd, the pirate. The swords could be heard clashing, and soon a heavy body fell, jarring the house, followed by groans and voices. This within three feet of where the spectators sat.

An old gentleman, who had come many miles to communicate with the spirit of his daughter, sat in the medium's lap, and the spirit purporting to be his daughter came and patted him on the cheek, the pats being heard distinctly by all present, calling him "papa," and conversing in audible tones with him. The dark circle last but a short time, and at the conclusion the cord which bound the medium's arms was untied by some power, and came whizzing through the room a distance of fifteen feet, and was thrown around the neck of Mr Hilliard.

Next was held the light circle, for which William Eddy sat. He was tied and placed in the dark bedroom, a room some six by twelve feet, and a blanket tacked up to the door, while the audience sat in the circle room, which was lighted. In order to preserve harmony in the circles, singing was engaged in, and in which ail joined. Soon after the curtain was pushed back and the spirit of an Indian woman made her appearance. This is the spirit of Honto, she called, which frequently presents itself at these séances, and was recognised by those present. This spirit was dressed as an Indian woman.

The next spirit purported to be that of William Whith, late editor *The Banner of Light*. He was dressed in a nice suit of broad cloth, with a white vest, and his features could be plainly seen. The next was the spirit of a young lady, dressed in white, and recognised by her friends who were present. And then the spirit of a little child, which no one recognised. No less than sixteen different forms and differently dressed were presented, and seen distinctly by all present.

*Central City Register.*

———◆———

## 1873 – THE PHANTOM TRAIN.

In all ages the belief in apparitions, spectral visitants, and supernatural appearances, generally has existed to greater or lesser extent in this and other countries. Nor has this strange infatuation been confined to the ignorant or vulgar—some of our most accomplished scholars and those who have possessed the highest intellectual endowments, have been imbued with superstitious fancies. A great English novelist, poet, and dramatist, who has but recently departed from our midst, was a believer in table turning and spiritualism. Sir Walter Scott is said to have placed implicit faith in auguries, omens, and signs, and other manifestations, and his work on Demonology and Witchcraft proves that he was strangely superstitious.

A century ago our great lexicographer, Dr. Johnson, paid a visit to a lane running out of the Old Bailey for the express purpose of entering a house said to be haunted, and after the visit the doctor declared that he had every reason to believe that the home in question was haunted by the ghost of Mrs. Veal. Numbers of other persons were deceived in the same manner, and for a long time the public mind was agitated to an extraordinary degree by the Cock Lane Ghost, as it was termed, and thousands flocked to the mysterious house.

This imposition—for it was proved beyond doubt to have been nothing else—was practised by one William Parsons, his wife and daughter, by means of a female ventriloquist. During 1760 and 1761 it was carried on at 33, Cock Lane, London, and was at length detected. Parsons and his wife were condemned to the pillory and imprisonment in July, 1762. In the present day persons are allowed to practise imposition of every description with impunity. Had Parsons lived a century later, the probability is that he would have retired with a fortune, and have been considered an exceedingly clever fellow. Poets, painters, and dramatists have frequently availed themselves of the supernatural—it is a licence they are, perhaps, justly entitled to.

Shakespeare introduces a ghost in many of his plays and all ideal or allegorical painters, both ancient and modern art, have represented ghosts, fairies, gnomes, water nymphs, and fabulous beings of every description in some of their works. The engraving above is reproduced from one which appeared in an American illustrated newspaper; it represents a singular superstition believed by many persons in that country at the present day. The following account is reprinted from the American paper:

### The Phantom Train — The Dead Lincoln's Yearly Trip Over The New York Central Railroad, as Related by a Night Watchman.

A writer in an Albany paper relates a conversation with a superstitious night watchman on the New York Central Railroad. Said the watchman, "I believe in spirits and ghosts. I know such things exist. If you will come in April I will convince you."

He then told of the phantom train that every year comes up the road with the body of Abraham Lincoln. Regularly in the month of April, about midnight, the air on the track becomes very keen and cutting. On either side it is warm and still. Every watchman, when he feels this air, steps off the track and sits down to watch. Soon after the pilot engine, with long black streamers, and a band with black instruments, playing dirges, grinning skeletons sitting all about, will pass up noiselessly, and the very air grows black. If it is moonlight, clouds always come over the moon, and the music seems to linger, as if frozen with horror. A few minutes after the phantom train glides by. Flags and streamers hang about. The track ahead seems covered with a black carpet, and the wheels are draped with the same.

The coffin of the murdered Lincoln is seen lying in the centre of a car, and all about it in the air and the train behind are vast numbers of blue coated men, some with coffins on their backs, others leaning on them. It seems then that all the vast armies of men who died during the war are escorting the phantom train of the President. The wind, if blowing, dies away at once, and over all the solemn air a solemn hush, almost stifling, prevails. If a train was passing, its noise would be drowned in the silence, and the phantom train would ride over it. Clocks and watches always stop, and when looked at are found to be from five to eight minutes behind. Everywhere on the road, about the 27th of April, the time of watches and trains is found suddenly behind. This, said the leading watchman, was from the passage of the phantom train.

THE PHANTOM TRAIN

We shall find it difficult to account in any rational way for the strange statement made by the night watchman. "In certain diseases of the brain, attended with excitement," says a writer on the subject, "persons exhibit a remarkable capability of reproducing and combining images of external objects; and whoever will consider carefully the mental phenomena produced by the different and opposite conditions of the brain in such cases, the one produced by the operation of a physical agent and the other from the influence of disease, will have no difficulty concerning the origin of spectral illusions, either with the consciousness that they are illusions, or with a temporary or permanent persuasion that they are real existences, and whether arising from external or internal causes, or from both combined."

The case of Nicholai, the celebrated bookseller of Berlin, affords a curious illustration of the long continuance of vivid spectral illusions, without the slightest belief in the existence of the apparition. Some minds, such as Nicholai's, have a strong tendency to form vivid pictorial images of everything that interests them; and we suspect that the night watchman on the New York Railway had a similar tendency. Certain states of the body and certain affections of the mind powerfully predispose to the intense renovation of past impressions, however those impressions have been produced, and whatever their nature, the immediate exciting cause of the renovation being often some external object acting upon the senses, or upon the imagination, under circumstances favourable to the illusion." A large class of spectral illusions are referable to this head, of which the following may be taken as an example:—

A gentleman was benighted while travelling alone in a remote part of the highlands of Scotland, and was compelled to ask for shelter for the evening at a small, lonely hut. When he was to be conducted to his bedroom the landlady observed, with mysterious reluctance, that he would find the windows very insecure. On examination part of the wall appeared to have been broken down to enlarge the opening. After some inquiry he was told that a pedlar, who had lodged in the room some time before, had committed suicide, and was found hanging behind the door in the morning.

According to the superstition of the country, it was deemed improper to remove the body through the door of the house, and to convey it through the window was impossible without removing part of the wall. Some hints were dropped that the room had been subsequently haunted by the poor man's spirit. My friend laid his arms, properly prepared against intrusion of any kind, by the bed side, and retired to rest, not without some degree of apprehension. He was visited in a dream by a frightful apparition, and awakening in agony, found himself sitting up in bed with a pistol grasped in his right hand. On casting a fearful glance round the room, he discovered, by the moonlight, a corpse, dressed in a shroud, reared erect against the wall close by the window.

With much difficulty he summoned up the resolution to approach the dismal object, the features of which, and the minutest parts of its funeral apparel he perceived distinctly. He passed one hand over it, felt nothing, and staggered back to bed. After a long interval, and much reasoning with himself, he renewed his investigation, and at length discovered that the object of his terror was produced by moonbeams forming a long bright image through the broken window, on which his fancy, impressed by his dream, had pictured with mischievous accuracy the lineaments of a body prepared for interment.

Powerful associations of terror in this instance had invested the recollected images with uncommon force and effect. We do not for moment doubt but that the phantom train depicted in our illustration is attributable to some such a cause, and that the imagination of the night watchman has been excited in a similar manner. The peculiarity of constitution expressed by the term predisposition, whether corporeal or mental, is not only deeply indicated in the production of a general tendency to the formation of these phantoms, but it often determines even the specific character which each assumes. Since the predisposition varies in each individual, the same morbid cause may conjure up images the most diversified.

The daughter of Sir Charles Lee saw about two o'clock in the morning the apparition of a little woman between her curtains and her pillow. She was her deceased mother; that she was happy, and by twelve of the clock by that day she should be with her. Thereupon she knocked up her maid, called for her clothes, and when she was dressed she went into her closet, and came not out again till nine, and then she brought with her a letter sealed to her father, brought it to her aunt, the Lady Everard, told her what had happened, and desired that as soon as she was dead it might be sent to him. She desired that the chaplain might be called to read prayers, and when prayers were ended she took her guitar and psalm book, and sat down in a chair without arms, and played and sang so melodiously and admirably that her music master, who was then there, was lost in admiration, and near the stroke of twelve she rose and sat herself down in a great chair with aims, and fetching a strong breath or two immediately expired.

In this case a spectral illusion occurring in a tender and susceptible frame produced such a powerful impression upon the imagination as absolutely to destroy life. Numbers of other instances could be cited to prove the danger of giving way to a diseased or distorted imagination.

In regard to ghosts it is observable that they were remarkably abundant in this country during the interregnum after the civil war in 1649. The melancholic tendency of the rigid Puritans of the period, and their occupancy of old family seats, formerly the residences of hospitality and good cheer, which in their hands became desolate and gloomy; and the dismal stories propagated by the discarded retainers of the ancient establishments, ecclesiastical and civil, contributed altogether to produce a national horror altogether unknown in other periods of our history.

We cannot conclude this article without declaring most positively and emphatically that ghosts and phantoms of every description are mere chimeras, produced by an overheated brain, or some other physical derangement of the system. Those who profess to "call spirits from the vast deep" are nothing more than quacks, charlatans, or impostors.

We have given the engraving of the Phantom Train in this week's paper to show how well the distorted imagination of persons can conjure up and people the air with phantoms. In many respects the illustration in question bears a striking similarity to Hans Holbein's celebrated "Dance of Death."

*Illustrated Police News.*

---

# 1873 – TRAGEDY AT A SÉANCE.

A terrible tragedy occurred in Birmingham on Sunday night. A séance, or spiritualistic service, was being held in the Athenaeum Assembly Rooms, Temple Row, and most of the prominent believers in spiritualism were present. In the course of the service, a medium, Benjamin Hawkes, a toy dealer, of New Street, addressed the audience. He averred that at one séance he and Peter the Apostle had clasped hands, and that he had felt the firm grasp of Peter's hand in his own. From this manifestation he went on to argue that it was quite possible to understand how Thomas, called Didymus, thrust his hand into the side of "The Personification of Divine Love." The instant these words were uttered the speaker fell back on a chair behind him, dead. The meeting broke up amidst the wildest excitement.

*Fife Herald.*

---

# 1874 – A REFLECTION.

Not a little alarm and curiosity was created last week in the neighbourhood of West Street, Reading, at the reported appearance of a spectral visitant in a large empty dwelling house, which until recently has been occupied as the Inland Revenue Office. People alleged that they could see "something" strange in the empty house on the 25th, and several hundred persons collected at the spot. Eventually, stones were thrown at the supposed apparition, resulting in the breaking of some fifteen or twenty panes of glass, and the police had considerable difficulty in suppressing the disturbance. The following night a crowd was again collecting, but an efficient body of police caused them to move on. The building was again watched, but fortunately no disturbance occurred. It is a singular fact that some years ago a similar superstition prevailed, and a disturbance was then created in respect to this very dwelling. The police have been over the house, and find nothing suspicious, and it is surmised that the singular appearances reported to be seen are simply caused by the reflections on the conservatory doors.

*Dudley Guardian.*

---

# 1874 – AMERICAN GHOSTS.

A story of ghosts and ghostly manifestations given to the world by an American paper, the *Des Moines* (Iowa) Register:-

"Ever since the Third street spook raised such a rumpus, ghostly visitors (it says) appear to have become numerous. Closely following the sudden demise of the uncertain spirit that disturbed the denizens of the Fourth Ward, were heard rumours of ghost power running sewing machines. Several citizens well known testify that the wheels were turned by some unknown and invisible agency. This was followed by unnatural lights blazing the walls and looking as green as an evening paper man afflicted with yellow jaundice.

On Cherry Street a resident reports that invisible bells are tinkled at unseemly hours. The tintinnabulation is like that of a Chicago charm bell, and is heard in different parts of the house, but never very close to any person. When anyone goes to the place where it has been heard, the tinkling appears to be just at the back of him. A house on Locust Street is afflicted with a bright light shining in a certain place on the wall of a bedroom. The light is plainly visible at a distance, but disappears whenever anyone gets close to it. Another peculiarity is that it shines as brightly during the day as at night, although it is necessary to close the shutters and darken the room during the sunlit hours in order to see the spook in all its brilliancy.

A Tenth Street dog sees ghosts, but whether of man, beast, or book peddler it is not explained. The animal will suddenly start from sleep and make a fierce attack upon some invisible foe, frequently following it round the house, growling and barking all the time. It has indulged in this phantom fighting for over two years. The phenomenon always occurs in daylight. One night last week a prominent citizen was awakened by the music of his piano, playing most sweetly to the tune of "Robin Adair." His daughter, the only musician in the house was absent at the time, and he hurried to the parlour to see who it was thus charming the night with the sweetest melody of the time. Arriving there he found the apartment empty, and the piano closed and locked.

A lady residing in the East Des Moines became very much interested in the Third Street ghost, and made several visits to the locality where it was reported to be boarding. One evening, accompanied by several other ladies, she was at the house, returning home about ten o'clock. Two of the ladies went into the parlour with her, and sat down to talk over the ghost. Suddenly a large music box on the mantel commenced to play, continuing through five tunes, the instrument being geared for ten. When it ceased the box was examined, and found to be entirely "run down." It was replaced on the mantel, and a moment later it commenced to play again, continuing until all the tunes were played.

In another house the gas in a certain room is frequently lighted by invisible matches. The person occupying the apartment has often gone to sleep after turning off the gas, and awakened hours after to find it brightly burning. Again it would be turned off, and at daylight the blaze would be as vivid as ever. This is a good natured spook, for a comparison of the gas bills before this phenomenon commenced, and since its existence, shows no increase in the amount consumed. A lady of eminent social position and undoubted truthfulness assured the author a few days since, that her buried child frequently appeared to her when she visited the room where he died. In the course of the conversation the lady said that her sweetest moments were during those silent intervals with her lost darling. Every feature of his face appears to her perfectly natural, and he always seems to clasp in his little hands a favourite toy that lay on his bed when he died. Strange to say, the mother never remembers how the image is dressed."

*Monmouthshire Beacon.*

# 1874 – LONDON GHOSTS.

One might have imagined that the biggest, busiest, and noisiest city in the world would have escaped the visitation of ghosts of every kind. But this is very far from being the case. Thousands of the enlightened inhabitants of the great metropolis, though they may have enjoyed opportunities of witnessing Professor Pepper's wonderful creations, are deeply saturated with the spirit of superstition that they succeed in making ghosts, sometimes out of common place material and sometimes out of no material at all.

The deluded people who believed, long ago in the Cock Lane ghost, have communicated their delusions to their descendants. Upwards of a year ago the papers contained accounts of the night wanderings of the sheeted Camberwell ghost, which had a fancy for frightening servant girls out of their wits at house corners and in suburban lanes; but the police at last succeeded in tripping up the heels of this nocturnal prowler, who turned out to be an Irish navvy, and a pretty severe fine imposed by the magistrate put a finishing touch upon the Camberwell ghost.

Another supernatural being, less material than the one just mentioned, has recently, however, made its appearance, and this time in a house of a decent greengrocer, residing in Tottenham Court Road. An exclamation, "Here's the ghost!" and an uplifted finger, directed to a front window, drew together, in no time, an immense crowd of excited people, who blocked both pavement and the roadway. A case of assault, which inevitably grew out of this block, led to the matter obtaining the publicity of a police court – the place where London ghosts are generally "laid" by magisterial fiat.

In answer to Mr. Newton, who sits at Marlborough Street, the greengrocer, in whose house the phantom had appeared, stated that his second floor lodgers had fire in the grate, but no lamp alight, and it caused the reflection of a figure on the celling! This was all. Here was the friendly, familiar domestic ghost with whom we have all been well acquainted from earliest childhood, and yet there was something in its appearance, as casually seen from the street, that made the playful, flickering firelight shadow seem a dreadful ogre to an excited London crowd. With all our boasted enlightenment, we have yet a good deal to do in "laying" the ghost of superstition.

*Whitby Times, and North Yorkshire Advertiser.*

# 1874 – SEANCE AT THE CRYSTAL PALACE.

Yesterday afternoon an extraordinary, and to most present an incomprehensible, entertainment was given at the Crystal Palace to a select few who had been invited to witness it. The entertainment consisted of what were termed light and dark séances, given by Miss Annie Eva Fay, a young lady from America, who is attended by Colonel H. C. Fay, of Ohio, on her visit to this country. The séances were given in the saloon at the rear of the royal box, in the centre transept, and the place had been fitted up by Mr. Wilkinson, general manager of the Palace, under the conditions which he had himself imposed – that neither the Colonel nor Miss Fay should superintend or direct the work, though at liberty to see its progress from time to time. Several of the visitors entered the room some time previous to the séance, and thoroughly satisfied themselves that no machinery, wires or other apparatus existed in connection with the platform or any other part of the room.

Colonel Fay having come up on the platform, said that the kind of manifestations which were about to be shown had previously been performed in this country and in America by two performers, but this was the first time that a young girl alone had exhibited such phenomena in this country With regard to the way in which they were accomplished he did not wish to set forth any theory. He meant simply that his hearers should see what was done and judge for themselves. Some might say the power at work was electricity; some that it was the OD force; others that it was magnetism. He did not wish to give any view of his own, but left the question of the power in the hands of a discriminating public. Let them take the facts for what they were worth— some of them had astounded scientists, puzzled conjurors, and confounded philosophers.

Mr. Attwood and Mr. F. A. Woods were then chosen to act as a committee to watch the performance from the platform, and Mr. Wilkinson being called upon, said the fitting up of the place had been done by him under the conditions above mentioned. Miss Annie Eva Fay was then introduced, and two staples, the lower of which held a ring, were then securely fastened under the inspection of the committee into an upright post, in front of which was placed an ordinary camp stool. Miss Fay then had her hands tied securely together behind her back with narrow strips of cotton cloth, the knots being not only securely made, but also sewn up carefully by Mrs. Attwood with a needle and thread. She then sat down on the camp stool; her hands were securely tied to the ring on the lower part of the post, and a narrow band of cotton was passed round her neck, and tied tightly to the upper staple so as to prevent any forward movement of the head. Her feet were then tightly tied together with a long rope, the end of which was given to one of the audience to hold.

The committee being appealed to, declared that Miss Fay was tied up perfectly secure. A strip of black cotton tape was then placed loosely round Miss Fay's neck, the ends hanging straight down in front. A curtain was then raised by Colonel Fay and held in front, he asking that a knot should be tied on the tape. In a few seconds Miss Fay called "Light," the colonel dropped the curtain, and the tape was seen to be tightly knotted. The committee examined and found all the bonds perfectly secure. A tambourine, a small mouth harmonium, and a couple of bells were then placed in her lap, and on the curtain being raised the tambourine was struck, the bells were rung, and the harmonium was sounded, the colonel explaining that this instrument was raised by the unknown power and placed in Miss Fay's mouth, so that she blew through it. A small finger ring was placed on her lap, and when the curtain was lowered was found in her left ear. A piece of paper and a scissors were laid in her lap, the sound of clipping was distinctly heard, and the rude figures of babies were cut out of it, which were presented to the members of the committee. A board, a hammer, and a nail were placed on a chair beside her. The audience, on the curtain being raised, heard the sound of hammering, and presently the chair was overturned. The curtain being dropped, the nail was found driven into the board. A glass nearly full of water was placed on the tambourine in Miss Fay's lap. The colonel asked that the glass should be lifted to her lips, so that she might drink, and on lowering the curtain about half the water was found to have vanished from the tumbler. A guitar which had been placed upon her knee began to play, and the curtain was moved as if it struck it behind, while now and then it was seen where the curtain rose a little above the platform moving about and strumming, though quite out of reach of Miss Fay.

It should be remarked that during the whole time the cord which bound her feet together was held tightly, and that as this cord prevented the curtain from touching the platform in the centre her feet could always be seen distinctly. A pail was placed in her lap, and when the curtain was lowered after not more than two seconds, the pail was inverted on her head. An open knife was laid in her lap, the curtain was raised; the knife closed was thrown over the curtain, light was called, and the bonds of cotton were found to be divided both at the neck and wrists. The knots were then examined and found to be intact.

Miss Fay was released from her bonds, and a circle of chair s having been formed, 14 of the audience, along with Colonel Fay, sat down to a dark séance, Miss Fay being seated in the centre on the camp stool. The various instruments above mentioned as well as a few fans were placed upon the knees of the sitters, each holding the hand of the person seated next him. The guitar was placed between the knees of the writer, who also held both hands of Colonel Fay in one of his, and can testify that during the séance the colonel did not move either of them. Miss Fay kept up a constant clapping of her hands, so that those around could perceive that she did not move; occasionally she ceased this and placed her hands on those of someone in the circle. The gas having been turned out, the different instruments were lifted and carried about, strummed, thumped, and rung, while soft hands were felt touching the hands, faces, and beards of the sitters, who, after a little time, were also treated to some very acceptable draughts of air from the fans.

In conclusion, the light was turned on again, and the séance ended.

*Morning Post.*

---

# 1875 – A RATIONAL EXPLANTION.

At the residence of Mr. D. W. Parsons, 31, Everton Crescent, strange noises had for some time past been heard during the night. These could by no means be accounted for, so servants declared their belief that the house was haunted. One of these, more gifted than the rest, had seen "an old lady" roaming through the cellars. "She made no noise but her eyes were awful!"

Ghosts, as a rule, return whence they came ere the clock ceases to strike the midnight hour. But the Crescent Ghost must have obtained extension leave, for the "old lady" continued her manoeuvring sometimes until near the break of day. Search had been made from time to time, but nothing was discovered which could throw light upon what then seemed to be a mystery. Behind the house the doctor had a well-stocked hen pen, where his poultry slept securely, until one morning the wire was found broken, and traces of commotion and havoc were plainly to be seen. As usual, and indeed in this case quite naturally, the cats were accused of having done the mischief. Each morning showed traces of either successful or unsuccessful attempts to plunder or destroy. Home cats were got rid of, vengeance vowed against all strange ones. A weasel was next supposed to be the culprit. Traps and poison were brought into requisition, but with no result.

At last the midnight robber was supposed to have been discovered in the form of a favourite cat belonging to the gentleman next door, she being detected one morning jumping over the wall and carrying off a young rabbit. Poor pussy's character was strongly defended by her master; but she was convicted and sentenced to imprisonment. Still it was plain that the ghost, or thief, or both, had not yet been banished. The noises continued and poultry disappeared. Traps of various kinds were again placed knowingly in position, and on Thursday morning it was ascertained that the cause of all the noises and other "devilry" which the doctor and his household had been so much disturbed was a visitor of the most unlikely kind to be found at large in the centre of the town of Liverpool – nothing less than a two year old fox caught at last by his hind leg, and dragging the trap behind him.

The rogue made for the cellars, where he had for so long made himself home. Closely pursued, and his retreat cut of, the chimney was before him, and here he for a time escaped. Various measures having been resorted to in order to compel him to "break cover," it was found necessary to get a sweep to do so, when he was finally captured and killed, a group wondering whence he could have come being "in at the death."

*Burnley Advertiser.*

---

# 1875 – THE WIDOWERS PROMISE.

A recent occurrence in Canada, says the *Ottawa Citizen*, affords a dreadful warning to widowers. The affair is described with great minuteness in the newspapers of the Dominion, and is of a character to make the hair of every man, under bonds to keep the peace with a wife in the cemetery, stand on end in the conventional way. In Hamilton, something over a year ago, lived an old couple named Kitchen, but the old gentleman is the only one now remaining, the wife dying suddenly some time since. She was a woman apparently inclined to jealousy, and, previous to her death gave convincing proof of this quality in her character, threatening to haunt her husband in case he ever became intimate with another woman. The old man promised, and for a period after the funeral kept the promise, but eventually yielded to that friskiness which appears to be widower's besetting sin.

A short time since, dressed in his best clothes, and feeling all the fire of youth in his veins again, the widower, in company with another man, drove off on a visit to a couple of ladies. They returned home late at night, and Kitchen became decidedly agitated as they approached an old church, in a graveyard attached to which his wife was buried. When opposite the spot "the white-robed form of a woman was seen to rise from the graveyard, and float through the air toward them." Kitchen screamed out in an agony of terror, the horse gave vent to a wild snort of fear, and ran down the mountain at breakneck speed, and the apparition continued to follow them, floating through the atmosphere in terrible proximity to the faithless widower. The other man stated that it "looked like the corpse of a woman, with the death-clothes son."

The face was quite dead and expressionless, and the eyes were closed; one hand was extended toward Kitchen, almost touching his head, and the other pointing toward the abode of the ladies visited.

Eventually the vehicle was smashed to pieces against a tree, and by the time the two men had recovered from the shock the ghost had disappeared. That is the story, and now young ladies haven't a chance with any widower in that region who promised his first wife that he'd remain single.

*Dundee Courier.*

## 1876 – A GHOST IN CHURCH.

A weird story comes from a little village not far from Modbury. It is a bleak raw night, the choir of the parish church have assembled for the purpose of practice, and their voices are making sweet melody in the sacred edifice, when a sharp-sighted chorister thinks he sees a door move, and a few seconds of anxious watching confirms his supposition. By this time the attention of the whole choir has been directed to the slowly opening door, and soon in the dimly lighted space a figure indescribable, draped in white, appears before them, and with solemn march goes slow and stately down the aisle and mounts the pulpit; thence it returns and vanishes into the night, whilst they, distilled almost to a jelly with the act of fear, stand dumb and speak not to it.

Thus far we have been able to borrow from Horatio's description another supernatural appearance; but the sequels differ. No sooner had the strange visitant disappeared through the doorway, than shrieks, faintings, and groans relieved the terrified choir, and a flight—a veritable *sauve qui pent* —followed. The night, as has been said, was dark and gloomy, just the one for eccentric spirits to select for visiting former scenes, and to make the spectators all the more positive that the white robed figure was a ghost. Indeed, the villagers are convinced that the apparition was that of one recently deceased—one whom they all knew and respected.

The mysterious occurrence had a marked effect upon those who witnessed it, and a doctor was in attendance upon one of them the following day, but we do not know whether the incident of the previous night had anything to do with the ailment.

Good ghost stories are becoming scarcer every day, and at such a season as Christmas a new apparition is very opportune. Under these circumstances, residents in the district are to be congratulated upon their rare fortune.

*Western Morning News.*

## 1876 – EXTRAORDINARY SPIRITUAL PHENOMENA.

A most extraordinary manifestation is said to have been witnessed by a number of persons in Middleton. On Friday night last according to the statement of a number of witnesses, the figure of a woman was seen flitting or travelling along the telegraph wires. The figure was at times indistinct and shadowy whilst at others it was more palpable to the sight. Many conjectures are afloat as to whose disembodied spirit it was that visited the earth and scared people in their peaceful habitations.

*Illustrated Police News.*

## 1876 – GHOSTS AND APPARITIONS.

The reader will find in this week's *Police News* a series of engravings of well authenticated ghost stories, or in other words, remarkable spectral illusion. It is not necessary to enter into discussion upon the question of apparitions and spiritual visitants. It will, however, be as well to note that at all ages and at all times the belief was more or less popular that the spirits of the departed had the power at certain times and under particular circumstances to revisit the earth.

An apparition may be described as the preternatural appearance of some departed spirit. Many have boldly asserted that this supposition of spectral visitants involves no absurdity or speculative impossibility.

Dr. Henry More and Dr. Glanvil with Mr. Baxter, have severally endeavoured to establish the reality of apparitions. It is, however, sufficiently evident that we can demonstrate the actual truth of the popular belief upon the subject from abstract considerations; the issue of the question must necessarily depend on the evidence adduced to prove the matter of fact, and can only be determined upon the testimony of several witnesses in every case, because it is well-known that fever and intoxication will leave behind them for a considerable time a diseased imagination, under the operation of which people have supposed that they have heard voices and seen objects which unquestionably had no reality out of their own minds. "It is not true," observes a writer, who takes a practical view of his subject, "as is generally supposed, that we see with the eye, hear with the ear, and taste with the tongue. The true seat of sensations is the brain, and the eye, ear, and the tongue are adapted to receive impressions from external objects, which impressions are transmitted from the organs by an appropriate apparatus to the brain, where they become sensations."

In order that the brain may carry on these operations, that is, in order that it may receive the impressions conveyed to it by the nerves from the organs of sense, in order that it may convert these impressions into sensations, and in order that it may duly combine and revive them, it must be in a sound state. The chief agents which nourish the brain in a sound state are its organic nerves and its circulating vessels. Like every other organ the brain is maintained in a healthy condition by the organic process of nutrition, over which the system of nerves termed organic preside. If these organic nerves become disordered, disease may take place in the substance of the brain, and this disease may assume a variety of forms far too great to be enumerated here, the slightest of which may be incompatible with sound thought. This

state accounts in a great measure for the many strange phantoms and superstitious fancies with which numbers of persons have been afflicted. Superstition is ever prone to explain the mysterious, or to account for the questionable by hunting for some supernatural cause, and hence then popular love for and strong faith in the miraculous.

The large centre illustration represents a popular ghost story, which the inhabitants of the district in which it is said to have taken place declare to be substantially correct. The figure on the ground represents the toll keeper who was murdered by some person or persons unknown many years ago, and as each anniversary of his murder comes around, the ghost is said to have stood at the gate and pointed to the prostrate form on the ground. This is one of the most popular traditions of Sussex. Numbers of travellers have declared that they have seen the ghost, and so impressed were the inhabitants with the truth of the story, that the toll house was disused shortly after the murder, so that it had a neglected, weird-like appearance.

The three top cuts are representations of goblins and sprites which are said at stated intervals to pay visits to human beings for the purpose of tormenting them. The small cut on the left hand corner is the figure of death paying a visit to a miser, who is gloating over his hoards. The two cuts at the bottom of the page are also of a spectral character; one represents the spirit of a departed wife appearing to her husband and reproving him for his faithlessness. The other, a

EXTRAORDINARY SPIRITUAL PHENOMENA.

Midnight Warning, represents the spirit of a brother, hovering around the couch of his sister to watch and protect her in the hour of danger and temptation.

*Dundee Courier.*

———⟶⟨◉⟩⟵———

# 1876 – THE GHOST OF OLD JOEY.

Some few evenings ago, while a party of spiritualists were gathered around the mystic table for the purpose of manifestations, several mysterious raps were heard on the table. Somebody suggested that a slate should be handed to the spirit and it was held beneath the mahogany table top. Great was the astonishment of all present on beholding the name Joey Grimaldi written on the slate in a fair round hand. In another minute, old Joey put in an appearance habited as a clown. After ogling and twisting his face into various contortions, he sang many of his old favourite songs and performed several of his well-known and mirth inducing tricks much the same as he was want to do when delighting the town as the prince of clowns.

*Illustrated Police News.*

———⟶⟨◉⟩⟵———

# 1876 – THE HAUNTED MANSION IN BERKELEY SQUARE.

There is in Berkeley Square a fine old mansion, which up to the present time, and for very many years past, has been constantly pointed out as "The Haunted House." Like many other mansions in the aristocratic locality its yearly value, if let, would be about £500 per annum. It has, however, long been closed to all comers, and has been allowed to grow externally into a neglected and deserted appearance. Numbers of persons have been in the habit of visiting the square for the purpose of even seeing the exterior, because the report has been so very generally current that strange unaccountable rappings and noises have for years been heard in the house, and that after midnight a strange mysterious figure has been seen about the rooms. The reputed story of the spirit rappings in the mansion has, since the conviction of Dr. Slade, been greatly revived and a good deal cited.

It is stated by many of the very old inhabitants of the locality that the story of the haunted house in Berkeley Square has been talked of as long as they can remember, and that they have heard their fathers say that there was some talk of a frightful tragedy there at one time, and talk of a ghost, and that the noises at the house used to be dreadful, but what the particulars were they could not recollect. They further assert that they have often heard that after the tragedy no one dared sleep in the house as there were such constant rappings. That at last the old landlord had to take the old house down, and a new one was then put up, but the noise continued, and nobody dare sleep in that place and that it was empty for some time.

At last a gentleman, who believed that the noises came from some explainable cause, got permission to sleep in the house one night accompanied only by his valet. He was to sleep in one room where the noises were principally heard, and his valet was to sleep in another, but on the following morning the gentleman was found dead in bed. The noises have since continued, and a strange figure has often been seen flittering about.

Such are the traditions which have recently attracted so many persons to visit Berkeley Square for the purpose of seeing the large mansion known as the haunted house.

The following authentic particulars may serve to show how such traditions probably grow and fill the minds of many with unfounded superstitious beliefs.

The London newspapers for August 3rd 1762, give an account of a very remarkable and celebrated trial for murders from which, no doubt, the present tradition first took its rise, and has created frequent riots in Berkeley Square.

The two murders were committed in the year 1758, but not in Berkeley Square, but about three quarters of a mile distance, namely, in Bruton Street, Hanover Square, and for five years remained a terrible undiscovered mystery. At that time there resided in Bruton Street a widow woman named Sarah Metyard, who obtained her livelihood principally by letting apartments and also by employing parish apprentice girls in knitting ladies' mittens. She had five of these girls from the parish whose ages ranged from eight to ten. They were scarcely ever allowed to go out, but were confined night and day in a small suffocating attic. They were hard worked, constantly brutally flogged, and half famished. She also had a daughter, seventeen years of age, whom she served very little better.

One of these girls, who had been reduced to a mere skeleton, one day managed to slip unobserved down the stairs and make her escape into the street, but was immediately overtaken and brought back upstairs, where she was again flogged in a terrible manner, then tied up in an empty room for three days without the slightest bit of food. The old woman, seeing the child's head hanging down as though she had fallen asleep, ordered the daughter to go and wake her up with another flogging. The girl did so, and under the last torture the poor child breathed her last. The old woman then told the other children, in order to account for the girl's absence that Annie Naylor had run away again.

At night, she divided the body for the purpose of trying to destroy it by burning; but after burning the two hands she desisted on account of the smell, and eventually hid the parts away in a box upstairs, where they remained for two months. The smell became so bad that she eventually carried the parts away in a bag to throw them into the Thames. For this purpose she threw them into a gulley hole in Crick Lane, at the back of the Temple. The water, however, did not carry them into the river as she expected, and the following morning they were found.

They were considered to be the remains of an anatomical dissection, and Mr. Umbreville, the then coroner, declined to hold an inquest. The unfortunate deceased had a sister who was one of the other girls employed by the old woman, and this girl happening one day to say that she knew her sister had not run away, but was dead, the old woman after questioning her as to how she knew it, destroyed her too.

Four years after the murders of the children, the old woman's daughter, Sarah Morgan Metyard, went to live in the service of a Mr. Rooker, a tea broker. He, for a long time, had had apartments in the old woman's house, but coming into possession of considerable property he went and took a house at the top of Hill Street on the corner of Berkeley Square, and knowing how cruelly the old woman treated her own girl, he took her daughter there to reside with him.

The old woman for many days and nights used to go in the most furious manner to demand her daughter out of the house. As she was refused admittance she used to create an uproar by knocking with stones on the door. The daughter, who was in possession of the terrible secret relative to the murders, used to endeavour to intimidate her mother's comings and creating the disturbances by opening the bedroom windows and calling out, "Mother, remember the gulley hole and the perfumed box. You know it is you that is the Click Lane ghost." The mother used to retaliate by calling out, "And you are another ghost, you slut. It is you that is the Click Lane ghost, and not me."

Thousands of persons used to assemble nightly in Berkeley Square to witness these scenes between the two women, and frequent riots took place at the corner in Hill Street. By and by the crowds used to ask each other what the women meant by calling each other the "Click Lane ghost." Mr. Rooker then asked the girl to tell him what these frequent allusions meant. The girl then told him that her mother had murdered Annie Naylor and that those were her remains that had been found in the gulley hole in Click Lane five years before. The mother, on Mr. Rooker's information, was arrested but she also implicated her daughter and both women were soon afterwards executed at Tyburn.

It is not difficult to see that this probably, was the first origin of the "fearful tragedy" – the ghost story and "noises at the house" – spoken of in the vicinity of Berkeley Square as being talked about by the parents of the oldest inhabitants for as long as they can remember.

The mansion, however, at present pointed out as the haunted house stands about six doors from where the reported house formerly stood, but this, too, has a very curious history, which has led to the present curious excitement and a revival and mixing together of the remembrance of other occurrences. There are, however, numbers of persons who positively declare that they know many who have seen and heard the noise at that very house, and that though the house is shut up, spirit lights are now sometimes seen floating about, and that the subject ought to be investigated in the interests of the believers in spiritual phenomena.

The following may be relied upon as the real facts upon which the excitement, since the Slade conviction, has been revived. About thirty years ago this house was taken by a medical gentleman who was fond of scientific investigations. He had only been there about three months, when he invited some friends to witness the effects of provings on himself, but to their horror he died under the administration, and, after his death, the house became vacant for some time.

It was afterwards taken by a very wealthy – but exceedingly eccentric – gentleman, named Myers. When he had purchased it he ordered extensive additions and alterations to be made to the place from an approved plan. He also ordered it to be fitted up in the most costly manner with antique furniture. His peculiarities took many forms, but one of the chief ones was that he would not be seen by anyone, especially by tradespeople or the workmen. During the fitting up he kept servants in the house, but lived somewhere else in the neighbourhood himself. The servants were under strict orders to be in bed every night by ten, locked in their respective rooms. His cheques for payment were always regularly sent, but if the work was not done strictly to order he reserved to himself the right to knock it down. He would never go to investigate the work, only at midnight, and that he acquired the name of the mysterious man. Dressed in a very eccentric manner, of an antiquated style, he used to let himself in with a private key and be seen through the windows in the dead of night from the square, going all about the place like a spectre, with an old fashioned horn lantern in his hand.

Crowds used to assemble nightly to see this strange, mysterious figure going about the rooms, and eventually he got the name of the ghost. It is stated that he had been engaged to be married, but to his disappointment it had been broken off. He eventually went to live there where he kept himself in strict seclusion, but keeping up as long as he could the habit of walking the rooms at night until he eventually became bedridden, and the walking of the alleged spectre ceased. The old gentleman died about two years ago, but the house has been shut up to all visitors for a nearly a quarter of a century.

The old servants are still permitted to live in the house for the purpose of taking care of it, as it is stated that there is likely to be some heavy legal dispute as to whom the whole of the valuable property should go.

They, however, positively aver that all the years they have been there they have never heard any noises in the house but what they could account for, neither have they ever seen any spirits excepting such as were safely corked in the bottles.

*Illustrated Police News.*

THE GHOST OF BERKELEY SQUARE.

# 1877 – SPRING–HEELED JACK JUMPING ON NEWPORT ARCH.

A correspondent sends the following account together with a sketch of a scene at Newport.

"For some time past," says our contributor, "the neighbourhood of Newport, near Lincoln, has been disturbed each evening by a man dressed in a sheepskin, or something of the kind, with a long white tail to it. The man who is playing this mischief has springs to his boots, and can jump a height of 15 or 20 feet. The other night he jumped upon a college, and got into a window on the roof, and so frightened the ladies that one has not recovered from the shock.

Some other people were so much frightened by this object, that every night a large mob of men, armed with sticks and stones, assemble and attempt to catch him, but to no avail. The nuisance became so great that two men got guns out and chased him.

The picture represents him jumping up the Newport arch, a very old Roman building built in 45 A.D., as he was jumping up he was shot at, but so tough is the hide he wears, that the shot did not penetrate it, and running over the house tops on the other side he escaped, but soon appeared in another part of the town.

He was again chased, and as he was running on the wall of the new barracks was shot at by a publican, but the shot did not appear to take effect. He has also done other tricks and which we think worthy of a picture in the "*Police News*"

*Illustrated Police News.*

---

# 1877 – THE HAUNTED MILL.

A sad instance of giving way to superstitious fears occurred on Friday last week at Newport. It would appear, from what our reporter has gathered, that a shadow has been cast on an oak fence which runs by the side of a large windmill, representing a death's head and crossbones. This shadow was only to be seen occasionally, and a report was current that the mill was haunted, some dreadful crime having been committed within its precincts. On Friday night, Robert Pugh and James Owen, two working men, were so alarmed at the appearance of the ghastly shadow that, after a few moments of suspense; they both fled precipitately from the spot. The effect on Pugh was of a most serious nature. His mind has

SPRING-HEELED JACK JUMPING ON NEWPORT ARCH

become affected, and the chances are that he will never recover his reason.

*Illustrated Police News.*

———◦———

## 1878 – GHOSTLY MANIFESTATIONS.

Great alarm has prevailed in the village of Goathurst, a few miles from Bridgwater, during the past fortnight, in consequence of the belief that a farmhouse there, in the occupation of Mr. John Shattock, a well-to-do yeoman and representative of the parish at the Board of Guardians, was haunted. It is alleged that every night loud raps were heard at the front and back doors, that articles of furniture and crockery were shifted from one portion of the premises to another, and that although many of the inhabitants and some members of the county constabulary were on the watch both inside and from without, and a large mastiff was stationed just outside the front door which was rapped at, the "manifestations" continued, and no clue could be obtained as to who or what was the cause of them.

It is positively asserted "by some of the more respectable inhabitants" that the knocks at the door, apparently from the outside, have been heard by them

THE HAUNTED MILL

while they have guarded all the approaches to the premises, and that immediately on hearing these raps they have fired pistols in the direction of the door, but without effect. The alarm was increased by a straw-rick close to the dwelling house, and belonging to the same owner, having taken fire and been totally destroyed, the ignition having taken place quite unaccountably, and whilst the neighbours and friends of the farmer were on the watch.

The district superintendent of police, who visited the premises by night on two occasions, had, however, it seems, after the manner of police officers, formed a certain "theory" of his own, and this has resulted in the apprehension of a girl named Ann Kidner, aged fourteen years, a domestic servant in the employ of Mr. Shattock, on a charge of setting fire to her master's ricks. It is suspected that this girl, although she strongly protests her innocence, is concerned in the "manifestations," if she has not been the direct and sole cause of them.

*Pall Mall Gazette.*

## 1878 – JUST DESSERTS.

An Aberdonian recently saw a ghost while walking along a lonely highway at midnight. The ghost stood exactly in the middle of the road and the wayfarer, deciding to investigate, poked at it with his umbrella. The next instant he was knocked into the ditch, and on getting out he philosophically concluded not to poke a white horse when its back is turned.

*Derbyshire Times & Chesterfield Herald.*

## 1878 – PHANTOMS OF THE SEA.

The illustration is engraved from a sketch furnished us by a mariner named James Oxleigh, who has endeavoured to realise what he and his associates saw, while in an open boat off the coast of Africa. Oxleigh thus describes the awful appearance presented by what he terms the "phantoms of the sea."

"I dare say," observes the narrator, "that our people at home may be after thinking that me and my companions had grown superstitious-like, or that our weak brains were wandering through want and hardship – and to say the truth, we had enough of both – but such was not the case. We all of us had our wits about us. As we passed one of the small islands near Madagascar, there all at once arose therefrom gigantic shadowy figures, which presently formed themselves in a solid group, terrible to look upon. They were immeasurably bigger than the island itself, and running from this group was a long line of smaller figures, which seemed to be creeping along the surface of the water, and heralding the approach of their more gigantic companions.

It was a sight once beheld never to be forgotten, and the whole five of us in the boat were speechless with terror. I send you a sketch of the strange uncouth beings, which in some respects resembled the prints of the witches in "Macbeth."

*Illustrated Police News.*

## 1878 – "SPRING HEELED JACK." IN READING.

Coincident with the publication of the public annuals with their thrilling ghost stones, considerable excitement has recently been caused at the east end of the town of Reading by the alleged nocturnal appearance of a ghostly visitor, who, from the wonderful leaping propensities with which he is attributed, is familiarly known as "Spring Heeled Jack." The most marvellous tales have been told of the antics in which he has indulged, the stories causing great alarm amongst the more timid and superstitious inhabitants of the locality. The rumour is supposed to have been first circulated by a foolish old woman who declared that she had seen someone jump out of the road and over a high wall. The rumour soon spread, and as it passed from mouth to mouth gradually resolved into a most circumstantial account of the personal appearance of the spectre, and of his doings. There was in reality not the slightest truth in any of the reports, but many persons believed that someone was playing a practical joke, and went in search of the perpetrator armed with thick sticks, but the ghost discreetly remained invisible. Amongst other things it was stated that Mr. Farmer, the lodge keeper at the Cemetery, chased "Jack" round the Cemetery, and in doing so had hurt himself by falling over one of the tombstones, but like the rest of the story, this was also without foundation.

*Swindon Advertiser and North Wilts Chronicle.*

# 1879 – AN AGGRIEVED SPIRIT.

A strange ghost story comes from the Principality. There is a friendly society at Pontardowe, in the Swansea Valley, among whose rules is one that the funeral allowance on account of a deceased member shall not be paid in cases of suicide. One of the members recently died by his own hand, and the club accordingly refused to pay the death money. For this reasonable and just refusal the members are now complaining that they are subjected to serious persecution from an unseen and, presumably, a ghostly agent.

The manifestations began on a recent Sunday, when one of the officers, returning home over a lonely road, was assailed, as he asserts, by the spirit of the late member, who failing to obtain a satisfactory reply to his demand for the money, in a somewhat unspiritlike manner assailed the unfortunate man and "tore his clothes to ribbons."

Such, at least, was the account he gave, in tones of horror, at the first public house he came to after this terrific encounter. But the ghost does not appear to have been satisfied with the demonstration. On the following Tuesday evening, whilst the members were assembled in the lodge room, the usual knocks were heard at the door as of a brother seeking admittance. The door was opened, but no one was to be seen. The members, however, are all very certain that they heard the voice of the deceased utter the words, "Pay my widow my funeral money, and then I shall be at rest."

PHANTOMS OF THE SEA

The meeting precipitately broke up, and the members are now puzzled to know what to do with such a determined deceased brother.

*Birmingham Gazette.*

medium and his wife were nonplussed at the exposure of the fraud, and the company was thrown into confusion, there being several believers present.

*Cumberland and Westmoreland Herald.*

## 1879 – EXPOSURE OF A SPIRITUALISTIC SEANCE.

Four "sceptical journalists" report an exposure of a spiritualistic séance which was held at Boston and which they attended for the purpose. The operators were Nelson and Jennie Holmes, whose tricks and practices had a considerable effect in impressing the late Robert Dale Owen with the phenomena of spiritualism, but who had for several years disappeared from public view in consequence of a public exposure. Hearing that the operators had returned to their old courses, though in Boston instead of Philadelphia, the four journalists attended a séance on the evening of the 17th ult., and took their places in the "charmed circle" round the table in a darkened room.

The first apparition was a "festive Indian maiden," but her voice was recognised as that of Mrs. Holmes. A spirit named "Dick" was next summoned, and ordered to play a guitar and rap the audience upon the head with it, which he did. One of the sceptical party, however, had managed to keep his hands free, and when the guitar touched his head he reached out quickly and seized "Dick" by the hand – "and a very substantial hand it was," remarks the reporter in the *Herald*, for it struggled vigorously, and succeeded in freeing itself before the lights could be turned up.

An announcement was then made that there were "sceptics in the room," but the séance was continued, and Rosie, the Indian girl, once more introduced. In answer to the audience, she said she was 4 years old, and went to school in the other world; but on being pressed with further questions lost her temper, and declared that "she didn't come there to furnish brains for anyone," and retired.

A young gentleman of 20 came to relieve her, and said he died in Chicago a good many years ago, but he also evinced displeasure at the questions of the audience, and would not answer. Next came an Irish girl, who professed to know Celtic, but failed to reply to a question in that language; and afterwards a number of ethereal beings commenced floating about the room, playing musical instruments. The journalist who had seized "Dick," however, waiting his opportunity, suddenly started forward and caught a spirit by the waist, when it was found that he had captured Mrs. Holmes. The

## 1879 – GHOST OR NO GHOST.

The people of Rochford, near Tenbury Wells, have lately been mystified by some spiritual manifestations of a most decided character. The "spirits" seemed to be of a remarkably mischievous and noisy disposition. Cows were mysteriously untied in their sheds, weights were removed, and for several days and nights showers of stones fell upon a farm house, which was specially favoured by the "spirits;" other stones descended the kitchen chimney, and doors were rattled and slammed at night, until the inhabitants came to the conclusion that the house was bewitched. Two policemen were sent there,—to arrest the spirits if they presented themselves in bodily form—and they found stones flying in all directions and the boards of the barn shaking violently.

A boy employed on the farm represented that he had been knocked down by the stones, and the people sent him into an upper room out of the way of the supposed unearthly visitors. They, however, seemed to follow him, for no sooner had he got upstairs than a terrible disturbance was heard overhead, doors being slammed, windows being broken, and a number of unearthly noises being heard. Then it was thought advisable to send the lad away from the house. Strange to say, the "manifestations" at once ceased. The villagers think that if he pleased that boy could a tale unfold, and that if he did they would talk less about ghosts than of mischievous youngsters.

*Isle of Wight Times.*

## 1879 – OLD FASHIONED SUPERSTITIONS.

Nineteenth century bustle and scepticism are fast elbowing out the way all the old fashioned superstitions of our childhood. Not only are we amazed and indignant when we read of the Russian *moujik* burning old men and women for witchcraft—a pastime we gave up in the days of the Stuarts—but have even brought ourselves to look on with complacency while the respectable ghosts of the days of Peel, or even Palmerston, are being frightened away into their own quiet ghost land.

Fast on the wane is the interest that used to be taken in the vagaries of our restless ancestors, and wearied incredulity follows the narration of the eccentric doings of the beautiful lady dressed in white, with the pale face and the hair, or the stout old gentleman with the plum coloured inexpressibles, who will be always on the trot. Yet there was a time when the family ghost in many respectable families used to be considered quite as much part and parcel of the old house as the old oak trees that grew up with his history, or the old walls that have grown grey as they watched for generations his eccentric revels. His portrait in the picture gallery was invested with a deeper respect than that with which we scanned the lineaments of his compeers around him, and of all the branches of the family tree, that from which the ghostly generation sprang was most interesting to us. Then, the periodical wanderings of the visitor from the world of spirits were sworn to by such a crowd of unimpeachable witnesses. He or she was recognised by the time-honoured garb that no fashion affected and no custom changed. All the sleepless years the beautiful countess disturbed her posterity with her midnight peregrinations she never dispensed with that trailing white satin robe whose awful *frou-frou* used to curdle the blood in the veins of the young people of many generations. After centuries of dissipation out of bed old Sir Marmaduke's doublet was as irreproachable as on the first night he ever donned it; his lace ruffles as white and spotless; and, though nights of chill and damp must have sadly tried it, the feather of his cavalier hat ever stoutly maintained its curl.

And if love of myths and marvels, once as strongly impregnated the Teutonic as in the Latin races, used to disarm the criticism of tolerably educated men and women not so many years ago, and make them view with indulgence rather than scoffing the tales and traditions of the enchanted world, what wonder can it be that the ignorant peasant, living far from the stirring of life cities and business, possessing naturally more imagination than common sense, retains still longer his ghostly friends and acquaintances? In mountainous countries especially, where the phenomena of nature are more remarkable and more curious, people naturally turn more kindly to superstitions of all kinds. The woody defile knows its nocturnal visitant, the waterfall that trips down the hill has its disembodied protector, the weird mountain peak its disagreeable witch, or, it may possibly be, its benignant and agreeable fairy.

Usually, however, in the interpretation of the vulgar, the visits from the world of spirits are pregnant with an unpleasant spirit of prophecy. Their idea is, or used to be, that the ghost only comes to beat up recruits. For instance, in many parts of Wales there used to exist—it may not have quite died out yet—a strange superstitious belief in what the peasants called "corpse candles," or

"dead men's lights." Someone was sure to be called away prematurely, it was said, when these mysterious lights were seen to hover and flicker. Old Richard Baxter, by his own showing, thoroughly believed in these disagreeable phenomena, and he has inserted as most true and authentic a story of this apparition in his quaint and curious "*Certainty of the World of Spirits*." which, he tells us himself, was written for the confusion and conviction of all atheists and Sadducees. "Being about the age of fifteen," says Baxter, "dwelling at Lanlyar, late at night, some neighbours saw one of these candles hovering up and down along the river bank until they were weary in beholding. At last they left it so, and went to bed. A few weeks after came a proper damsel from Montgomeryshire to see her friends, who dwelt on the other side of the rivet Ystinik, and thought to ford the river at that very place where the light was seen. But, being dissuaded by some lookers-on to adventure on the water, which was high by reason of the flood, she walked up and down the river bank, even as the aforesaid candle did, waiting for the falling of the water, which, at last, she took; but too soon for her, for she was drowned therein."

However, if it is amazing to us that a divine of Baxter's capabilities should have had a childish and confiding belief in "corpse candles," that a matter-of-fact, dry lawyer and judge like Hale should have feared witchcraft and burned witches, what possible excuse can we make to ourselves for our folly adhering scrupulously, as we do many of us in these days of science and scepticism, to superstitious avoidances, which rest on even less solid foundation than a belief in ghosts or witches? There is hardly a country in Europe, save Turkey, where there does not reign unchecked that ridiculous dislike to making one of thirteen at dinner. We have heard that at Paris there positively existed at one time a society called the "Quartorzieme," whose *raison d'etre* and business it was to supply this deficiency of the dinner table as it occurred. Of course the idea is that one of the thirteen will die within the year, or, to go more fully into the superstition, that death will make the fourteenth, and mark his prey to carry away with him to the land of spirits.

The gay Parisian, however, thinks it better on reflection to look upon the unpleasant situation from an Epicurean point of view. As the Egyptian regarded the coffin carried round at the feast as a powerful hint to make the best of his opportunities, and to revel all the more merrily because life was short, so the Frenchman took the visit of the ghostly fourteenth merely as a warning of the brevity of time, and that we must all die someday.

*The Globe.*

## 1879 – THE HAUNTED COTTAGE NEAR CHARD.

A Plymouth paper says:- "In March last an old man named Churchill was murdered in a cottage near Chard. For some time after the execution the building remained uninhabited, but it was let to a labourer and his family, but the incomers soon found they could obtain no rest. They state that the murderess, "Kitty," has been frequently seen to glide about the premises in ghostly attire, and that old Churchill has been distinctly observed to look in at the window, with hideous countenance. This, added to the appearance of blood on the floor of the room in which the tragedy was enacted, supernatural movements amongst the furniture and other articles, and unearthly noises in the immediate vicinity of the cottage, so unsettled the occupants that they at last abandoned the dwelling, which is now regarded as haunted."

*Illustrated Police News.*

## 1879 – THE MYSTERY OF THE HAUNTED KITCHEN.

A strange story reaches us from Newtown. It appears that for some days past most extraordinary noises have been heard in the kitchen of a tradesman's house in the town. The cook and housemaid were seriously alarmed, being under the impression that the house was haunted, and nothing could persuade them to the contrary. Eventually the boards of the kitchen were removed by a carpenter, when, to the surprise of all the occupants of the house, a wretched, emaciated-looking man was discovered in almost a dying condition in a vault beneath the kitchen. The poor fellow appeared to be on the verge of starvation, and would certainly have died had he not been discovered in the extraordinary manner already described. He has been rescued from his prison house, and is now under the doctor's hands. At present it has not transpired how he got into the vault.

*Illustrated Police News.*

THE HAUNTED COTTAGE NEAR CHARD.

# 1879 – THE WOMAN IN GREEN.

A house in Mayfair belongs to a noble lord. It was let some years ago to a Brazilian Minister, whose wife died there. This house being recently in the market, was purchased by a friend of the owner. On this the wife of the owner wrote to the friend, and begged her to rescind the purchase, the reason alleged being that she would have no peace in the house, as a ghostly woman in green had the unpleasant knack of wandering about the staircases and rooms, and occasionally passing through a window and airing herself on the balcony. The peculiarity of this ghost is that she appears by day as well as night. Many attempts have been made to grapple with her, but they have all proved futile. Now I do not believe in ghosts, but who is this mysterious visitant that actually prevents the sale of a house in London.

*Dundee Evening Telegraph.*

# 1880 – AN UNEARTHLY VISITOR.

Owing to widespread dissemination of a rumour that a ghost has been espied taking its nightly promenades amongst the ruins of the houses demolished by the Metropolitan Board of Works, under the provisions of the Metropolitan Improvement Act, on the site abutting on Whitecross Street and Golden Lane, London, for the last week nightly vast crowds have assembled in the hope of getting a peep of the unearthly visitant.

The disorder, obstruction, and violence consequent on such a gathering in a neighbourhood consisting mainly of low lodging houses, thieves' kitchens, and houses of ill-fame, and crowded with the vilest and most criminal classes of the metropolis, has caused much anxiety to the authorities, and it has been found necessary to place a large number of extra members of the G division of police on the spot, and this step was taken none too soon, as on Saturday night the scene of riot and ruffianism was beyond description.

According to the police the "appearance" was first observed by a Mrs. Taylor, residing in Hartshorn Court, which runs parallel with the City of London Baths, and whose rooms overlook the site in question. Her version is that she was looking through her window when she saw a female form rise suddenly from the ruins. It was clothed in white, with long black hair down the back.

THE MYSTERY OF THE HAUNTED KITCHEN REVEALED

She went into violent hysterics, and the neighbours and police were sent for, when she explained the cause.

On the next night, a watch was kept, and several persons, including a policeman, aver to the genuineness of the apparition, one witness adding that the ghost had a bright red mark on the temple. This theory has also other supporters, and on each night one or more persons are said to see it. It is the recollection of some of the inhabitants that a woman residing in Black Boy Court—a portion of the site—some 40 years ago mysteriously disappeared, and was supposed to have been murdered; and in support of this theory the body of a woman, with a fracture of the temple caused by an axe, was discovered on the demolition of the Court in question.

The police authorities assert that the rumour was got up by the thieves in the neighbourhood for the purpose of plunder, and the respectable inhabitants are about to memorialise the Board of Works to take steps, by utilising the land for building, so as to put an end to the nuisance.

*Glasgow Evening Post.*

———◦◉◦———

# 1880 – BATS AND "VAMPIRES."

A Hampshire newspaper gives currency to a story, which, but for a timely discovery, might have gone far towards reviving hobgoblin belief amongst the simple-minded country folks concerned.

One afternoon during the late cold weather a cottager's wife placed her child, a baby a few months old, to sleep in its cradle, which stood in a room adjoining that in which the family lived. There was an old-fashioned fireplace in the chamber but no fire, so for the sake of a little warmth the woman placed on the hob a lighted paraffin lamp. Peeping into the apartment at dusk to see if baby was still sleeping comfortably, judge of her dismay when she beheld a black and winged creature uttering moaning sounds as it slowly flapped round and round the room, and finally alighted on the coverlet of the cradle, close to the child's face With a shriek the affrighted mother flung the door wide open, on which the imp-like creature, squeaking its displeasure at being disturbed, rose heavily from the child's bed, and after one turn round the chamber dashed at the lamp in the chimney, which was extinguished with a crash, and then it vanished.

The terror-stricken parent caught up her infant, and hurried with it to a neighbour's house. It was found to be quite uninjured excepting that on its throat there was a slight puncture, from which a tiny drop of blood had issued. The verdict was prompt and unanimous – the babe had been attacked by a vampire! Nor could that blood-curdling conclusion have been easily disturbed had not the child's father, on his return home, bethought him of examining the chimney, where he discovered the monster in a hole near the top.

It was a harmless bat of the long-eared species that had probably been lured down into the room by the light and heat of the lamp, while as for the sanguinary evidence which bespoke the vampire, it was found that the child's nightgown was fastened at the neck with a pin, the point of which had pricked the skin when the mother so hastily caught it up.

It is not all countries, however, that are so favoured that when in such a case as that above quoted the unwelcome intruder is discovered to be "only a bat" all alarms on the score of vampires are at once dispelled. There are inhabited parts of the earth where the bat is by nature a blood-sucker. On the banks of the River Amazon for example, and in Brazil, Mr. Bates, the well-known naturalist and explorer, on one occasion made the acquaintance of a large number of the unpleasant creatures alluded to, and who took the liberty of introducing themselves as bedfellows. It was on his arrival at Caripi.

At midnight the intrepid traveller was awoke by the noise of countless bats sweeping round him. They had extinguished his lamp, and when he relit it the place was alive with their flapping wings. Having a stick at hand he endeavoured to disperse them, but they extinguished the light again and defied him. On this and up to this time having no experience of bats but such as fed on insects, Mr. Bates covered his head with his blanket, and composed himself for sleep. In the morning he discovered that his confidence had been abused. He found several bats in his hammock, and a punctured wound on his hip, which had bled very considerably. Next night Mr. Bates lodged somewhere else!

*The Graphic.*

———◦◉◦———

# 1880 – THE PUBLIC SPIRITED GHOST.

Not content that Knock, and other Irelandish places, together with Lourdes, Paray le Monial, and other wonder-working spots across the "silver streak," should enjoy a monopoly in the supernatural line, London has at last set up a ghost of its own. It is a particularly independent and public spirited ghost, for instead of arranging with some respectable "medium" to show itself off to select circles only, it exhibits free of charge amid the ruins of some demolished buildings that have been pulled down for street improvement purposes in Golden Lane. It is altogether a new and improved sort of spectre, more worthy of the nineteenth century than the puny wraiths who give precarious exhibitions of themselves only with the aid of cabinets, and in the dim religious light of the séance room. This robust spirit is of the good old fashioned, orthodox, melodramatic order, and seems to know its way about.

It has, of course, a story behind it, and does not come fooling around without reason, as too many professional ghosts do in these degenerate days. Forty years ago a woman disappeared from a court in Golden Lane, and nothing more was heard of her until this court was lately pulled down, when there was discovered under the floor of one of the houses the body of a woman, with the mark of a wound on the temple. What could be more proper then, and more in accordance with what was to be expected, than the appearance at midnight, amid the ruins, of the form of a woman, clad in white, with long black hair streaming over her shoulders and down the back, and with a bright red mark on the temple?

The "poor ghost" was first seen by a woman, who very properly fainted, while the neighbours, with great presence of mind sent for the police. They too saw the ghost, but for some reason or other did not take it up. Yet their testimony proves beyond doubt the reality of ghosts—for no one would think of denying their existence now that some policemen have really seen one, any more than Mark Twain could question the genuineness of the Mormon Bible, after he had seen a man who had positively "hefted" those apocryphal scriptures.

Meanwhile Golden Lane is crowded every night, and, perhaps, after all, the constables may more usefully employ their energies in arresting the rogues and vagabonds who mix plentifully with the throng, and who, probably, know more about the ghost than anyone else. Indeed, if the Golden Lane spectre turned out to be an accomplice of the pickpockets, and shared the plunder every morning, no one would die of surprise.

*Portsmouth Evening News.*

———◆———

# 1881 – SOME TRUE STORIES ABOUT GHOSTS.

In the centre cut in the front page of this week's POLICE NEWS the reader will find several engravings as far as can be done of the scenes with ghostly visitants as described by the correspondents to the Daily Telegraph. The centre subject "Bound by a Spell," represents a scene described to us by the chief actor. Mr. James Morant, a young man of a highly sensitive organisation, became enamoured of a young lady whom he hoped someday to make his wife. Whenever he was on the eve of a proposal he asserts that the spirit of an old woman, who had nursed him in his infancy, appeared to him. The purpose of her visit being, so he argued, was to warn him against compromising himself. Mr. Morant declaring that the spectre has appeared to him frequently, and it exercised so powerful an influence over him that he refrained from proposing to the lady in question, and has now good reason to congratulate himself upon having done so. She has been married and divorced, since which time the ghost has not made its appearance.

A gentleman who signs himself "A Believer," writes as follows:- "About fifteen or eighteen years ago I had driven a young lady friend from the village of Sandhurst, in Berkshire, to Windsor, where we spent the day. It was about this period of the year, and on our return at night the moon being at its full, was shining brilliantly. On turning out of the Bracknell Road, into the village, we had to pass a house which in former years had the reputation of being haunted, but on the occasion I am referring to such a subject as ghosts was very far from my thoughts. I was chatting with my companion till we came to the meadow at the back of the so-called haunted house, when we both saw standing in the middle of the meadow a figure of most brilliant white. It seemed to me to look like a man without a head, and with a remarkably white frock on the rest of his body. I stopped the horse I was driving and gave the reins to my friend, and was about to descend and go into the field to see what the object was, when, before I had time to alight, it began to approach us, and came within a few feet, when it so suddenly disappeared as to cause us both to be much more alarmed than at the sight of the spectre."

"A. Ross" says:- "My ghost story is this. I had gone to bed, slept well all through the night, having given orders to be called earlier than usual, as my mother was to set out, after breakfast, by train, on the Highland Railway, to the far North. I woke suddenly, remembering it might be time to rise when I distinctly saw a figure standing in a corner of the bedroom. It was clad from head to foot in armour, the visor down. I felt my heart beat fast with fear, still I gazed, and could take in the proportions of the figure, and recognised it as the eldest brother of a very intimate girl friend of mine, but no relation. I closed my eyes, unable to overcome the awfully mysterious impression the apparition imparted to me. When I looked again it had vanished. I got up, dressed and on going downstairs found my mother prepared for her journey. An indefinable dread prevented me disclosing to her what I had seen that morning. I accompanied her to the railway station, impressing on her to telegraph on her arrival at Inverness. That evening her telegram reached me – the words to this effect-: "I arrived all safe and well, Young Munro died this morning" And so it was; but why his apparition visited me I know not. The death was sudden and unexpected, at his Highland residence. His family relations were at the time in the South, and he died before any of them even heard of any illness to cause uneasiness."

"An Observer" says:- "When, once upon a time, I was reading for a difficult examination, my tutor left me one night at about eleven o'clock, after some hard work, saying, "You can finish that problem before twelve." His empty chair was beside me. After about half an hour, I perceived that his figure was in the chair again exactly as he used to sit beside me. He was leaning his head on his left hand, with his eyes directed to the paper before me. I was greatly interested in this apparition, which, of course, was the result of excitement in my work. I need hardly say on looking at the figure for a little time it vanished, leaving nothing but the chair, and that I closed my book and went to bed. The tutor is alive and hearty to this day."

In the letter signed "Ancient Briton" we have the following:- "Permit me to add a further instance, also within the range of my personal experience. In the summer of 1857, the Mutiny year, I was at home from India for some few months and at the country house where I was then staying, on a calm warm night in July, dozing, neither asleep nor actively awake, I distinctly saw a coffin and in it the corpse of a valued friend of mine, lying in a bedroom of a bungalow at Mattra. The features of the dead were exactly in the condition that might be looked for after death by one who was an old friend, in whose memory his living countenance was enduringly familiar. He was an officer in the 9th Bengal Cavalry, and I had left him in India, in May, in good health. I now felt assuredly that he must have died, and my anxious glance at the obituary of the Calcutta Englishman, received by the next mail. Revealed his name, rank, and date of decease at Mattra, in exact fulfilment of the preceding fatal intimation."

Observes another correspondent:- "After the death of a female relative, whose husband at the time was lying paralysed, the room in which she died gave birth to all kinds of noises – the furniture was moved violently about, while the room itself was locked and the key in my possession. This lasted until the death of her husband, when the house resumed its normal condition. These sounds were not heard by one pair of ears, or by the inmates of this house only. And here I am reminded of another fallacy in the reasoning of ghost scoffers. They say that a man, by prolonged concentration of thought on one particular object, may project a picture of that object on to the retina. But from this view how is the following explained? A

friend of mine came home one evening and told me that he saw his father walk down the corridor leading from the boxes of a certain theatre. He was much surprised, as he imagined his father to be some miles in the country at the time. The next day he received intelligence of the death of his father at the hour when the saw him in the theatre. His father was in perfect health when he saw him last."

A "Firm Believer in Ghosts" says:- "The first night I slept in the house I was awakened in a remarkable manner, and I saw a figure standing not far from the bed, looking very calm but very sad. It distinctly looked at me and then vanished. I was too awed to wake my husband. This occurred over and over again. On going about the house and up and down the stairs I have repeatedly passed the same figure. On coming down from my bedroom I have seen the drawing room door open, and the figure pass out and go down the stairs before me. Not only myself, but everyone in the house was cognisant of its presence. It was the cry of servant after servant, "This house is haunted; there is someone walks down the stairs every evening." Not one of the children would sleep alone. Occasionally we heard slight noises, but in general it was a quiet passing in and out. At first we were frightened, and slept one night at a hotel, but the latter part of the two years that we occupied the house we became familiar with it. At another house we saw it once, but for the last five years we have seen nothing at all of the apparition."

Another correspondent furnishes us with an account of a ghost, which his servants and children assured him they had seen. He affected to disbelieve them. One night it appeared to him on the stairs, passed by him, and glided into his bedroom. He followed it and locked the door. While in the act of fastening the door he looked round and the figure had vanished.

A girl gives an account of seeing the ghost of a man in armour. She took no notice of the apparition at the time, but some time afterwards received intelligence of her mother's death.

We are in receipt ourselves of a ghost story, which will be found illustrated on the left hand side of the page. A Mr. Johnson declares that he saw a hazy figure standing at the foot of his bed. His wife was asleep at the time, but he would not wake her, He gently got out of bed, still keeping his eyes on the figure, and when within a few steps of the same it instantly vanished and left him in utter darkness. He declares that the room was made luminous while the figure was visible.

*Illustrated Police News.*

# 1881 – GHOSTLY MUBIO.

(From the New Yok Post).

Spiritualism which is represented by those who believe in it to be vastly superior to Christianity, differs, of course, from the latter in its revelations as to the state of music in the other world. The church has always held that the angelic host sings and plays on the harp and trumpet in a way altogether beyond the reach of criticism. But Spiritualism, on the other hand, shows us that the state of musical culture among ghosts is no better than that which characterises an Indiana country town.

The average ghost plays only the most execrable instruments, and sings only the most empty and aggravating songs. As for producing a decent note with a trumpet, or playing the simplest melody with the harp, the ghosts of spiritualism have never even ventured to make the attempt. When a "materialising séance" is held, the medium always requests the circle of believers to sing, alleging that under the influence of music ghosts materialise with comparative ease. But what are the songs that are sung in spiritual circles? The "Sweet Bye and Bye" is a fair sample of them. They are invariably the illiterate sentimental songs popular among people who know absolutely nothing about music. They are sung through the nose with the mechanical sameness of the barrel organ, and with a dragging of the time that is simply maddening.

One would think that if the singing of the "Sweet Bye and Bye" could induce any ghost to materialise it would be a large one with a heavy club, and a wild desire to brain the singers. Unfortunately, this is not what ordinarily happens. The singing is followed by the appearance of ghosts who are in the best of tempers, and apparently satisfied with the "music" which has lured them from the other world. Of course this is fatal to our respect for ghosts. If a ghost will deliberately come to earth to hear people whose voices are as cracked as their brains sing the "Sweet Bye and Bye" they are wholly unfit to be noticed by persons of any sort of musical culture.

This being the kind of musical taste which prevails in the other world we need not be surprised to find that not a single ghost has yet materialised who can play on any decent instrument. What is even worse is the fact that the entire ghostly world seems to be given over to the accordion. Occasionally a ghost will strike the strings of a guitar so as to produce a discordant noise, but the accordion is positively the only instrument which ghosts will play in public. If spiritualism is true, it is evident that the first thing a disembodied spirit does is to learn to play on the accordion. Men who in this world would have smitten to the earth the wretch who should have tried to place

an accordion in their hands will, in their ghostly state, take up the instrument from the medium's table, and proceed to encourage its asthmatic wheezing.

It is certainly very strange that we should thus deteriorate after death. The late Daniel Webster was confessedly one of the greatest men of any age. He never played on any instrument, and, in fact, had no liking whatever for music, but his views of the accordion were such as became a statesman, a Christian, and a gentleman. Yet, now that he is dead, he has devoted himself with much assiduity to the accordion, and when he condescends to materialise for the benefit of a roomful of spiritualists— as he frequently does—he is pretty sure to say, "Gimme that there accordion and I'll play a little suthin," whereupon he plays the "Sweet Bye and Bye." "Mollie Darling," or "Beautiful Spring." George Washington is equally bad, and even Shakespeare has repeatedly shown that he shares the ghostly fondness for accordions.

Inevitably this casts a gloom over the future world. If, when we are dead, we sink to the accordion and find pleasure in the "Sweet Bye and Bye," we are decidedly better off here than we will be hereafter. So far as we can learn from materialised ghosts, there is not a harp nor a brass instrument in the other world, and if there were there is not a ghost who could play on them. Were we to adopt the hypothesis that only the ghosts of bad men had the power to return to earth, and that their familiarity with the accordion is acquired while undergoing punishment, we might feel a little encouraged, but, in point of fact, the ghosts of the very best and noblest men play the accordion, so that the hypothesis suggested is dearly untenable.

Our best plan is to decide that spiritualism cannot be true. It is far more probable that mediums lie and that spiritualists are deceived than it is that Daniel Webster and Dante play the accordion. Let us cherish our old belief in celestial harps and angelic trumpets, and hope that in the future life we shall be free from the sight and sound of the accordion. Perhaps the fallen angels, having dropped and broken their harps, torment miserable sinners by singing the "Sweet Bye and Bye," and accompanying themselves on the accordion, but surely in any other part of the universe of ghosts that wretched instrument and revolting song must be unknown.

*Blackburn Standard.*

# 1881 – THE GARSTANG GHOST.

Not a bad title for a farce would be "The Garstang Ghost and the Palpitating Postman;" yet it may be doubted whether the unfortunate functionary who has just been so frightened by a ghost at Garstang that he has given up his situation rather than face the nocturnal visitant again will discover anything farcical in his alarming experiences. The facts of his case seem sufficiently well authenticated. He declares that a few evenings ago, as he was quietly pursuing his way along a lonely road near the village of Garstang, absorbed in his occupation of letter-carrier, a ghost stopped his way, and worried him with many mysterious signs not to continue in his present courses. The

terrified postman immediately acted upon the ghostly injunction to the extent that he at once turned tail and fled.

He has since resigned his official position, not so much, it is believed, from any desire on his part to obey the advice tendered from another world as from an irresistible repugnance to continue his ghostship's acquaintance. The act certainly goes far to prove the reality of the postman's terror, if it does not completely establish the objective existence of the ghost.

Other proofs in the late direction are, however, not wanting. Brief as was the period during which the postman permitted himself to gaze upon that dreadful apparition, he carried away with him a very clear notion of its principal

THE GARSTANG GHOST

THE PALPITATING POSTMAN

characteristics. These would seem to be abnormal stature, a horrid pallor of hue, and a variety of terror-striking gestures.

His description of the Garstang Ghost is borne out by the testimony of another unimpeachable witness. A young woman of the district has also had one dreadful look at the spectre. She happened also to be out in the haunted lane when evening "had in her sober livery all things clad." As she walked along perhaps in maiden meditation, not altogether fancy free, her affrighted eyes beheld the ghost. There it was, of fearsome height, clothed in white, and performing portentous movements with its arms – so she afterwards declared. This witness's testimony is invalidated to a trifling extent by her confession that directly she saw the awful sight she threw her apron over her head and ran home. Having got there safely, she instantly went to bed, where she has since remained, in proof of the truth of her story. The reality of the Garstang Ghost is thus very fairly substantiated; and if it should manage to appear in the midst of the young men who are now looking for it, and, at the same time, elude capture, it will certainly deserve to rank with the respectable fraternity of shades who in times past have revisited the glimpses of the moon, and usually with so much dramatic effect.

We may doubt, however, if the Garstang Ghost will achieve any such distinction. The present is not a time favourable for the appearance of spirits of the good old-fashioned sort. Perhaps the discipline to which spirits have of late years been subjected by professional spiritualists has robbed them of the gaiety of disposition which once prompted them to disport in rural lanes and frighten country bumpkins. It is easy to understand that a poor ghost condemned to rap tables at the bidding, and for the profit, of a very poor sort of social adventurer must lose all heart for either lighter or more serious business of its existence. The modern spirit is, in truth, in bonds; its original occupation is gone, to be replaced by such undignified exercises as beating tambourines, or tweaking noses at a dark séance.

Special exception, however, must be made in favour of the apparitions whose business it is to intimate their own divorce from bodily existence in some distant land. The amount of direct, circumstantial, and, to all appearances, perfectly trustworthy evidence to be obtained on this subject is really astonishing. Any number of people may be found whose character for veracity has never been impeached, and will most solemnly aver that on a specified occasion they, being of perfectly sane mind, saw distinctly the counterfeit presentment of a dear friend or relative; and that subsequent testimony proved that at the same moment such friend and relative expired at the Antipodes. Sometimes, though rarely, the ghostly appearance is seen by two people at the same time, and there is one well authenticated instance of a dog enjoying the same privilege, and being nearly driven beside itself by what it saw. But

these are only occurrences which can be said to make even a pretence with leavening with the truth the modern mass of ghosts and imposters. In ancient times, when ghosts appeared they invariably did so with a purpose; their solemnity in their manner and a dreadful import in their words puts to shame the frivolous manifestations of their degenerative descendants.

Indeed, the commonplace ghosts of today are degenerate creatures, unworthy the traditions of their species. They apparently have no better mission than that of frightening simple-minded folks out of their wits. There is no consistency, no moral resolve apparent in their behaviour. They bring no criminal to justice, they guide the way to no guilty-hidden treasure.

Some years ago a Spring-heeled Jack – the most vulgar and unromantic ghost imaginable – took to playing pranks in one quarter of London, to the great alarm of its feminine inhabitants. But its success brought into the field a crowd of rivals who were speedily found out, and the originator of the deception retired from business in disgust. At another time, the residents in a fashionable suburb were thrown into a state of great consternation by the exploits of an invisible knocker of double knocks. A watch was set, but, though the knocks continued, the knocking agency could not be discovered. People lay in wait in their passages or just round the corner, and the moment the ominous double knock came, rushed impetuously out and caught nothing.

So far as we remember the perpetrator of these practical jokes was never discovered, for the reason that he left off performing when detection became probable. Ghosts of the type of the one now troubling Garstang have always been common enough. A striking similarity is to be observed in their general appearance and bearing. They are white in colour, indefinite in shape, and perform odd motions. In most cases, a closer approach would prove them to be white horses or cows straying on unaccustomed pastures. On some occasions they are, of course, silly people masquerading in white sheets. If the Garstang Ghost be of this stamp, it is impossible not to wish the young men, who, armed with sticks, are looking for it, all success in their search. It is indeed difficult to understand what pleasures even the most malicious can find in frightening superstitious or timid people into serious illness, or out of their employment.

Fortunately the liking for this sort of practical joke has diminished of late years. If it were to die out entirely society would doubtless survive the loss. The bolder and more stalwart of the inhabitants of Garstang have now the opportunity of hastening this desirable end by unmasking the supernatural disturber of maiden reveries and of the more prosaic fancies of the belated postman.

*Illustrated Police News.*

# 1881 – THE SHROPSHIRE GHOST.

Great excitement continues in Church Stretton and neighbourhood, as the men engaged in clearing the Copper Hole Shaft are approaching the bottom, in their search for the missing body of Sarah Duckett. The task has been one of great difficulty as the pit fills with water during the night, and little work could be proceeded with until this had been bailed out. The place has been visited by hundreds of people, and the road on Sunday looked as though it were the highway to a country fair. The men expected to reach the bottom of the shaft in a day or two, and the interest in the experiment increases with every foot gained in depth. Many rumours of the discovery of human remains have been circulated, but up to the present time nothing has been found calculated to allay the public anxiety as to the fate of the missing woman. Several ladies and gentlemen in carriages daily visit the works.

As has been already been stated, Sarah Duckett left Sondly, a small village near Church Stretton, seven years ago, to go to Australia. She remained away over eighteen months, and then returned. She came to Church Stretton station, and was seen one night walking up the Hazel Road. Since then no trace of her has been found.

On a Ludlow correspondent visiting the Copper Hole Shaft near Church Stretton, on Monday, he found the man Roberts at work with the other labourers clearing the shaft of the rubbish and water. The men had reached a depth of 21 ft., and had some 15 ft. more soil to remove before reaching the bottom. Roberts told the correspondent that he saw the apparition of the missing woman, Sarah Duckett, twice the night he was coming from Church Stretton. The second time he went back to try if he could see anything of it. It was in the same place, with the face towards the road, when he passed. Three more respectable persons assert that they have also seen the missing female.

Miss Duckett had an account at the Church Stretton Bank, which is still on the books. She is supposed to have had money with her when she came back from Australia. It appears that for some reason, Miss Duckett when out of a situation, did not make her home with her relations, but stayed always at the Hazel or Toll bar. It is reported that after her mysterious disappearance the cellar at the Toll bar was filled up. Miss Duckett, on the night of leaving Church Stretton station called at the cottage of one Beddoes, on the Old Hazel Road. Many of the inhabitants of the town are impressed with the idea that foul play has befallen her, and trust to the clearing of the copper hole to solve the mystery.

THE APPARITION.

Sarah Duckett was about forty years of age, 5ft. 3in. or 5ft. 4 in. high, of stout build, dark brown hair, dark complexion, and dark eyes; dressed at the time of her disappearance in a dark dress, with dark shawl and cotton bonnet. The copper hole is almost a mile away from the railway station, almost at the foot of the Caradoc range of hills. The boxes belonging to Miss Duckett were found warehoused at Church Stretton Railway Station, where they have been about five years.

*Illustrated Police News.*

## 1881 – THE SHROPSHIRE GHOST STORY CONTINUED…

The venue of the Shropshire ghost story has now been changed to Worcester. It will be remembered that after the well at Church Stretton had been fruitlessly excavated it was stated that the deceased woman was actually living at Martley, in Worcestershire. However she has not appeared in the flesh, and a day or two ago a letter was received from the clergyman of Eaton-under-Heywood, near Church Stretton, by a surgeon at Worcester, stating that the relations of the deceased woman, Sarah Duckett, had reason to believe that she died in Worcester in 1876, Accordingly the registrar at Worcester, on searching the registers for the last seven months in 1876, as desired, found an entry of Sarah Duckett, aged 45, who was entered having died at the Worcester Infirmary.

*Northampton Mercury.*

## 1881 – THE SULTAN PUBLIC HOUSE.

For the past few weeks the Sultan public house, next door to the Prince's Theatre, Lake Road, has been closed, the tenant having left. On Wednesday, by some unexplained means, a story got wind that the place was haunted, and that a ghost was frequently to be seen at the windows. This was further circulated yesterday, with the result that hundreds of people came to see the spiritual visitor, and judging by what has occurred today, the crowd may reasonably be expected to be immensely increased tonight. One of the numerous tales afloat was to the effect that a man and woman, with their throats cut from ear to ear, were found in the cellar. There was, however, no foundation whatever for

this and the other absurd stories, which have evidently been concocted by some imaginative or weak-minded individual.

*Portsmouth Evening News.*

## 1882 – A GHOST INVESTIGATION SOCIETY.

Ghosts, dreams, presentiments, "apparitions at the moment of death or otherwise," are at last to be made the subject of formal inquiry by a philosophical society established for the purpose. It is called the Society for Psychical Research, and was founded by Mr. Henry Sidgwick "for the purpose of inquiry into a mass of obscure phenomena which lie at present on the outskirts of our organized knowledge." In a letter addressed to us by Messrs. Edmund Gurney and Frederic Myers—secretaries to the literary committee of the society – these gentlemen appeal to the public to assist the investigation. They say, "Should any of your readers, now or in the future, be able and inclined to send us an account, or to put us on the track, of any phenomena of the kind, they would greatly oblige us; and would also (as we think we may fairly say) be rendering a real aid to the progress of knowledge in a direction where such aid is much needed." An assurance follows that "nothing will be printed or published, either with or without names, except with the full consent of the persons concerned."

Now this, it strikes us at starting, is a very proper engagement; indeed, for some most interesting cases it must be absolutely indispensable. All that is known about ghosts up to the present time goes to show that they visit the guilty more often than the innocent; and no person responsible for the wanderings of a perturbed spirit, however willing he might be on scientific grounds to assist the objects of the Psychical Research Society, could be expected to do so at the risk of giving a hint to the police. And yet it is in this field that the society might probably find its most useful phenomena; and they will do well to spare nor thought nor pains in winning the confidence of haunted homicides. It will be a hard task, no doubt, especially at the beginning of the society's labours. The spectre-dogged murderer can never be so desirous to assist inquiry as to profit by remedy; and many months, many years perhaps, will pass away before the society will be able either to soothe or to confirm the terrors of men haunted by ghosts of their own providing.

We are all much mistaken if it is not amongst the blood-stained that the more serious and meaning apparitions stalk. More should be learned from the coming and the going of these ghosts, and their effect on their victims and creators, than from visitations of any other kind; and here, no doubt, we have the explanation of the society's pledge that "nothing will be printed or published, either with or without names, without the full consent of the persons concerned." It is very delicately put —so delicately as in itself to inspire confidence; and there is reason to hope that the secretaries, Messrs. Gurney and Myers, will be rewarded with many a story, told in the ear, of no mere stomach born apparitions, about which all interest is quite exhausted, but of the haunting sprites of troubled souls fore-damned. That is the sort of thing to get true psychology out of; but we are afraid that to gather much in that field of research the society begins a little too late. Not that there are fewer persons now who, having done their man, their woman, or their child to death, ought by rights to be haunted —for doubtless that is not the case; but in our days hell has been abolished, and much it is doubted whether there is any one to judge the quick and the dead. Therefore there are fewer troubled souls; and it is not to be supposed that the number of ghosts to murderers is nearly as great relatively as it used to be fifty or even twenty years ago.

For the same reason, even the dreams of the guilty— (and the Psychical Research Society also inquires into dreams) —are likely to be much duller nowadays—much less rousing to the faculties of both dreamer and student; but that also the Society must put up with; regret is useless on that point. Dreams enough there are of the strangest even to this day; and we are inclined to think that there is little less belief in them. Say what they may, few men are really staunch in the negation of apparitions. The family ghost obtains much credence still, long after the churchyard ghost has lost its last believer. Indeed, belief in family ghosts seems to have extended of late; but that may be accounted for in some measure by the wide circulation of society journals. But when we speak of apparitions we do not refer to the old-fashioned ghost who establishes himself about a man's person or his premises, but of the momentary apparition of one who is far away, and on the instant in danger or dying. This is the apparition which, when all's said and done, few men deny with absolute conviction; for in this region of the psychical many things are told which confound the incredulous, and bring the Joyce-fed scoffer to a pause. Here, we take it, Mr. Sidgwick's society will find wonders pouring in upon them, with authentication undeniable; and here will their speculations be most largely exercised.

As to dreams, it is doubtful whether anybody who dreams himself feels sure that there is not something supernatural at times in the visions of the night, or is quite satisfied that the verification of their prophecy is always a matter of coincidence. What could we not ourselves say about dreams if time and space permitted in this world

of limitations? And what work the Psychical Research Society will have before them ere the month is out! We do not doubt that at this moment —it is midnight—hundreds of pens are hard at work over hundreds of ghost stories, miraculous presentiments, prophetic dreams, warning voices, death bed apparitions, these and more kinds of wonders than the society seeks information about.

Did the Psychicals think of this when they issued their circular? Have they taken premises large enough to contain the manuscripts that are now in course of preparation for them? Have the members of the society been adequately reinforced for dealing with the flight of letters and papers they are calling into existence? And—another thing; what means have they discovered for detecting the inventions of the gamesome fabricator? That is a serious question; and at present we see not how it can be solved. However, that is a matter for the philosophers of the Psychical Research Society, who from the nature of their studies are better equipped, perhaps, for the business of discrimination.

*St. James's Gazette.*

<hr>

# 1882 – THE GHOST OF SARAH DUCKETT.

The Church Stretton Copper Hole ghost story has just been revived in that neighbourhood in a remarkable manner, and all the fears of the superstitious people resident in the district have returned. A young man a few nights back – who had laughed the loudest and ridiculed the most when the "ghost" story was at its' height, declaring that if he had seen something resembling even his satanic majesty, much less the ghost of inoffensive Sarah Duckett, he should have something to say to it – was returning from Church Stretton, when as he relates; he perceived a woman following him at a little distance. Thinking he should have company, he stayed for her to come up to him but, although she appeared to continue walking, she did not seem to gain ground; neither could he hear the footsteps, but only ''the rustling of her dress.''

After stopping a number of times for this singular "follower" to overtake him, and always with the same unsuccessful result, his bravery deserted him, and he walked rapidly on towards Hope Bowdler. Coming to a part of the road called "The Pykes," he states that he "summoned up courage" to stand again determined this time to have some conversation with this strange woman. She then ''glided'' noiselessly towards him, and, when within a few yards, stood and slowly removed her cotton bonnet from her head, holding it towards him.

He states that he saw "the bonnet plainly and the strings dangling from it." The woman then passed through the hedge and vanished from sight.

The young man reached home in a pitiable condition from fright. The "scare" appears positively greater than ever. The appearance of this alarming visitor was not confined to the young man from Hope Bowdler, for an old man going along the lane leading to his cottage one night found his passage barred by the ghost, and fainted outright. A youth on horseback was so scared by its presence that, putting spurs to the animal, he never drew rein until he reached the village of Lechotwood. And I hear a lady received a more serious injury to her nervous system through imagining she saw the ghost through her parlour window.

It is surprising how many people around Church Stretton solemnly shake their heads and observes that "Sarah Duckett's death hasn't been clearly proved yet, after all." If it has not, it certainly seems a pity that someone cannot come forward to "clearly prove it," to the satisfaction of even the most superstitious neighbour.

*Illustrated Police News.*

# 1883 – SUPERSTITIOUS SCARE AT SHREWSBURY.

Manifestations of an extraordinary nature have been frightening the good people of Shrewsbury and the adjacent villages. A reporter has interviewed the mother and the neighbours of the child and has obtained the following narrative:-

Mrs. Davies said, "On last Thursday evening, Emma went down to the house of her brother Edward living in Wharf Road, While there she was helping her sister-in-law to hang out some clothes, but the collars and other small articles jumped off the ledge as fast as she could put them on, while those put on by her sister-in-law did not move. They went into the back kitchen, where there was a bucket filled with soapsuds and directly Emma passed it, it moved several yards and upset. Then just as they got into the kitchen the Bible flew off a table on to the hearth, and a pair of boots were hurled over their heads against the mantelpiece, while the mat was thrown from the door into the middle of the road. The coat hammer was also thrown into the road, and when it was fetched back it went again. Emma then walked home, and told me they had sent her home, as the things had begun to fly about like they did at "The Wood." I was baking at the time, and I thought perhaps the bread

THE GHOST OF SARAH DUCKETT-SHROPSHIRE

would not bake, as it would not at "The Wood." I told her to stay outside.

Afterwards I went out to cut sticks, and my daughter went up to the door. She at once shouted, "Mother, there is a lump of coal on the table." I went in the house and found a large piece of burning coal on the table opposite the fire, and I put it on the fire again with the tongs. I was very much alarmed, and told Emma to go out. She went out through the back door, and just as she passed a bench a large stein filled with water which stood on it leaped after her, and, falling on the pavement near her, broke into atoms. I told her she had better fetch her father, who works at Petton, and she started.

On the way, however, she became suddenly ill, and she was brought back in a trap. She screamed frightfully, and directly she came in the house a large flower pot began to clatter. I called in a neighbour to look at it. It moved

to the edge of the sill, and I pushed it back. My husband then came home, and said he would not believe that such things had taken place. Shortly afterwards another piece of coal shot of the fire. Three or four neighbours were in the house at this time, and we all agreed to go outside, and take my daughter with us. There were a lot of people outside. We had just got out when there seemed to come a shower of stones, broken tiles, bricks, and soil. Some of them struck the windows, some fell on the slates, and one large lump of soil fell on my shoulder. We did not know where they came from. We at once went inside the house again, and just then there was a burst as if bottles were breaking. I suppose that was the upstairs window breaking. Then the clothes brush flew over our heads and wont under the fire. It was put back, but it again jumped into the hearth, and was put back three times afterwards. Emma was at this time in the kitchen.

SUPERSTITIOUS SCARE at SHREWSBURY.

A Primitive Methodist hymn book jumped off the table three or four times into the hearth, and there are the black marks on it. A knife that had been left on the table was also hurled across the room. None of us except the little boys went to bed that night (Thursday). There was a lot of Primitive Methodists here, and we had a prayer meeting. The girl seemed to be very much frightened, and trembled violently when the things were moving. On Friday morning pieces of bricks and soil continued to fly about, and we did not know where they came from. A neighbour, Mrs. Kynaston, who was sitting in a chair in the house, was struck in the arm, and two or three pieces afterwards came through the doorway. My daughter drank a good deal, but we could get her to eat nothing scarcely.

On Saturday morning, about half past two, she went to bed and slept until about nine. She jumped nervously in her sleep. While she slept everything was quiet, but directly she awoke a little work box flew of the chimney-piece right across the room to the stairs door. There was a tremendous row, as if the roof had fallen in. The noise upset the woman who lives in the adjoining house, and she had to go away. The girl then got up, and as she was coming towards the door a large looking-glass fell from the dressing table, but it did not break."

It is, however, said that the police and the doctors have been investigating the matter, and have acknowledged themselves fairly nonplussed for any explanation of it. The patient, or victim of the malignant agency, a young girl of thirteen, is described by Dr. Corke, of Baschuche, as being in a very nervous and excited state, but not a designing girl. But wherever she goes this ghostly persecution follows her. When she is at home the domestic furniture goes into convulsions, and knocks about the house in the most singular and unaccountable manner. It would be well if this were the worst. But the wicked shade who has revisited the glimpses of the moon is guilty of downright outrage. He breaks the windows, shatters the tea things, tears the buttons off articles of dress, and actually throws knives at people. To this complexion have these unwelcome manes come at last. It is the first time, we believe, that edged weapons have been used in these displays.

In the case of the Cock Lane ghost, for example, where a girl twelve years old, daughter of a man named Parsons, was haunted exactly as Emma Davies is said to be haunted, the prodigy did not go beyond certain scratchings and knockings, with the occasional apparition of a woman surrounded by a blazing eight. This child baffled for some time the observations of the distinguished persons who undertook the exposure of the imposture. Thus, although the girl was removed from her home, and successively watched in several houses where there could be no possible collusion of the kind she was suspected to have had with her family, and though the number of watchers who surrounded her bed had been increased to twenty, the knockings and scratchings still continued, and questions were answered by the same sort of telegraphy.

And after all it was a mere want of punctuality on the part of the ghost which furnishes the pretext for the theory that the imposture was exploded. As a mere point of justice between Miss Parsons and her familiar on the one hand, and the learned sceptics on the other, it remains that the ghost, having promised to attend in a vault at a certain hour, and there manifest its presence by a knock upon a coffin, failed to keep the appointment, whereupon it was forthwith concluded in effect that the ghost was as apocryphal as Mrs. Harris. Why a denizen of the other world should be expected to observe a respect for his engagements, which is the exception in this world, is a question not worth discussing now; but if the inquisitors had not subsequently foiled a bit of board in the girl's bed and decided that this was the machine she produced the eldritch sounds upon, there would be ground for the complaint that the Cock Lane ghost did not get a fair hearing.

*Illustrated Police News.*

———✺———

# 1883 – THE PSYCHICAL RESEARCH SOCIETY.

Some of the stories accumulated by this society appear to illustrate the transference of thoughts or impressions without signs or words, and in certain areas, if such an idea could be allowed, from distant relatives or friends. Anybody who has dipped into the voluminous literature of "second sight" and warning dreams must be aware that one class of stories seems to stand out with some distinctness from the mass. They are those where persons at a distance were suddenly conscious, while asleep or awake, of the presence of a friend or relative who at that instant, as after facts appear to prove, passed beyond this life. To say that these stories are absolutely authentic would be to prejudge the whole question, but they seem to a certain extent fortified by the evidence of respectable rational witnesses.

Hitherto these tales have been taken to mean the return of the dead. The society, however, resolute to trace the matter to the bottom, are investigating the theory that these may simply illustrate the transference of thought or vivid mental impression from the living person at the point of death to a distant friend. In other words, the story may be removed from the domain of the supernatural and become a physiological possibility, suggesting a great extension of the natural powers at a moment of intense excitement or strain.

Everybody is familiar with the exaggerated hearing of fever patients, and that peculiar sympathies knit together persons of exceptional susceptibility has been incidentally established more than once. The experience of Louis Blanc and his brother lacked the dramatic completeness of the "'Corsican Brothers," but it resembled it in kind though not in degree, and several other cases are noted in the records of medicine and psychology. There is also in almost every family some legend or dream or presentiment fulfilled. Many of these would melt away no doubt before the tests of a thorough research, but that would be the world's gain.

The question for inquirers would be first; How many would stand the investigation? with the further problem; To what cause can we trace the established phenomena? There are men of science who unscientifically refuse even to regard the subject. They take their stand on Materialism, and decline to accept what they cannot handle, analyse, or touch. They are backed by Agnosticism, or even sometimes by a blank Atheism, which denies another life and rejects all evidence of supernaturalism as forged. This is not the truly philosophical spirit.

True science has no eternal negative; it faces all facts and is ready to listen to any theory which professes to be built up on evidence. That certain phenomena are mysterious or irregular in their recurrence does not prove their non-existence. There are phases of certain diseases that occur perhaps only once in fifty years, but medical men who have never seen them in their own practice accept them on the evidence of others. This especially applies to the mysteries that lie on the middle line—if there be a middle line – where mind and body seem to touch and overlap; where the wise physician hesitates to say whether the impression is a mental effect from a physical cause or vice versa. Here, above all, there is room for hesitation, modesty, and further research.

It is characteristic of all honest investigation that the earlier inquirers have to pile up heaps of facts before they, as if it were by accident, discover some law or theory that rules, explains, or harmonises all. Some of the most important discoveries in the world have been made by men groping about for other objects. The quest for the Philosopher's Stone and for the Elixir of Life kept chemical science alive in the dark ages. Thousands of workers, including himself, the most patient of all, laboured without light to build up the basis of Darwin's edifice, and now we know the value of the millions of facts. It is this hope of a retrospective sanction that animates all really scientific men. The path they tread may be difficult—heavy underwood beneath their feet, tangled growth above. Yet this only shows that the road is new, and that a road has to be made. Herein is the best incentive to real enthusiasts. They leave to others the beaten paths, where scientific students plod on with ease, almost in single file, heaping unnecessary experiments on one another, and proving again and again old theories and old truths. They, on the contrary, strike out in a direction hitherto neglected, rescuing perchance from superstition credulity a domain where they simply seek for truth. The most sceptical may wish such pioneers every success.

Their offence, no doubt, in the eyes of some is that they refuse to accept the negative dogma of the Atheist. He says, "There is no future life; the dead do not rise again; we have dissected bodies and found no soul." But, to put it on the lowest ground, it is utterly unscientific to take this Materialist gospel without proof. And, where is the proof? The Materialists refuse to examine any facts that seem to establish anything beyond matter; yet we are glad to say there are men more purely scientific who forbear to reject without trial the Christian hope which at this season soothes many a sorrowing heart.

Christmas is a time of joy to millions. To some, however, the bright red jewels of the holly will be seen through tears, because one beloved face forever present to the memory is invisible to the bodily eye. Such mourners cling to the religion that teaches them to hope and pray, and respect the science that does not scoff at such belief. Nor is the expectation of a future life confined to Christianity. In all ages, amongst men of all creeds, a belief that those who have gone before live on has been and is cherished—whether it takes the Buddhist form of life in another frame, or the impression, strong with the Chinese, that the spirits of their ancestors are about them still. The Materialist, who recognises nothing but matter, or the Atheist who denies the soul and scoffs at the whole realm of the supernatural, opposes himself to the instincts, traditions and the hopes of universal mankind.

To investigate calmly and without prejudice every account that bears even remotely on this essentially human aspiration is, we are told, the purpose of the Society for Psychical Research. It should from this point of view receive the help and encouragement of every religious man. The Churches are interested in anything that promises to give a solid basis of modern fact for the supernatural elements on which their creeds are built. That, however, is not the object of the inquiry. It simply aims at truth; and its ultimate outcome is a matter of secondary consideration. What light may be thrown on science itself, on theories of medicine, on physiology, or on mental disease by a thorough examination of facts, or alleged facts, nobody can predict; but, as Tennyson's Princess says, "Knowledge is knowledge," and must be pursued "unfearing consequences."

*Daily Telegraph.*

# 1883 – THOUGHT READING AND THOUGHT TRANSFERENCE.

The following somewhat extraordinary letter signed "John A. Rowe," appears in this morning's *Chronicle*:-

Sir,

Under the above heading, a letter from the prolific pen of T. P. Barkas, Esq., appears in today's issue the *Newcastle Daily Chronicle*. He calls attention to the existence of the "Psychical Research Society," "composed of gentlemen eminent in literature and science," and hopes, "if any of your readers have mesmeric sensitives under their control." they will allow him "to try some crucial experiments in thought reading and clairvoyance, in order that the facts may be placed in an orderly and authenticated manner before the society for psychical research." Perhaps you will permit me to offer the Psychical Research Society, through Mr Barkas, the following extraordinary experience, which in my opinion cannot be covered and explained by thought transference merely.

About three years ago I was invited by a friend living in Newcastle to witness a private exhibition of mesmeric phenomena. About ten sitters were present, ladies and gentlemen well-known to each other, and the proceedings took place in a luxurious and well-lighted drawing room. A Mr. Ogle, now, I understand, living in Sunderland, was the mesmerist, the sensitive being an illiterate miner whose name was probably mentioned, but whom I have always spoken since as "Dick," this being the name which he was repeatedly addressed by the mesmerist. I will not weary Mr. Barkas by relating the ABC phenomena of mesmerism, which we at first witnessed, and with which he is so familiar; I will describe the test which I suggested, and which corroborated the phenomena witnessed and related by Professor Gregory, M.D., in his valuable work on "Animal Magnetism."

The faculty of clairvoyance was being exhibited by the sensitive professing to describe events happening at the moment on the Town Moor and other places not very remote from where we sat. "Can the sensitive see and describe events transpiring in, say, a neighbouring town?" I asked. "Yes" was the reply. "Let him then say what is happening at this moment in a house in North Shields." The address was demanded and given, when the sensitive described very accurately the interior of portions of my house, and, more remarkable still, what the inmates were doing. A "young woman" was declared to be in a front bedroom (the bedroom being correctly depicted), sitting by the side of a bed in which sat a "chubby faced boy." The boy was alleged to be eating a crust. Then the "chubby faced boy" was seen crawling over the large bed towards a smaller one, where lay a baby, the object of the chubby one being to give the younger, fum fum, as the Chinaman says. Looking at my watch and finding it nearly 10.30 p.m., I observed to my wife, "It will be well to remember the time, for it is scarcely possible that what has been stated can be true, seeing the children are put to bed not later than seven o'clock."

On returning to Shields I questioned the astonished maid servant, who admitted keeping our little boy (then between two and three years old) up until about half past ten, "because he was lively!" "He did not have his supper in bed, however, but was sitting in bed for a time sucking his thumb! Neither did he crawl over the bed to beat his sister; it was to coax her to play!" I have every reason to suppose that this domestic, who is now a blessing to some other household, was for a time somewhat cautious in her methods when we were absent; but as she was a strict religionist it is probable she attributed my knowledge to a source not angelic. On the whole though she was not a bad girl.

Well, sir, what I wish to say is this;—Will your talented and esteemed fellow-townsman Mr Barkas, or the members of the Psychical Research Society, be good enough to elucidate this mysterious phenomenon? Of course I have a theory of my own, but I will esteem it a favour to hear from superior authorities, what in their opinion were the methods pursued by the mesmerist, or sensitive, or both, in order to reveal to me, and my friends at Newcastle, what was transpiring at my house at North Shields.

P.S.—Perhaps it may anticipate queries from those who doubt psychical phenomena to say that the sensitive and mesmerist were utter strangers to me and mine, and are nearly so still.

*Shields Daily News.*

---

# 1884 – A GHOSTLY DIRECTORY.

The London Society of Psychical Research has discovered that there is an enormous number of ghosts in England. Haunted houses are as plentiful as boarding houses, and some of them are densely packed with ghosts. Before the society began its researches it was supposed that there were very few resident ghosts in England. Proprietors of haunted houses carefully concealed the fact that they had ghostly tenants, lest it should hinder them from obtaining flesh-and-blood tenants, and people who had been compelled to abandon houses because they were haunted feared to mention the fact lest they should be ridiculed. Thanks to the society we can now form some idea of the ghost population of England. It is estimated that in London alone there are thirty thousand ghosts who reside permanently in their respective haunted houses besides a floating population of about three thousand ghosts who visit London without the intention of remaining there.

There are many persons who would like to make the acquaintance with ghosts, but hitherto they have had no means of finding out the residence of desirable ghosts. It is true that a man could, if he chose, advertise for a ghost, but it is more than doubtful if any ghost would see and answer the advertisement. Moreover, were anyone to advertise for a sober, middle-aged, evangelical ghost—"one who does not break furniture and who never frightens children preferred"—the advertisement would immediately be ridiculed by graceless newspapers.

With a view of supplying a long-felt want, the Society for Psychical Research is now preparing a ghostly directory, giving the names, residences, business, and general reputation of all the ghosts in the United Kingdom. Anyone desiring to make the acquaintance of a ghost has only to consult this directory. In it he will read of "James Smith, No. 2 Bloomsbury Square. Born 1665; murdered, 1720. Quiet and gentlemanly ghost; walks in the two-pair front bedroom, with a knife in his heart" or of "Crazy Jane, No. 64 Minories. Age unknown, shrieky and chain rattling ghost; performs every night at one o'clock a.m., but is rarely visible. Can be recommended to married men whose mother-in-laws frequently visit them."

In this directory anyone can find just the style of ghost of which he may search, and although the compiler of the directory does not guarantee the character of his ghost, and cannot be held responsible if they prove unsatisfactory, great confidence can no doubt be placed in the honesty and care with which his work is performed. The compiler in question is without doubt one of the boldest men now living. Has he reflected that no man has ever yet compiled a directory free from mistakes? Does he know that the man whose name is omitted from a directory, or whose name spelled incorrectly, or whose residence or business is incorrectly stated, hates the directory compiler with a hatred that cannot be appeased? Such a man can call on the compiler of the directory, or write to him and denounce him as a forger and an idiot, but he cannot proceed to acts of personal violence without danger of falling into the hands of the police.

There is, however, no limits to the ways in which a miss-spelled or miss-represented ghost can wreck vengeance on the unfortunate compiler of the Ghosts' Directory. That the compiler will make mistakes is a foregone conclusion, in which case he is certain to be haunted to an extent that will make life a burden to him. If he makes only fifty mistakes he will make at least fifty deadly enemies among the ghosts, and he should ask

himself, "What will life be worth to a man haunted by fifty simultaneous, infuriated, and utterly irresponsible ghosts?"

No words can fitly express the bravery of the compiler who incurs this tremendous risk, and he will certainly be a madman within a month after the publication of his directory—unless, indeed, he is a madman already. *Dundee Courier.*

---

# 1884 – A MODEL GHOST STORY.

A very singular story, which forms one of the sensational topics of the day, is the best authenticated of the many stories of the supernatural that have been lately told. Only a short time ago a young and well-known artist, Mr. A. was invited to pay a visit to his distinguished friend, Mr. Izzard. The house was filled with guests, but a large and handsome room was placed at his disposal, apparently one of the best in the house. For three days he had a delightful visit, delightful in all particulars save one – he had each night a horrible dream. He dreamed – or was really – suddenly awakened by some person entering his room, and on looking around, saw the room brilliantly lighted, while at the window stood a lady, elegantly attired, in the act of throwing something out. This accomplished she turned her face towards the only spectator, showing a countenance so distorted by evil passions that he was thrilled with horror. Soon the light and the figure with the dreadful face disappeared, leaving the artist suffering from a frightful nightmare.

On returning to his city home, he was so haunted by the dreadful countenance which had for three consecutive nights troubled him that he made a sketch of it, and so real that the evil expression seemed to horrify everyone who saw it. Not a great while after, the artist went to make an evening visit on Mr. Izzard; that gentleman invited him to the picture gallery, as he wished to show him some remarkable old family portraits. What was Mr. A's surprise to recognise among them, in the likeness of a stately, well-dressed lady, the one who had so troubled his slumbers on his previous visit, lacking, however, the revolting, wicked expression.

As soon as he saw it he involuntarily exclaimed, "Why, I, have seen that lady." "Indeed, said Mr. I., smiling,"that it hardly possible, as she died more than a hundred, years ago. She was the second wife of my great-grandfather, and reflected anything but credit on the family. She was strongly suspected of having murdered her husband's son by a former marriage, in order to make her own child heir to the property. The unfortunate boy broke his neck in a fall from a window, and there is every reason to believe, that he was precipitated from the window by his stepmother."

The artist then told his host the circumstances of his thrice repeated experience or dream, and sent for his sketch, which, so far as the features were concerned, was identical with the portrait in Mr. Izzard's gallery. The sketch has since been photographed, but, from its hideous expression, is far from pleasant to look upon.

*Illustrated Police News.*

# 1884 – AN AUTHENTIC AND EXCITING GHOST STORY.

That our nature is prone to be superstitious, and apt to be wrought upon by idle fancies, has been proved beyond all controversy; this is evidenced by the accounts which appear from time to time in the public newspapers of accredited ghost stories. People of almost every denomination have given credence to tales about unearthly visitants. Had it not been for the few who were ready and willing to expose the fallacy of spiritualism and bring to the bar of justice those who were making a good harvest out of it, half the nation

AN AUTHENTIC AND EXCITING GHOST STORY NR IVY CHURCH LANE.

would have been by this time devout believers in it; but the exposure, together with the strong arm of the law, have done much to scare this foolish delusion from the minds of the weak.

We will now proceed to present to our readers the last ghost story, as nearly as possible in the words we have received it, from an eye-witness who was himself intimately acquainted with the person who formed the leading character, an illustration of which will be found on the front page of this week's *Police News*. It appears the ghost took up his quarters in a very old country church, situated in one of the Midland counties. The edifice had sunk into decay; the windows had long departed, leaving but portions of the masonry standing, which was thinly covered with ivy. There was easy access to many parts of the building, as no doors remained, so that the curious were able to scan at leisure the few remaining objects of interest. Seats and pews had long since disappeared, leaving but fragments of stone and earth for flooring. There were several tablets on the walls, on which were written inscriptions which were easily deciphered. In summer time it was the resort of many children from the adjacent village, though many aged couples in the winter of their existence found it a place for quiet meditation; but as the winter approached the place was deserted.

Somewhat late one evening a week or so ago, two strangers called in at the White Lion Inn, and were served with some ale; when those persons who happened to be in the White Lion, as well as the host himself, were struck with their appearances. They were pale, and appeared to have been scared. Some resultory conversation took place, and in the course of a few minutes the strangers told the landlord and others that they had seen a ghost while passing through a narrow path of the churchyard. The landlord smiled, and looking up at the old Dutch clock in the parlour, and then at his watch, said the time hadn't arrived for ghosts to walk, for it was only half past eleven o'clock.

However, the two strangers persisted in their assertion, stating that it brushed close beside them, and that the face was awful to look at, resembling Death's head, giving it an appearance as if it had just left the sepulchre. This brought about a general conversation, and as the old church graveyard wasn't more than half a mile, several of the parties present, with the strangers, determined to visit the spot. The two latter could not be persuaded to enter the graveyard, so they consented, one and all, to remain at the palings outside. They hadn't long to stay before a figure clothed in white, and holding a lantern in one hand, moved stealthily among the tombstones in a peculiar manner, as if wanting to get back to its charnel house, but had missed its way. It then took a direction to where the men were standing. "See," said one, "It is making towards us. Probably it may want to speak with us."

Two or three of the party were disposed to take to their heels, but persuasion mastered the thought, and they held close together. The figure advanced slowly but closely to where they stood, till the face was discernible; and a more awful, sorrow-stricken countenance could not be imagined. Close up to the palings it came, when it raised its left arm in a manner as if inviting them to enter, at the same time making its face look strangely hideous and forbidding. It then turned from them, looking about in the same manner as before.

Them after some little time, the light in the lantern was extinguished, and the figure was all but shut out from view; but by close observation they perceived that it had entered the church, and was lost to sight. At times this strange figure would be absent at intervals for two or three nights together, and then again put in an appearance. In all haste we made tracks for the beer house, when one and all told their story, declaring they had truly seen a ghost.

Night after night the apparition was seen, but it kept nearer to the church, not venturing, as at first, near the palings, the people continually adding to their numbers, so that the visitors at times may be said to have increased to several hundreds.

We must leave the ghost for the present for the purpose of introducing a new character upon the scene in the form of a pantomime actor, and well known to the villagers for his drollery and comic acting, who said that as no one was disposed to face the ghost he would do it himself, in the following manner, and, as he himself stated, would soon bring him to account and frighten him considerably more than he had frightened others. So, having gained a spacious room at the Inn in question, he promised to be with them again in the evening, urging upon the landlord to assemble as many people as he possibly could, but with strict instructions to be as quiet and unseemly as possible, so as not to cause suspicion or to give intimation that anything unusual was taking place. The room was soon crammed with eager faces; never was the little village roused to such a state of excitement. A figure, closely wrapped in a mantle, presented itself before the audience. Momentarily he let fall the vestment or covering and the form of a theatrical demon was disclosed. The make-up had a startling effect on the village folks, who had never witnessed anything like it before. The writer goes on to aver that the actor was well-known far and wide, and had fulfilled many theatrical engagements with much success – but we have strict orders not to publish his name – being a good elocutionist and endowed with a fine, rich, deep voice, with good judgement in using the same, and made a very impressive character.

His appearance represented the demon elder seen in the opening of extravaganzas, profuse with yellow, crimson, and green foil, which now and again, when brought into contact with the gaslight, made the figure look extremely hideous and terrifying, especially the face, with small horns on the top of the head, and the cloven hoof. After amusing the company with droll ditties, recitations, and a demon dance – all of which was most rapturously enjoyed – he made his obeisance, and was shortly with us again in his usual attire.

The following evening arrived, by which the demon had made up his mind to test the faithfulness of his co-operator. Closely wrapped in a dark mantle he managed to conceal himself behind a tombstone unobserved. The mob outside were now waiting anxiously for the appearance of the ghost, and their enthusiasm was intense when they saw the spectre form emerge from one of the openings of the church with lantern in hand. The people with one accord, and with a low hushed voice said, "See where it comes!" One shivering mortal, standing next to me said, "That's a real ghost, mark my words I would not be in that other man's shoes for a trifle; In all hours of the night too, I've seen it; I've come with one or two of my mates purposely. What man on earth do you think would walk about now and again among the tombstones on a night like this when everyone is comfortably wrapped up between the sheets?" "It's my opinion," said another, "that when he falls across that 'ere chap he'll knock him into a cocked hat." "You can dry up," said another. "You fancy yourself awfully good at chatting, but you haven't got the pluck of a – well, you know what I mean. You talk about cocked hats; why don't yer go into the yard and knock that ere fellow – spirit I mean – into a cocked hat? You aren't up to it." "Up to it or no," said another, "When he falls across that ere chap he'll convert him – that is, make a ghost of the fellow like himself, and no mistake, and then they will bunk it off together, and we will hear no more about 'em" Others were prone to laugh, but it was not genial.

The mob was now upon the tiptoes of anxiety. A last a yell went up in the air. The ghost had momentarily held up the lantern, and before him was revealed the form of his most unexpected foe. The light thrown upon the tinselled gentlemen produced a marvellous effect. The glowing colours, as it hit them – well it was too much for his weak antagonist. The lamp fell from his hand, which the other dexterously caught without its going out, and putting it on the stone slab beside him. The characters now before the audience made out a peculiar and very interesting picture, and the people became more at their ease, perceiving the attitude of Grim Brimstone and the mute, death-like appearance of the ghost.

The former placed his hand upon his shoulder, and with a sepulchral voice spoke as follows:- "That his time had come, and that he must fly with him into inky darkness and space, for he was lost to all purpose in this world, and that his Satanic Majesty had ruling power to seize all such who could find no quiet below as the grave had seemingly held its tenant worthless, and so disgorged them up again. Wherefore would you go?" said his stout antagonist. "Nowhere. You have no place, and your sins can't be purged away by prowling about this graveyard. See yonder there, a hundred faces looking at you awe-stricken, though I am invisible to their sight. This, therefore, can't be endured. You have sold yourself to Satan so irresistibly, you must follow me, and before another moon and croaking sounds of hungry vultures, you will be hurled into the bottomless pit of darkness and despair"

With a look of terrible agony and painful remorse, and utterly deprived of the sense of speech, he seemed upon the eve of giving up the ghost then and there, if the other hadn't momentarily seized him in his arms, and by a dextrous effort removed the mask from his face, and hinting in a more human voice that the game was played out.

The lamp that was still left burning gave forth the picture and the situation, so that the mob gave a terrible yell time after time; in fact, they had become absolutely frantic, and I began to feel sympathy for my more unfortunate spirit. With the quickness of thought I doused the glim, and hastened him out by a back way into a narrow avenue or lane at the back of the church where there were no people assembled, till we arrived where stood a number of small cottages, in one of which I had the good fortune to house him and myself for the night; for had he been indiscriminately let loose upon the howling mob, ten chances to one he would have been torn to pieces.

Quietly housed, but not so the people outside, for from the peculiar noises made, with various ejaculations, such as, "Bring him out!" "Where is he? Where is he?" "Hand him over!" "Let us tear him piecemeal!" (and various other adjectives were used) which tended to show the multitude were not in the best of humour. However, time must wear them out, howl as they may; for on no consideration was I disposed to give up my prisoner, for my prisoner he certainly was, and I considered I had greater claim to him than anyone else. Having divested ourselves of our outer garments and had a wash up, we, seating ourselves before a warm fire, I questioned him why he acted so foolishly, and carrying on the game for so many nights in succession, absolutely disturbing the village from its propriety. "Well, I can't say exactly why I should have acted so foolishly. I didn't give it thought. I must have had ghost upon the brain, and imagined the people would be rather interested than otherwise." "That may be a very easy, way to put of it," said I; "but if I hand you over to the police to be dealt with according to law, the probability would be you would get six months' hard labour as a rogue and vagabond, and I'm not certain yet that I shall not do so; and, mind you, I'll stand to no nonsense" – at the same time showing him a revolver. "You see I am well prepared."

Perceiving he had no loophole to get out of, he fairly made up his mind to yield to fate and to the generosity of his keeper. We permitted the time to wear away as pleasantly as possible. In the meantime I was cogitating in my mind what I should do. Shall I let him go? If so, what account can I render of myself'? It will not be satisfactory to the people. "The fact of the matter is this, I shall have to give you into custody." "Oh! Don't do that," said he; "I shall be ruined for life. I had no ill intention I can assure you, and as I am a person of means, will £30 square the matter? The inhabitants of this place are poor people, so that you could exercise your authority, and command respect by apportioning out the money, giving each a portion. This would tend in every way to pacify them. If you will kindly accede to this entreaty, I assure you on my honour I will not be so foolish as to play the ghost again. I have the money with me." He counted out thirty golden sovereigns and laid them on the table. "Agreed," said I, and having ascertained that the whole of the money was genuine, I pocketed it with the intention of going straight to the pub and handing the same to John Barleycorn, to apportion out the money to his numerous customers as the ransom for the ghost's release. This, I am pleased to say, had the desired effect, so that the village of Ivy Church Green was soon brought to a state of blissful tranquillity.

*Illustrated Police News.*

# 1884 – LEGENDARY WHITE LADIES.

Whilst the learned members of the Society of Psychical Research are anxiously looking out for ghosts, another class of scholars are industriously explaining them away. Even the royal ghosts do not escape in this Democratic age, and thus M. Karl Blind found in the pages of *Cassell's Magazine* undertaking to show the unreality of the "White Lady of the Hohenzollerns."

It will be remembered that this *Weisse Frau* was said to have been seen in the palace at Berlin just before the late illness of the German Emperor. Fortunately he recovered; had his sickness ended fatally the lingering superstition would have received confirmation. The appearance of the Ancestress is always held to be the forerunner of death to one of the royal family. The White Lady is not the sole property the Prussian princes, for there is also one who's coming at the Vienna Hofburg is a sign of woe to the Hapsburgs. Other princely families of the Fatherland, not to be behind their move formidable relatives, have also a ghostly woman in white announce their doom. Once at Karlsruhe the fair apparition was not only seen but captured, and turned out to be a man.

In nearly every case the White Woman has a name, and that name is Bertha. This, in the opinion of M. Blind, is the key to the mystery. Bertha is the Teutonic equivalent of the Scandinavian Freia, who was the Goddess of Love, the Mother of Life, and the Mistress of Death. The kingly races claim a supernatural origin. The Anglo-Saxon, the Norwegian, and the Danish princes alike boasted of Odin as an ancestor. So the Teutonic ruling families have mythical Berthas in their pedigree. The legendary mother of Charlemagne is called "Bertha with the large foot," and "Bertha with the swan's foot," and this connects her with the beliefs of the pre-Christian German people by whom Freia-Bertha was regarded as a Swan Virgin, or even as a swan.

But the myth became vulgarised. "Under a new deterioration of the tale, a goose foot is substituted for the swan's foot. The goose foot, again, is changed into a flat foot, a large foot—nay, into a club-foot. And so out of a white-robed goddess; Freia-Bertha —an Elder-mother of All Life and a Mistress of Death, who was originally a Swan Virgin—we get Bertha's ancestresses of kings, as well as White Ladies who are harbingers of death in royal palaces."

The walking stick with which the ghost now taps is believed by M. Blind to be a degenerate form of the distaff which the goddess bore. There is a tradition that the Ancestress built the Castle of Neuhaus, and that she promised the workmen at the finish a festive treat. The poor are still annually fed in her remembrance on Maundy Thursday. But the food provided is that which in heathen days was sacred to the goddess Bertha. This is all very ingenious, but terribly iconoclastic. The old fashioned heathen deities, who have degenerated into mere ghosts, are now being driven off the earth by rationalising "folklorists."

*Edinburgh Evening News.*

# 1884 –"SPRING HEELED JACK" IN DARLINGTON.

For some days the wildest rumours have been afloat in Darlington regarding some mysterious being who has been playing antics in the ghost line for nearly a week. First he was seen in Neasham Road, then he paid a visit to Eastburn, and latterly he has honoured Rise Carr with his presence. It is said that he is on a visit to various towns in the North. From a simple ghost he has developed into a kind of supernatural being. He can stride several yards at a time, leap hedges and walls like a greyhound, and one person actually declares that he has darted across the Tees at Yarm! At any rate, whatever he may be, the result is that in Darlington women and children scarcely dare to move out at night.

Owing to the nervous condition of several timid females in Darlington our representative there has been led to make some enquiries concerning the "Ghost," and as the result we can assure all those who are in trepidation on the subject that the wild rumours now afloat have more existence in the imaginations of persons than in real life.

The most difficult thing our representative had to do was to find any person who had really seen the ghost. After about an hour's inquiry he at last found the man he sought. This was Thomas Nellis, a workman at the Bridge Yard, Neasham Road. Nellis informed him that on going down Neasham Road he distinctly saw a man in white standing near Mr Tree's gate. On Nellis saluting him he received no answer. Nellis at once walked up, and the ghost took to his heels. He thinks the white part of the performance is either produced by a light or white sheet. At any rate the moment Nellis approached the white disappeared, and he distinctly saw in the dusk a man about six feet high. He chased him down the field, but the ghost was very fleet of foot, and by the time they reached the bottom Nellis was forty yards behind. Nellis is of opinion that the man is assisted in running by some mechanical apparatus fixed to his boots, enabling him to take strides of immense length.

One thing he is certain of, that it is a man, so that it is to be hoped that this announcement will dispel the fears of those persons who are in terror of a visit from the Eastburn apparition. The ghost is not yet in the Darlington police cells, as currently reported, although it is expected he soon will be.

*Daily Gazette.*

---

# 1886 – GHOSTS IN THE BIRMINGHAM BOARD SCHOOLS.

During the past fortnight crowds, ranging in number from five hundred to three thousand, have assembled around various Board schools in Birmingham, obstructing the traffic and necessitating the presence of large bodies of police. The excitement has been occasioned by the report that a ghost was visible in certain of the Board schools at different portions of the night. So firmly has this notion taken hold of the popular mind, that last night an immense assemblage congregated round Dartmouth Street Board Schools awaiting the appearance of the

ghost. They sat upon the walls, filled the playgrounds, and, when the caretaker attempted to eject them, assailed him with stones; and though, in the struggle, he knocked several down with a broomstick, he was overpowered, and the crowd continued their demonstrations until dispersed by the police and the rain.

Within a fortnight, the Birmingham Board Schools at Summer Lane, where the ghost is said to have first appeared, at Smith Street, Kilkington Street, Thomas Street, Aston, Windsor Street, and elsewhere, there have been supposed appearances of the spectre, and in each case the police have had the utmost difficulty in dispersing the crowds. The nightly assemblages have awaited the appearance of the ghost in the belfry of the school, and several assistant masters have testified to seeing some person hopping thence across the roof into the playground. The practical joke which is thus being played has been the source of great annoyance to residents in the vicinity of the schools and the police, who, hitherto, have been unsuccessful in capturing the perpetrator.

*Shields Daily News.*

---

# 1886 – THE GHOSTLY LEG.

The following is a Japanese story founded upon the dreadful custom of burying one or more men beneath the foundation of a new palace, castle or fort with the idea that it conduced to the strength and solidity of the building.

One day a human leg was seen protruding from a wall in the residence of the Prince of Kaga. It was the ghost leg of one of the buried victims. Its appearance naturally caused great consternation, but one of the retainers, more daring than the rest, seized it. It kicked him into the middle of next week and no one had the courage to repeat the experiment. Its condition suggested that perhaps it wanted to be washed. The leg, with a satisfied flourish, thrust itself into the tub that was brought but kicked the whole thing over when it found that the water was cold. By repeated experiments it was ascertained that the leg really wanted to be bathed in warm water by a maiden, and after having been gently washed and carefully dried it waved a graceful farewell to the assembled company, and retired for the night, appearing every evening after for the same purpose, but always refusing in the same emphatic manner cold water and the touch of a masculine hand.

*Glasgow Evening Post.*

---

## 1886 – THE SPECTRE IN THE FOREST.

A story reaches us from Virginia which seems on all-fours with many similar narratives that have appeared in the public newspapers in this country. It appeared for some months past the villagers and farm folk belonging to a small hamlet in Virginia are so positive that a ghastly and unearthly visitor haunted a neighbouring forest that few cared to be in its precincts after nightfall. At length, however, the mystery was cleared up. Two travellers were passing through the forest a few evenings ago, when all of a sudden they came upon what they deemed to be a spectre, which the foremost traveller challenged, but receiving no answer, fired at it. Upon closer inspection our travellers found that the whole affair was an optical illusion. A mist was rising through the shrubbery, and between two trees, whose branches overlapped each other, there was depicted what our artist has shown in the illustration accompanying this article.

*Illustrated Police News.*

---

## 1887 – GHOSTLY GLASS.

The death of an aunt had called me to the city. The funeral over I was weary and lonely and overcome by a

THE SPECTRE IN THE FOREST.

disagreeable foreboding of future uncertainty—something which always attacks me after a funeral. I went to the room assigned me, lighted the gas, then sat me cautiously down in a "sleepy hollow" and looked about me.

I say "sat me cautiously down," because I am a country girl and know very little about the springs and contrivances which go to furnish a fashionable city house—as in truth, my story will certainly prove to you.

When I left my home in Cloverdale, I had decided to remain in San Francisco for two days, for I hate the city; it stifles me, makes me nervous and hurts my eyes. Besides, the city pavements weary my feet, and I seem to lose all my pride and strength under so many eyes and in such a crowd. My cousins, when they came to us in the summer, complain of weariness from perfectly opposite causes, and I suppose it is natural to weary of that which we are not used to.

Well, sitting there in that blue satin "sleepy hollow" I looked about me and sighed at the grandeur of my surroundings. There were two immense rooms, divided by blue satin curtains and white lace draperies. I had no desire to look behind these curtains, for it looked very dark and uninviting. I did not like to feel that the room was there. I wished from the bottom of my heart that they had given me of one of the servants' rooms, instead of doing me so much uncomfortable honour.

The rooms were the back suite, which overlooked the city. I pulled aside the lace and satin, opened a blind and was at once fascinated by the brilliancy of the view. Lights flickered and floated as far as I could see, and in the southern extremity of the city there was an immense curve of lights; then there were lines of lights; then there were lights in every conceivable shape; and when I looked at the star filled sky and then at the lamp lit earth, I could not tell in my rapture where earth left off and the heavens began.

At last I turned from the window and stood still in the vast place, and felt, I am sure, very much like a mouse in a church.

Suddenly the thought occurred to me that my aunt's rooms were adjoining these which they had given me; that but a few hours before her still body had lain there, and, in spite of myself, I shuddered.

I am afraid my imagination was getting the better of me, for the more I allowed myself to think, the larger seemed to grow the rooms. The long lace draperies seemed like huge ghosts looking down upon me. The fireplace looked like an immense mouth, opened to take me in. The bed in the corner, which was an ancient French affair, with a dubious looking roll at the head instead of a pillow, looked to me like a tomb. I could not help fancying that in that bed I should look like the stone figures on the pillars at Westminster, with nose and toes turned upward, and hands folded on the breast, as I had seen them in pictures. Again I shuddered and longed for my comfortable bed at home, with which I felt at least acquainted.

At last I saw what I took to be a French plate mirror. Forgetting for a moment my discomfort in the prospect of seeing myself in real plate glass, I hurried across the room, stood in front of the awful mouth and peered into the mirror.

I looked and was amazed. I looked again, but it was the same. Puzzled and alarmed, I sat down on the nearest chair to get my breath. I put my hands to my face, to make sure I had one. Yes, it was there, and being assured of this, it gave me courage to look again, and I did so, but the mirror obstinately refused to cast back any reflection. It reflected the room, but not me.

"Am I then," I said "of so slight importance that city mirrors refuse to let me see myself on their surfaces?"

Again I looked, and felt very much like the man who sold his shadow to the demon. I felt more lonely and chilled than before.

Then I determined to go over every article in the reflection of the room and see if that were perfect. Yes, there was the tomb-like bed in the corner, there the chiffonier, there the "sleepy hollow," the hassocks, the, long, ghostly curtains, the table in the centre of the room. Slowly I turned my head over my shoulder and started on seeing no table. Again, I looked in the glass. Yes, there stood a queer little table.

This decided my next move. I pulled the bed clothes down from the tombs, I slipped out of my clothes as only a country girl can, and slid in under the blankets, and hid my head, thinking—as women and ostriches ever think— that a head hidden is a head safe.

In spite of my fears, I must have gone directly to sleep, for the next remembrance I have is of looking about me in that surprised, dazed way that nearly everyone has upon waking up in a strange room.

I sat up in bed and thought a moment. Some clock in the house struck one, but this gave no comfort, since I knew that most clocks have a mean little habit of striking the half hours; so that hearing a single stroke in the middle of the night leaves me in doubt whether it is one o'clock or half after some other o'clock. But I had slept, and felt ready to laugh at anything, especially my fears of the first part of the evening.

I had just decided to get up and turn off the gas I had left burning, when I was startled by a slight noise, which seemed to be in the very room where I was. I thought of the dark room adjoining mine. I thought of burglars, fire, and then I thought of my dead aunt, whose room was next to mine. And then I thought of the mysterious table in the mirror.

Pulled one way by curiosity and the other by fear, I crept out of bed, very clear of the centre of the room, where the table ought to have been, I found my way to the ghostly glass.

I can now fully understand how one must feel before he can truly say, "My hair stood on end." I certainly felt the roots swimming about under my scalp when looking in that awful mirror, as I saw, standing by the table, a woman.

I dare not stir; my heart gave a heavy thud like strokes against my sides, my knees trembled, and I saw that long, lank, black robed woman unlock the drawer and take from it a glittering mass of jewels and thrust them into a great baize bag that hung on her arm. Then she closed the drawer and glided away behind the curtains into the dark room which I had not dared to enter.

I had just strength enough to tumble, once more, into bed, which I did not again leave until morning, when I hurriedly dressed and hastened down stairs. One by one as the family entered the breakfast room they exclaimed, "Oh, Kate, how pale you are!", and "Did you sleep at all last night?" "Why, cousin Kate, have you seen a ghost"?" I only smiled, determined to tell none of my fright but Aunt Lou, who, I was sure, would not laugh at me.

After breakfast Aunt Lou said, "Girls, I have a litter of gifts your aunt gave me before she died, and we will all go up to her room, and there I will divide among you her little valuables."

Generally girls cannot be kept long in sadness, and these cousins of mine were six strong, so it was anything but a quiet group that followed Aunt Lou up the broad stairs to "aunt's room."

Mai pushed in her head and cried out: "Why, the gas is burning." And "Oh, Kate!" cried another, "did you see the funny glass in the room you slept in?" But I did not answer, for Aunt Lou was reading a letter, which I did not take much interest in until she read something about "diamonds," "the square table" and "trap in prayer book pocket."

Then I looked wildly at the simple sheet of plate glass over the mantel piece, and cried out, "Oh, my stupidity Dear Aunt Lou, you'll never see the diamonds again, for last night, looking through that piece of glass, I saw a woman – a tall, lank, black robed woman – unlock the table and take out the diamonds!"

"What do you mean?" they cried in a breath; then they made a rush for the drawer, which was empty.

Then they all looked at me, and Aunt Lou said, "But why did you not call us, my dear child?"

"Because aunt I thought, I didn't know— indeed, aunty dear, the mirror deceived me, and I thought -I thought, the woman was an apparition, and oh, please, I think I should like to go home."

Before I left they had found some clue to the diamonds, which gave me some comfort but I shall hereafter stay at home where mirrors, though cracked and wavy, can at least be depended upon.

*South Wales Echo.*

# 1888 – A HAUNTED HOUSE IN DUBLIN.

A house in Clanbrassil Street, Dublin, is reported to be haunted. Within the last few months four tenants have occupied it, but left soon after taking possession. The landlord gave the fourth tenant the house rent free for twelve months if he would "live the ghost down," but he failed. The ghost is said to approach with a great noise, and smashes the furniture.

*Dundee Courier.*

# 1888 – THE SPECTRE OF THE BROCKEN.

After months of weary waiting the miserable summer has given place to a spell of delightful September weather. For nearly a fortnight we have been having fine bright days, with as many hours of bright sunshine in one day as we had in a whole week about Midsummer; the nights, too, are clear, with copious dew, and in most parts the mornings and evenings are veiled in thick autumnal mists which may be seen in the earliest stages to rise from the ground, and, gently wafted along by the all but still atmosphere, spreading over the surrounding country, enveloping it in a white, damp shroud. In all mountainous districts these conditions are highly favourable to the production of one of the most beautiful and oftentimes weird of natural phenomena, one which in former ages impressed those who witnessed it as being the manifestation of tutelary spirits, and, with the lively and picturesque imagination of our forefathers, fantastic myths soon surrounded it.

The scene witnessed on Carnedd Llewellyn, in North Wales, a few evenings ago would have been looked upon less than a century ago as some supernatural exhibition doubtless full of meaning as a portent of approaching events. The mountain was enveloped in mist, and as the sun was sinking in the west three travellers who were on their way across to Bethesda were suddenly confronted with what is known as the Spectre of the Brocken. At first a semi-circle of prismatic colours was seen in the mist, and in the centre the shadow of a man was visible. The sun setting lower and lower the semi-circle gradually increased to a complete circle, and the ghost-like shadows assumed enormous proportions.

As the travellers moved along or in any way altered the position of their limbs the huge shadows responded to every action, and faithfully copied every movement, but, of course, on a vastly increased scale, so that the spectacle was altogether a most diverting one. Ignorant people would have been alarmed and, perhaps, frightened out of their wits on being brought face to face with such an apparently diabolical presentment, but Mr. Woodall and his companions do not seem to have been terrified at the spectral appearances, which they rightly judged to be their own selves reflected on the wall of mist in front of them.

We look with awe upon a giant seven or eight feet high, but what must be our feelings when we see for the first time our own forms enlarged 10 or 20 times, and everything about us increased in the same proportion. In the Hartz Mountains, where the phenomenon was first noticed, and hence the general name of the Spectre of the Brocken, the monstrous demon was represented as stalking about the mountains crowned with oak leaves, his walking stick a pine tree taken up by the roots, large enough "to be the mast of some high admiral." On many of the local medals and coins the shadow has been represented as that of a substantial goblin.

Although there can be no doubt that the spectre has been witnessed for ages, the earliest account of it which has been discovered is that published by Silberschlag in 1780, He saw the shadow of the Brocken itself on the fog just as the sun touched the horizon, the movements of the people on the top of the mountain were imitated, each person being like an enormous Cyclops, the hut on the Brocken took the form of a palace, the people's legs were twisted pine trees, their arms masts, and pocket handkerchiefs sails. Haue, the traveller, made no less than 30 ascents of the Brocken with the object of seeing the spectre but the atmospheric conditions were unfavourable, and it was not until May 23, 1797, at sunrise, that he was rewarded for his energies. The mist was sweeping by to the westward, and the rising sun threw a colossal shadow on it. Have thought the shadows must be from 500 ft. to 600 ft. high, and over four miles distant, but in this he was probably mistaken. A violent puff of wind nearly took his hat off, and he lifted his hand to catch it, the spectre did the same; he stooped, and so did the foggy ghost; whatever he did the figure in the distance imitated it, and Haue came to the conclusion that the spectre was nothing else than his own shadow reflected on the fog by the sun behind him.

Since then the sight has been witnessed in most parts of the world, but more particular observation has brought to light the fact that it is as a rule accompanied by prismatic circles surrounding the images. The Ettrick shepherd did not fail to note the curious phenomenon in the dense mists of his native hills. He found that "After one ascends through the mist to within a certain distance of the sunshine, a halo of glory is thrown round his head, something like a rainbow, but brighter and paler." He seems to have frequently seen the spectre, but one morning when the fog was more dense than usual,

he was alarmed by the apparition of a giant blackamore at least 30ft. high; his first idea was to run away, to hide himself, but thinking of the hundreds of sheep under his care he took off his cap in his perplexity and began to scratch his head with both hands; the monster did exactly the same, "but in such style, oh! there's no man can describe it. His arms and fingers were like trees and branches without leaves. I laughed at him till I actually fell down upon the sward, the figure also fell down and laughed at me. I then noted that he had two collie dogs at his feet, bigger than buffaloes, I arose, and made him a most graceful bow, which he returned at the same moment — but such a bow for awkwardness I never saw. It was as if Troon Kirk steeple had bowed to me. I turned my cheek to the sun as well as I could, that I might see the figure's profile properly defined in the cloud; it was capital. His nose was about half a yard long, his face at least three yards, and then he was gaping and laughing so that one would have thought he might have swallowed the biggest man in the country. It was quite scene of enchantment. I could not leave it. On going five or six steps onward it vanished; but on returning to the same spot, there he stood, and I could make him make a fool of himself as much as I liked; but always as the sun rose higher he grew shorter, so that I think, could I have stayed, he might have come to a respectable size at last."

It will be gathered from this lucid description that the spectre varies in appearance and size according to circumstances— the density of the mist and the sun's position. With these requisites the curious phenomenon is to be observed in all seasons of the year, and at all hours of the day, but at sunrise and sunset especially. The apparition may be either the simple spectral figure, with sometimes a coloured fringe, or with a bow, or with a glory halo, the head of the spectre in each of the latter cases being in the centre of the concentric circles of prismatic colours. A modern authority appears to think that the vastness of the image is an optical illusion, that it is really close by and only life size, the idea of immensity being due to the shadow being scattered over myriads of the minute droplets forming the mist.

We are, however, rather sceptical as to the case reported as having been seen on a hill near New Radnor at 2 p.m. on August 21, 1851. It is to the effect that a young lady saw in a thin mist rising from a damp spot her own person reproduced in every particular— her dress, her handkerchief, her flowers, and her face appeared as vividly as if in a looking glass, the colour as well as the form being easily distinguishable. Two ladies in a carriage some distance away are said to have seen the figure and afterwards questioned the young lady about her supposed companion.

Another form which the phenomenon partakes is the beautiful appearance imparted by the sun's rays in the early morning to the trees on the summit of a hill. Under certain conditions they appear self-luminous, and look like pure silver, even the birds flying about near them seem so many flashes of white light, a curious and interesting instance of the effect of diffraction. Other variations of the effects of the rising or setting sun on a thick atmosphere may be referred to, but sufficient has been said to dispel from the minds of mountain climbers (a rapidly increasing class) any idea of dread in the presence of their own shadows, whatever be the dimensions of the latter. What is required is a calm and dispassionate description of the many forms of the phenomenon, unbiased by prejudice and terror; and tourists, if they keep their eyes open and their wits about them, have many opportunities for making accurate observations of a natural manifestation which alone is well worth the energy expended in gaining the mountain tops.

*Morning Post.*

---

# 1888 – THE TOWER GHOST RETURNS.

*(This story is a true story, in which the names only of the persons concerned have been suppressed. Its main incidents were known to the late Sir David Brewster, who communicated them to the late Professor Gregory, in whose work on "Animal Magnetism" they are noted "Case 65." But it is believed that no detailed account of the "Tower Ghost" has been yet published. The origin of this apparition is quite obscure, and no probable cause for it has ever been assigned. The results were, of course, due to simple terror, and not to say any destructive power possessed by the apparition. It is a curious fact in connection with this ghost that its appearance was not identical to everyone who saw it; that while to some it merely took the appearance of a mass of grey mist, to others, observing it at the same moment, it appeared as a fearful human form; while others, again, were unable to see it at all. This has been explained as the result of the varying degree of "sensitiveness" which is possessed by different persons, and by the different distances at which the appearance is seen, as well as by the decree of its intensity at a given moment. And, in the absence of any better explanation, this may perhaps be accepted.)*

"Well," said Colonel Blake, as he withdrew his cigar from his mouth and emitted a little cloud of tobacco smoke," the quarters aren't bad, at any rate, and, ghosts or no ghosts, I mean to make myself comfortable here."

"I don't suppose you'll be much troubled," responded the Rev. Mr. Orwin; "but it is quite certain that half-a-dozen of the men here believe that they have seen this apparition or vision, or whatever you like to call it and it is equally certain that many uncanny things have happened here—and do happen still."

And, after a pause, he went on:—

"Only yesterday, I was talking to Sergeant McMurdo about it, who is a stout fellow enough, and the last man to be frightened out of his wits by anything that has ever appeared to mortal eyes. He told me that the men get used to it after a time, when they find it doesn't do them any harm. But they never talk of it; and recruits are left to find out its existence for themselves. However, you now know all there is to tell you, so let us change the subject."

This conversation took place in a comfortable room in the Tower of London one evening in the late summer of 1821. The trial of Queen Caroline was in progress, and popular feeling ran high; for which, and other reasons the Guards at the Tower had been doubled. Colonel Blake had just taken his quarters there as Keeper of the Regalia, and he had brought his wife and daughter and a young son with him. This was his first evening in his new abode, and the resident chaplain had dined with the new Keeper and his family.

On the following day Colonel Blake, who was no believer in ghosts, made what enquiries he could as to the stories which had been told to him by Orwin. But he failed to learn much. He could hardly question the men personally, and though he closely interrogated Sergeant McMurdo, he could not get much satisfaction from him. He (the Sergeant) used to call it rubbish too, he told the Colonel, but knew better now. No; he had not seen anything in particular himself, but he had heard queer sounds, and certainly there were many uncanny things seen there. The guard had often turned out at the sound of a shot, sometimes to find the sentry in a fit or a swoon; and always the same story when brought round. After a time the boys seemed to get used to the ghost—for ghost there certainly was—and then they paid no further attention to it, finding that their musket balls did not hurt it and that it didn't hurt them. Still, they seemed to want a good deal of introduction to it before they reached that stage of familiarity which is supposed to breed contempt.

"I never mention it to the men," ended the Sergeant, "and never take notice of their stories. It's best that I should seem to know nothing of the ghosts. They do us no harm, and we do them none; so "live and let live," I says.

Dr. Splinters, the medical officer, pooh-poohed this particular ghost, and all other ghosts, after the manner of all approved scientists. He had never seen anything the existence of which he could not explain, except the spleen; and he didn't believe in anything which he couldn't understand. He admitted that he had been on several occasions called upon to attend sentries who had been found unconscious at their posts; but attributed their seizures to natural causes.

"These fellows are too well fed here, you see," he told the Colonel; "and their livers are consequently always going wrong. Then they get giddy, and think that they see things, and suffer from vertigo. Odd that so many of them should be taken bad? Yes, of course, it's odd; but sure to be some natural explanation. River air not so wholesome as it might be. Ghosts all buncombe, anyhow. Smart chap, perhaps, started the story to get off punishment. Example followed by less smart chaps— who couldn't invent for themselves—ever since. They always pull round after a couple of blue pills. Nothing like a blue pill to clear away the blue devils."

And the materialist medico laughed the short, dry laugh that was peculiar to himself.

So Colonel Blake was obliged to wait upon events. He had done what he could. Though no believer in ghosts, he was yet no scoffer, for he knew that there were things on earth not comprehended in his philosophy. Yet, strangely enough, he became conscious of regrets that he had brought his family to the Tower with him, which increased rather than diminished as the uneventful days passed by; and once he felt a strong impulse to send his family from him, if only for a time. Still, he could not say that he felt any presentiment of coming evil, and the ladies had given no sign that they were aware of anything unusual; and soon he came to laugh at the idea that he might have sent them away, and lived the solitary life of an unmarried officer.

Yet Colonel Blake was destined to pass the remainder of his life in unavailing regret that he had not acted upon that almost momentary impulse.

"Amy," said her father one very sultry evening, after the dinner things had been cleared away; "cannot you sing something for us? Or is it too hot for such exertion?"

"Oh, no, father," replied Miss Blake; "I will sing as much as you like."

And she sat down at the piano and sang several of the most popular songs of the day. Presently she closed the instrument, and moved towards the open window.

"It is warm tonight," she said, as she seated herself opposite her father.

"Piping hot, I should call it," emphasized her brother Ted, a boy of fifteen, as he laid aside the book which the gathering twilight rendered impossible to read.

"Reminds me of Madras," added Colonel Blake.

"Do you know," said Mrs. Blake, who was sitting by the table in the middle of the room, "that while Amy was playing, it seemed to me to grow suddenly cold. I felt so chilly that I was just going to ask you if you would close the window, when the feeling seemed to pass off. Silly me, is it not?"

And Mrs. Blake shivered as she spoke.

"Very strange," replied Colonel Blake, with concern; "I hope, my dear, you are not going to be ill. To me it seems that this is the hottest day that we have had this year."

And the Colonel thought, as the party relapsed into silence, that he would get Dr. Splinters to come over in the morning and look at his wife.

And so, for a time, the party sat in the warm twilight, listening to the regular tramp of the sentinels upon the terraces above and below, and the sound of their voices as they answered one another. Presently, the refrain of Amy Blake's last song was heard from below, as the sentry at the bottom of the staircase took up the air with a fine, though uncultivated, tenor voice. Right through to the end the man sang the song, which was one of those military compositions so much in vogue sixty years or so ago and as he finished, Mrs. Blake shivered again audibly.

"Ted," she said, "will you shut the—ah—h" And as she turned towards the door, which was open, she broke off suddenly.

Startled at the strained tone of her voice. Colonel Blake looked at his wife. An expression of wondering surprise, mingled with terror, was on her face, and her eyes were fixed on the open door.

Following her gaze, the Colonel leaped from his chair as his eye fell upon the door. For, rolling through it, into the room, he saw what seemed to be a volume of dense smoke.

"Good heavens!" he exclaimed; "there is something on fire!"

But as he spoke the smoke seemed to sharpen itself into a pyramid of dark, thick mist, which revolved quickly round its own centre.

"What do you see?" he asked his wife, striving to speak calmly, and keeping his gaze fixed upon the shapeless mass, which now seemed to him to contain something working in its centre. But his wife seemed too terrified to speak. She and her daughter could only stare—as a rabbit may stare at the serpent whose prey he is to be—unable to move or speak.

And all the time Ted, who saw nothing except the frightened faces of his mother and sister, looked on in wondering awe, unable to understand what was taking place. At last he cried out:-

"Father, look mother! What is the matter with her? Amy! Amy! What is it?"

But there was no answer, until a minute later Mrs. Blake threw down her head upon her arms on the table, and, finding her tongue at last, cried out in agony, "Oh my God, it has seized me!"

And, with a piercing scream, she swooned away. His wife's cry aroused Colonel Blake, who seized a chair and hurled it at the phantom with all his force. It passed right through the figure and crashed against the sideboard behind it. And now the at first shapeless mass had evolved from itself the fearful form of a gigantic man, clad in a leathern Jerkin, stained, as seemed, with dark stains. In its right hand the thing held by the hair a human head, which seemed to drop blood upon the carpet as it was borne forward; while in its left it grasped a bloody axe, such as the headsmen of the Middle Ages used to wield. And horrible as the thing was look upon, its face was more dreadful still. Such a demoniacal, scowling grin the Colonel could never have imagined until he saw it; it passed all description. And this apparition, still enshrouded in the thick grey mist in which it first appeared, seemed to the Colonel to glide slowly round the room, scowling upon him with that frightful grin as it did so, until it reached the door again. Then it disappeared, as it had come, through the open door.

Not till the thing had gone did Colonel Blake find himself able to move. After his one effort to rout the enemy, he had stood as though paralysed, unable to take his eyes from the phantom, whose fiendish look had almost frozen the blood in his veins. But Colonel Blake was no coward, and, as it disappeared, he rushed to the door to follow it. Before he could do so, however, the sound of a challenge from below, and a shot, followed a fearful shriek from outside, smote upon his ears. Then there was a moment's silence, and finally a heavy fall. The Colonel paused, horror struck, as he listened; and ere he could sufficiently recover himself to get downstairs, the measured tramp of the guard approaching fell upon his grateful ears. He stopped to listen, and heard the poor sentry, who had so lately been singing, challenged. But there was no response for the man was lying face downwards on the ground, utterly unconscious of his duty. The Sergeant shook him roughly, and, asserting with oath that he had been asleep at his post, ordered him under arrest. Then, having posted a new sentry, he went on to complete his round.

Colonel Blake drew his hand across his damp brow, and returned to the room where he had left his wife. There the sight of his son and daughter, bending over her lifeless form, seemed to bring him to himself once more. Raising his wife in his shaking arms, he bore her to her room, where, laying her on the bed, he left her with his daughter, whose terror at what she had seen had given way to anxiety for her mother, when she saw her stretched upon the floor, to all appearances dead. Next he summoned an orderly, and sent an urgent message to Dr. Splinters.

The rest of this true story is soon told. Dr. Splinters seemed impressed when he heard Colonel Blake's story, but, after his kind, would admit nothing, and said little. Mrs. Blake returned to consciousness under the influence of such restoratives administered; but as perfect quiet was enjoined upon her, no questions were asked as to what she had seen. She was never herself again, and when, some days after that terrible evening,

her husband ventured to allude to it, she shuddered so violently, and with such evident signs of real terror, that the subject was once dropped. She was, of course, removed from the Tower on the day following her attack; but though tended with the greatest care by her daughter, and prescribed for by the most eminent physicians of the day, they could not heal the mind diseased, and Mrs. Blake never rallied. She lingered on in a state of extreme dejection for six weeks of apathy, and then she died, quietly—the doctor said of inanition. Perhaps it wasn't only the necessity or nursing her mother that saved Amy from a like fate, by diverting her thoughts from what she had seen until the horror of that fatal evening had decreased.

As for the poor sentry who had been so frightened by what he saw, he was court-martialled on the next day for having been found asleep on his post. He declared that, whilst walking towards the stair entrance which led to Colonel Blake's quarters, he had seen a gigantic form glide out from the doorway. At first he had taken it for a huge bear, and viewed it with surprise, wondering at the same time as to how such an animal should be found in such a place. But as the thing passed close to him, and leaning forward glared into his face as it did so with the expression of a perfect devil, he described it, he had felt an inexpressible dread come over him. Nevertheless, as it passed, the sentry had raised his musket and fired into the figure; which, he said, had responded with a peal of unearthly laughter as it floated over the barbican. After that he remembered no more until he found himself under arrest.

The Court, of course, refused to believe this story, though it could not doubt the man's sincerity, so clearly was it impressed upon his hard white face; but Colonel Blake appeared on his behalf, and proved that the man could not have been asleep, as he had been singing, his (the Colonel's) family had been listening to him less than five minutes before. There was also in his favour the evidence of the discharged musket; and eventually the Court acquitted him, believing that he had been the victim of a sudden attack of vertigo. Colonel Blake, who visited the poor fellow after his acquittal, was shocked at the change which he saw in his face. From the ruddy glow of robust health it had given place to corpse-like pallor.

"Cheer up, my lad," said the Colonel; "your singing got you off so well that time that you will be wise to cultivate the habit."

"Colonel," he replied, "I have to thank you for saving my character but there will be no more singing for me in this world. When that fiend grinned into my face as it passed, I knew that my time had come."

And, in spite of the efforts of his comrades to cheer him up, and to rid him of his morbid fancies, the man died within eight and forty hours—another victim to the Tower Ghost.

Colonel Blake was never the same man again. The impression created on him by the events that terrible night never wore off, and, added to the death of his wife, to whom he was devoted, made him a prematurely old man. To the day of his death, he was most reluctant to speak of the Tower Ghost, though, as he always said, he would never deny the thing that he had seen.

*Western Gazette.*

---

# 1889 – A "HAUNTED HOUSE" AT GREENWICH.

A remarkable "ghost" story comes from Greenwich.

It appears that Mr. Peter Bothwick, in the employ of the South Metropolitan Gas Company, has resided for three years with his family at 14, Horse Ferry Road, Greenwich, a four-roomed house. Mrs. D. Bothwick had been troubled by hearing inexplicable noises, which her husband tried to explain away. The previous tenant, who occupied the house for twenty nine years, states that he never heard any noises, but his wife often complained to him that she had heard sounds like children falling out of bed. About two years ago the Bothwicks were away from home, and a neighbour states that during their absence he heard loud rapping in the house.

Twelve months later, in July, 1888, Mr. Bothwiock was in the country for a holiday, and on the 25th there were in the house Mrs. Bothwick, Mrs. Stedman, and Mrs. Lloyd. At ten minutes to eleven these three were in the back sitting room, which is divided from the passage by a wooden partition running to the top of the house, when they heard three hard blows as of a man's fist on the cellar door. Much alarmed, they rushed off to bed, and heard no more that night.

On Mr. Bothwick's return he put a new floor to the cellar, making it even with the passage. All went well until 25th July of the present year, the anniversary of the former manifestation. At twenty minutes to ten at night there were in the house Mrs. Bothwick and Mr. and Mrs. Lloyd, while a Mrs. Parkinson was in the next house, adjoining the passage. The three persons first named heard loud raps on the partition, and Mr. Lloyd went out, but saw no one, and searched the cellar with similar result. The rapping continued, sometimes appearing to be on the partition and sometimes under the stairs. It turned out that Mrs. Parkinson was not the person rapping, and on Mr. Lloyd giving a rap on the wall he was startled by hearing at the cellar door, close to his elbow, three knocks, which shook the partition, and were almost sufficient to knock the cellar door down. He opened the door on the instant, and searched the cellar, but found nothing. He knocked again,

and in reply there came three terrific knocks on the cellar door, which Mr. Lloyd had just closed. He immediately opened it again, and nothing could be seen, although a lamp in the passage shone into the cellar.

Shortly afterwards Mr. Bothwick and Mr. Parkinson, who had been out together, returned home. The knocking continuing, they made a careful examination of both houses, but found nothing unusual. Half an hour later two police officers arrived, and stayed some time. The knockings continued as before, at one time on the cellar door, at another on the stairs or at different parts of the partition. The people who were in the house also state that they distinctly heard footsteps on the floor above the passage, but on going up could see no one. The police considered the matter a practical joke, but could not suggest how it was done.

Meanwhile the knocking, which could be plainly heard on the other side of the road, had attracted a large crowd, and one of the men volunteered to communicate with the "spirit." A conversation somewhat to the following effect ensued:- "Are you a man?" No answer. "Are you English?" Three raps, supposed to mean yes. "Are you a woman?" Three raps. "Are you in great trouble?" Three raps. "Have the people in this house harmed you?" No answer. "You are troubling this house a deal?" Three raps. "Did your friends harm you?" Three raps. "Did they kill you?" Three tremendous raps. Mrs. Bothwick here exclaimed, "For gracious sake, let the man go away." He remained, however, at Mr. Bothwick's wish, and continued the questioning, with the result that the interrogator pronounced that a woman was troubling the house on account of some crime committed many years ago. The "ghost" would not answer any frivolous questions, such as "Will you come out and have a drink with me."

About midnight the knocking began to subside, and the crowd dispersed, but the Bothwick family would not go to bed. Mrs. Bothwick lay on the bed for an hour or so with her clothes on, and Mr. Bothwick sat on a couch till he went to work at six next morning, and two young men stayed with him. The rapping gradually died away, and ceased altogether about one o'clock. The Bothwicks determined not to remain in the house, and on the following Tuesday removed to Haddo Street, sitting up on nearly all the intervening days until midnight.

Two ladies, who appeared to be interested in the subject of spiritualism, called before they removed, and said they should have liked to hear the rappings. One of them said she did not suppose the "spirit'" would trouble anyone till next year, but it might, as it had been spoken to.

*Illustrated Police News.*

---

# 1889 – THE WRAITH OF TUMMELL BRIDGE.

A correspondent writes:—

Many years ago I had occasion to visit Tummel Bridge Inn at least thrice a year. I have driven the district in all seasons, and seen this wild and romantic district in all weathers. In the autumn of 1868 the shadow of Schichallion was thrown o'er the valley of the Tummel, one evening, ere I left the village of Kinloch Rannoch for Tummel Bridge. The sun had disappeared behind the western hills, leaving its gloaming gloom on Dunalister's birken show. Business for that day was at an end, and I leisurely allowed my horse to walk each snag and steep brae. After passing Dunalister the road slopes in keeping with the tumbling river. The road is narrow and winding, and in many parts very steep. With a mind at ease, a landscape unlit, the gargling of the stream, and the whirr of the startled grouse, I was contemplating a happy evening with my friend the host of Tummel Bridge Inn.

In this mood, and giving my horse rein, who knew his journey's end was near, I espied a form in flowing robes on the road before me. At first sight I imagined it was a gipsy, or one of that tribe who are to be met all over the country. I was astonished, however, at the figure keeping the same distance in front, although I increased the pace. The form kept ahead, and finally vanished from my view on a sharp turn of the road where a clump of natural birches grew on a small knoll. The incident would have passed unheeded, had not the following occurred that same night, and which has cost me not a little thought to unravel the mystery connected therewith.

Fifteen minutes or so from the time that the form had disappeared, I had arrived at the Inn of Tummel Bridge. The horse was unharnessed, stabled, and made comfortable for the night, the landlord and I had supper, and giving and getting the news of the district, discussing the affairs of Church and State, and in a happy, brotherly, and friendly manner spending the night. Not a sound disturbed us in our conversation till we were preparing to part for our respective apartments. All at once the barking and howling of dogs took place, of which there were with collies and terriers at least half-a-dozen in connection with the establishment. "What is the matter now?" I enquired of the landlord. The landlord, whose face I observed grew very pale, although usually sunburnt and ruddy, muttered some sentence or other in Gaelic, and then said to me, "Will you put on your boots and go out and see what it is?" The dogs still continued to bark, and when we got to the door, we found man servants and maid servants with lanterns lit searching the steading and outside premises.

There was nothing to be seen, and no one could account for the disturbance.

The servants and others gave their impressions in Gaelic, and the dogs got orders in the same language to cease their noise. The landlord, taking a lantern from one of the servants, asked me to follow him, which I did. He then told me that his servant informed him in Gaelic that it was a wraith he had seen. It had appeared in various forms of late, but tonight it came in pure white, and made straight for the Free Church Manse. The dogs had followed it to the door of the Manse, and the minister, who was a very old man and a bachelor, was away from home. The landlord had charge in his absence, and having the key in his pocket he went away, although drawing near the hour of midnight, to inspect the premises. There was no roadway proper, a grass covered path and tufts of heather led to the Manse, which proved to be a lonely, dreary abode.

When we got there that night, I remember the windows, doors, and floors were all patched and pasted over with old newspapers to keep out the wintry winds. There was not a vestige of life to be seen, and collie and terrier failed to trace the cause of the disturbance within the walls of the old Manse. We returned, as wise as we came, to the Hotel, but before going to sleep I remembered the form that I had seen at the foot of Dunalister's brae. Neither at that time, nor at any time, have I ever believed in warlocks, witches, or wraiths, and it was with mixed feelings that I read of the old minister's death before I again had occasion to visit Tummel Bridge.

The wraith has been seen after that time, but led to a house on the other side of the river, and on being told this circumstance I tried to throw off incredulity and had little difficulty in my own mind in making light of the wraith. Alas, however, death carried off one in the prime of her life—the summons came with suddenness—startling all the neighbours in that quiet and secluded spot. The year following, the landlord himself was carried off by death in a very sudden manner.

The late James Menzies of the Tummel Bridge Inn, was a comparatively young man, not over forty years of age. He was strong, well-knit, agile, and a thorough Highlander as his name implies. He was taken ill at Kenmore one afternoon, with great difficulty was able to be driven home, and in a couple of days breathed his last. His sister, who still conducts the Hotel, rehearsed all the circumstances regarding his death, which coincided in every detail with his own belief when in health and life. Having occasion to stay at the Inn often afterwards, I had my own thoughts and allowed others to have their own impressions of the wraith seen at Tummel Bridge. The most difficult part to understand was the part played by the dogs—their wild howling and barking—but they have an enemy in the mountain fox.

It is now sixteen years since I last visited the locality and I have often thought of the incident. The links that go to make up the chain of evidences for the wraith at Tummel Bridge are the weird, wild, lone and homely homes of a warm, kind, true, and illiterate people. They found their faith in the supernatural through the Gaelic. Theirs is the gospel of witch and warlock, and their belief is as much in the unseen as in that which is seen.

(This curious incident might have given to the world 16 years ago but for the reticence of our correspondent.)

*Perthshire Advertiser.*

---

# 1890 – THE HAUNTED SHIP.

The world abounds with ghost stories, but it is exceedingly difficult to get them at first hand; that is to say, from persons who have actually seen the ghosts. This may be the reason why they have fallen into discredit with the dubious.

I once, however, heard a story of the kind from one who came within an ace of being an eyewitness, and who believed in it most honestly. He was a worthy captain of the sea, a native of Nantucket, or, at any rate, a place noted for its breed of hardy mariners.

I met with him in the ancient city of Seville. Our conversation one day turned upon the wonders and adventures of the sea, when he informed me that, among his multitudinous cruising, he had once made a voyage on a haunted ship.

It was a vessel that had been met with drifting, half dismantled, about the sea near the Gulf of Florida, between the mainland and the Bahama banks.

Those who went on board her found her without a living soul on board; the hatchways were broken open; the cargo had been rifled; the decks were covered with blood; the shrouds and rigging were smeared with the same, as if some wretched beings had been massacred as they clung to them. It was evident that the ship had been plundered by pirates, and, to all appearance, the crew had been murdered and thrown overboard.

The ship was taken possession of by the finders and successfully taken to Boston, but the timid sailors who navigated her to port declared that they would not make another such voyage for all the wealth of Peru.

They had been harassed the whole day by the ghosts of the murdered crew, who at night would appear and perform all the usual duties of the ship.

As no harm had resulted from this ghostly seamanship the story was treated lightly, and the ship was fitted out for another voyage; but when ready for sea no sailors could be found to embark in her.

She lay for some time in Boston harbour, regarded by the superstitious seamen as a fatal ship; and there she might have rotted had not the worthy captain, who related to me the story, undertaken to command her. He succeeded in getting some hardy tars who stood less in awe of ghosts to accompany him, and his brother-in-law sailed with him as chief mate.

When they had got fairly to sea, the hobgoblin crew began to play their pranks. At night there would be such a racketing and rummaging, as if the whole cargo was being overhauled; and sometimes it seemed as if the ballast was shifted from side to side.

All this was heard with dismay by the sailors; and even the captain's brother-in-law, who appears to have been a very sagacious man, was exceedingly troubled at it.

As to the captain himself, he honestly confessed to me that he never saw nor heard anything; but then he slept soundly, and when once asleep; was hard to awaken.

Notwithstanding all these ghostly vagaries the ship arrived safe at the destined end of the voyage, which was one of the South American rivers under the line.

The captain proposed to go in his boat to a town some distance up the river, leaving the ship in the charge of his brother-in-law.

The latter said he would anchor her opposite an island in the river; where he could go on shore at night and yet be at hand to keep guard upon her; but that nothing should tempt him to sleep on board.

The crew all swore the same. The captain could not reasonably object to such an arrangement; so the ship was anchored opposite the island and the captain departed on his expedition.

For a time all went well; the brother-in-law and his sagacious comrades regularly abandoned the ship at nightfall and slept on shore; the ghosts then took command, and the ship remained as quietly at anchor as though she had been manned by living bodies instead of hobgoblin sprites.

One night, however; the captain's brother-in-law was awakened by a tremendous storm. He hastened to the shore. The sea was lashed up in foaming and roaring surges; the rain came down in torrents, the lightning flashed, the thunder bellowed.

It was one of those sudden tempests only known at the tropics. The captain's brother-in-law cast a rueful look at the poor tossing and labouring ship. He saw numbers of uncouth beings busy about her, who were only to be descried by the flashes of lightning or by pale fires that glided about the rigging; he heard occasionally the piping of a boatswain's whistle or the bellowing of a hoarse voice through a speaking-trumpet.

The ghosts were evidently striving to save the ship; but a tropical storm is sometimes an overmatch for ghost, or goblin, or even the ___ himself.

In a word, the ship parted her cables, drove before the wind, stranded on the rocks, and there she laid on her bows.

When the captain returned from his expedition up the river he found his late gallant vessel a mere hulk, and received this wonderful account of her fate from his sagacious brother-in-law.

Whether the wreck continued to be haunted or not he would not inform us, and I forgot to ask whether the owners recovered anything from the underwriters, who rarely insure against accidents from ghosts.

Such is one of the nearest chances I have ever had of getting at the fountain head of a ghost story. I have often since regretted that the captain should have been so sound a sleeper, and that I did not see his brother-in-law.

*Illustrated Police News.*

---

# 1890 – THE WRAITH OF RAVEN'S ROCK.

The precise date when the melancholy and tragic events recorded in this tale took place cannot be determined, but they occurred very probably in the year 1550. In the spring of that year the Laird of Glenmoriston took unto himself a handsome looking wife, who brought him a considerable dower. When the honeymoon was over the lady, as the custom was in those days, went to pay a visit to the neighbouring landed houses. The first house our heroine visited on this occasion was that of Fraser of Foyers. Here Mrs. Grant of Glenmoriston was most courteously received, and entertained for several days with Highland hospitality. On her departure, "Foyers" gave her very substantial presents, among which were quantities of smoked venison, wild boar, and salmon; a large pile of woollen stuffs, and a lot of butter and cheese. When the youthful wife reached her home her husband inquired how she had fared at Foyers. She replied saying, "Oh, most splendidly? A thorough Highland gentleman, every inch, is Foyers. But, between us both—I mean you and me—what do you think he asked? If I would marry him!" "Insolent hound!" said the Glenmoriston chieftain, "he shall live to rue his words."

It was in vain that the young lady tried to calm the storm which her licentious tongue had raised. Old Donald Grant, the piper, was instantly ordered to sound his war slogan or pibroch to summon his clansmen armed for battle. A trusty friend of Foyers at once left, via way of Fort Augustus, to warn him of the approaching danger. Glenmoriston numbered his men—150, good and true—and took to the road, resolved to exterminate Foyers and his retainers.

Whenever the messenger arrived at Foyers House the laird lost no time in preparing to make a desperate resistance, and receive honourable amends for his justly wounded honour. His followers were much the same strength as the Grants. Foyers, with consummate tact and strategic skill, led his company about three miles South West from the mansion, and not far from where Wade's Road now traverses the district, there being at that period merely a narrow and rough track for horsemen. Here Foyers exercised his men and harangued them, and told them of the gross insult that was flung at him, and told them to fight like heroes, and showed them not only that he was resolved to fight personally, but what he could do when the hour of action came.

At the conclusion of these words he flashed his huge claymore like lightning, slicing off clean a large piece of rock, which, our narrator told us, is there to this day, and that he often saw it. After this achievement Foyers made his men lie concealed in the large and deep heath behind the rock until they heard, "Forward!" In the course of half-an-hour the sentry reported the enemy in sight. Soon they were abreast of the ambuscade. Still no orders—not until the enemy got half down the incline which terminates at Loch Ness level. It will be at once apparent that the Grants were "trapped." They were exhausted after their long march, they were on very disadvantageous ground—it could hardly be worse—when there swooped down upon them like an avalanche Foyers and his clansmen.

The carnage was dreadful. Glenmoriston fled for his life, plunged into Loch Ness, and was about half way over when he was discovered. Foyers leaped into the water, like a sleuth hound in pursuit, and overtook Glenmoriston near Altsigh. Here a horrible duel took place—far more desperate than that of the "Saxon and the Gael." Glenmoriston was killed—Foyers severing his head; then he re-plunged into "the dark and stormy waters," and swam back holding the ghastly head by the hair in his teeth!

Seeing the direful consequences of her infamous lie, the demented widow fled to the forest, where she lived for seven years, and it is said that her wraith is seen now and again on wild and stormy nights and keepers and foresters alike declare that more than once they have seen and heard sounds around "The Raven's Rock" which made their very flesh creep—although they don't care to speak about them.

*Dundee Evening Telegraph.*

---

# 1891 – GRAVEYARD LIGHTS.

"Having been concerned in a most remarkable and altogether inexplicable adventure the other evening, which happened to me in Thomas Lane, Knotty Ash, I have been induced, at the earnest solicitation of many friends, to communicate the following particulars of the same to the Liverpool public as being of more than ordinary interest.

I was proceeding leisurely on foot to Broadgreen when, on passing the church at Knotty Ash, my attention was suddenly arrested by the strange and uncanny appearance of its graveyards. The time would then be shortly after midnight. The whole burying ground seemed alive and glistening with a thousand small blueish lights, which appeared to creep in and out of the different graves, as if the departed spirits were taking a midnight ramble. I stood petrified, not knowing what to make of it, at the same time experiencing a feeling of horror which suddenly took complete possession of me.

Just at this moment the moon, which had hitherto been more or less obscured by a moving panorama of passing clouds came, as it would seem, to my assistance, giving me for a very short time the benefit of her companionship. And now appeared the most startling phenomenon of all, a phenomenon which caused my hair to stand on end with fright, a cold numbness of horror paralysing me in every limb, for, advancing up the road directly opposite to me, came a funeral train, the coffin borne along with measured tread, covered with an immense black pall, which fluttered up in the midnight wind.

At first I thought I must surely be dreaming, and therefore pinched myself in the arm to ascertain if this were really the case, but no, I certainly was not, for I distinctly felt the nip, and was therefore satisfied as to my wakefulness. "What could it all mean?" I asked myself as the cortege gradually approached me, and I began to distinguish the general outlines of the bearers. These appeared to be elderly men and to have lived in a bygone age. All were dressed in the costume of the latter part of the 18th century. They wore the wigs, and some had swords, as well as walking sticks mounted with deaths' heads. I observed only one really young man among the crowd of followers, walking just behind the coffin. His youth, in comparison with the others, perhaps made me take especial notice of him. He was dressed in what appeared to be black velvet, the whiteness of his ruffles standing out in marked contrast to the sombre nature of his general attire. He carried a sword, had diamond buckles in his shoes, and wore his powdered hair in a queue. The face of this young man was deathly pale, as were also the faces of all the others accompanying him. Instead of the procession advancing to the gate at which I stood, it turned suddenly and entered the burial ground by the one situated at a few yards distance. As the coffin was borne through this gate all the blue spirit lights seemed to rise from the graves as if to meet the cortege for the purpose of escorting the body to its last resting place, these awful lights added considerably to the ghastliness of the scene as they floated over the coffin and heads of the mourners. Slowly the procession glided up the pathway, passing the main entrance of the church, and, continuing its way in a straight line, finally disappeared at the back of the edifice.

Where this most extraordinary funeral went to or what became of it, I cannot tell; but this much I distinctly aver, that coffin, mourners, and lights even the pale flickering moonlight all disappeared as mysteriously as they came, leaving me standing in the darkness, transfixed with astonishment and fright. Upon, gathering together my somewhat scattered senses, I took to my heels and never stopped running till I found myself safe in my own house. In fact, I scarcely remember how I got home. After recovering a little from the shock I immediately aroused a female relative who had retired for the night, and related to her the above particulars. She assured me that I must have been suffering from mental hallucination, but, seeing the great perturbation of my mind, and at the same time knowing my natural scepticism with regard to all so-called supernatural phenomena, she came to the conclusion that, after all. I might possibly have seen what has been described above.

The next day I made inquiries in the neighbourhood of Knotty Ash, and ascertained from a very old woman that she remembered a story in her youth having reference to the mysterious and sudden death of an old occupant of Thingwall Hall, who was hastily and secretly buried, she thought, at midnight, in old Knotty Ash churchyard. If so, was this a ghastly repetition or the event got up for my especial benefit, or was it a portent intended to foreshadow the coming of the Dread Visitor to myself? Now, as I have before stated, I am no believer in ghosts, but certainly this very remarkable experience of mine his entirely upset all my previous conceived notions of the subject, leaving me in a quandary of doubt. On the evening upon which I saw the mysterious midnight funeral at Knotty Ash, I was exceedingly wide awake; had met several cyclists on the Trescott Road, with whom I conversed, and had likewise refreshed myself at the public drinking fountain placed at the top of Thomas Lane. Strange that a few hundred yards further down the road I should encounter so ghostly an experience – an experience I shall never forget to my dying day.

*Liverpool Post.*

## 1891 – IMPENDING DOOM.

Two giant owls perch upon the battlements of Wardour Castle when the last hour of an Arundel of Wardour has come. If a Devonshire Oxenham is about to die a white breasted bird flutters over the doomed one's head. The Middletons of Yorkshire, as becomes an ancient Roman Catholic house, have a Benedictine nun to warn them of an approaching death. A weeping, mourning spirit warns the Stanleys of a reduction in their number. A hairy armed girl, called May Mullach, brings the like sad news to the Grants of Grant. The Bodach am-dum or ghost of the hills performs the same office for the Grants of Rothiemurcus.

The death of an Earl of Airlie is foretold by the beating of an invisible drum. So respectable a man as Dr. Norman McLeod, editor of *Good Words*, lent the weight of his testimony to it. In 1849 Lord Airlie died in London, and the household at Cortachy Castle, his seat in Forfarshire, were thus prepared for the news, and when his son died in Colorado, the ghostly drummer boy was heard just before his death. Lady Airlie heard it in her room, and was greatly prostrated, but one of the servants first heard it in the corridor. The approaching death of a Bruce is announced by the spectre of a women in white, who appears to the doomed scion of that ancient and once royal house.

*New Ross Standard.*

---

## 1891 – SPECTRE SHIPS.

In the south and west of England, and notably on the Cornish coast, there are many stories of spectre ships. Some of them sailed over land as well as sea. They were usually visible in tempestuous weather, and often manned by bad young men who did some desperate deed and then vanished. Sometimes these phantom barques suddenly carried off notorious wreckers, who had grown rich by luring ships ashore with false lights. Only some fifty years ago the captain of a revenue cutter reported that he had passed at sea, off the Devonshire coast, a spectre boat rowed by what appeared to be the ghost of a notorious wizard of the region. The question is, how did the revenue skipper know that the boat was a spectre? He does not seem to have boarded her.

The *Palatine* is an American spectre-ship. She was once a Dutch barque, but was wrecked on Block Island in the year 1752. After sacking her, the wreckers set fire to her and sent her adrift out to sea, although there was woman aboard who refused to land among such human fiends. Every year, on the anniversary of this shocking deed, the ghost of the *Palatine* is seen blazing away off the Point. And as Whittier says—

"The wise, sound skippers, though skies fine,
Reef their sails when they see the sign
Of the blazing wreck of the *Palatine*."

Whittier tells of another American phantom ship. A young skipper, who traded to the Labrador coast in the season fell in love with one of two beautiful sisters who lived with their mother in a secluded bay. Both the sisters, however, fell in love with him, and the elder was jealous that he preferred the younger. So when the skipper came, by arrangement, to carry off the bride of his choice, the sister shut her in her room and, closely veiled, went out herself to meet the sailor. It is not until they are far out at sea that the disappointed lover learns how he had been deceived. He turns back at once, but finds his own sweetheart dead. Neither he nor his ship ever returned home.

The Greyport legend is familiar to all readers of Bret Harte's works. He tells how some children went to play on board an old hulk, which broke adrift, floated out to sea, and was lost with all its innocent company. When the fogs come down on the coast, the fishermen still hear the voices of the children on board the phantom hulk that drifts along but never returns.

In the Gulf of St. Lawrence they tell of a spectre often seen off Cape d'Espoir. It is a large ship, crowded with soldiers, and on the bowsprit stands an officer pointing to the shore with one arm, while he supports a woman with the other. Then the lights suddenly go out, a scream is heard, and the ship disappears. This is the ghost of the flagship of the admiral sent by Queen Anne to reduce the French forts. The fleet was wrecked of this Cape, and all hands were lost.

On the Hudson River there is a legend of a spectral boat manned by Ramhout Van Dam, who, after drinking until midnight one Saturday, swore that he would row home, although it took him a month of Sundays. He never reached home, but he is heard at night desperately plying his oars on the river on which he is condemned to row till the day of judgement.

*Glasgow Evening Post.*

---

## 1892 – A GHOST HUNT IN DURHAM.

The villagers of Birtley, near Newcastle, have been much excited of late by strange sounds heard in the house of a miner named Wild. The walls and roof have been pierced to discover the cause, and the partitions have been smoked, but no discovery has been made. A correspondent telegraphs that he sat up with the ghost to a late hour on Tuesday night. He heard a cry at intervals, a faraway tremulous wailing sound, but saw nothing unusual. Local Spiritualists have expressed a desire to interview the shade, but Wild has declined this happy medium as a means of communication with the unseen. All kinds of stories are afloat as to the ghost, and crowds assemble nightly outside the house.

*Blackburn Standard.*

———◈———

## 1892 – A STRANGE COMPANION.

On the evening of the 9th inst., when returning home between 8 and 9 o'clock, I had my first experience of a real ghost.

I was walking in a northerly direction, the moon shining on my right side and back. On the side of the road there was a low hedge, along which I was walking, bounding a large lea field in course of being ploughed out. I observed a man walking across the field in the same direction I was going, and about 300 yards distant from me. I walked on until he reached the edge of the ploughed portion of the field; then thinking the person might be a friend I expected to come that way I waited, and the figure appeared to walk on the grass towards me. After waiting a few minutes, and observing that the man did not come up to me, I hailed him, but got no response. I was then satisfied that it was not my friend at any rate, and I proceeded on my way home.

To my surprise the person started in the same direction. I stopped, so did he, I waved my umbrella. My mysterious and rather auspicious looking companion replied by shaking his spectral "Drooko" at me. Being now fairly aroused as to the strange nature of the appearance, I turned and walked back along the road. My unknown friend also turned, still keeping the same respectful distance. I again stopped and turned homewards, but my friend was not to be shaken off; he immediately turned and accompanied me. By-and-by, however, he began to lag behind, farther and farther, until he finally disappeared.

Wishing to know if I could recall so mysterious a being, I retraced my steps a second time. A hazy and shapeless figure shortly appeared in the field, and as I proceeded it gradually assumed form and distinctness. The moon at this moment shining out clearly, I walked for a few minutes farther along, and I then saw the figure as plainly as I could have seen any person at the same distance from me.

As I have stated, the figure was between myself and the moon, and about three hundred yards away. On the other or left hand side there was a bright white cloud, and it occurred to me that the apparition might be due to a reflection from this cloud. But the singular part of the situation was that the hedge, which would be about three feet high, stood between me and the figure, and the figure appeared to walk along close on the surface of the ground. It would naturally have been expected that the hedge would have intercepted the rays of light whether they came from the moon or the cloud, and that the figure would have been distorted or appeared raised above the surface of the ground. The illusion was a perfect Pepper's ghost, but I was unable to discover in what manner it was produced.

I daresay these particulars may be of interest to some of your readers, and perhaps some of them may be able to offer an explanation of the matter. I have little doubt many real ghost stories have occurred under similar natural conditions, whatever these may be.

*The Scotsman.*

———◈———

## 1893 – ROYAL GHOSTS AT HAMPTON COURT.

During the past few days there have been numerous rumours of the reappearance in Hampton Court Palace of the ghosts which are supposed to haunt certain parts of the royal building. The spectres who are said to be exercising the minds chiefly of the domestics in the palace are reported to be those of Queen Anne Boleyn and Queen Jane Seymour. Nothing is heard just now of the apparition of Mistress Penn, or of Catherine Howard, which but a few years ago terrified some of the residents in the vicinity of the apartments formerly occupied by these personages. But it is asserted that the supernatural visitants in question have been seen gliding through doors and walls, that their footfalls have been heard traversing the rooms in the dead of night, and that they have disported themselves by carrying off the pillows from under the heads of those who were sleeping thereon. Two servants are leaving the palace in consequence of these uncanny visitors.

Queen Catherine Howard's restless spirit is said to be the most terrible of all the ghostly spectres which roam through the rooms, and concerning her there is some remarkable and almost convincing testimony. After the disclosures made to Henry of the alleged faithlessness of his Queen, the King was one day hearing mass in the Royal closet in the chapel. Catherine Howard, who was confined to her room, escaped, ran along the (now named) Haunted Gallery, the door of which is on the right hand side of the Queen's Great Staircase, and had just reached the door of the closet when the guards rudely seized her, and in spite of her piercing screams carried her back to her room, while her husband continued his devotions unmoved. This is the scene which is said to have been re-enacted again and again in the Haunted Gallery.

A tall figure, dressed from head to foot in white, has been seen going towards the Royal pew, and on reaching the door has rushed back with disordered garments, a look of despair on her face, and uttering at the same time a succession of unearthly shrieks till she passes through the doorway leading on to the Queen's staircase. Though the gallery is now locked and used as a lumber-room, yet the screams are still heard. On this point Mr. Law says he is enabled to adduce some recent and very convincing testimony from letters which he has received from a Mrs. Cavendish Boyle, who still lives in the palace in apartments adjacent to the Haunted Gallery, and Lady Eastlake. Mrs. Boyle states that she was awakened out of a profound sleep one night by a loud and unearthly shriek from the direction of the gallery, followed by perfect stillness. She did not mention the occurrence, not wishing to cause alarm, nor to lend encouragement to the idea that the palace was haunted.

Sometime afterwards, however, Lady Eastlake, who had stayed at the palace several times, told Mrs. Boyle that on a previous visit she was startled by a piercing shriek in the same place and also in the dead of night.

Queen Anne Boleyn and her successor in Henry's affections, Queen Jane Seymour, are also said to be frequent visitors in the spirit to the scenes of their gay revels three hundred years since. The former of these royal dames appears to be a very harmless spectre, and confines herself to promenading the rooms at all hours of the night. Some six years ago a Surrey damsel, strong and robust, received such a shock to her system, by the sudden and unexpected apparition of this long deceased queen, dressed in a light blue gown, that she left the palace an altered girl, and has been unwell ever since. And even today there lives in the palace a "queen of the kitchen" who avers she has seen the very same shadow, and who declares that nothing in the world will induce her to stay in a place , where "Ann Bullion walked, and ghosts were so barbacious."

Queen Jane Seymour's spirit is to be seen – or was – walking in the vicinity of her former apartments with a lighted taper in her hand, but according to more modern accounts she has developed a mania for pulling pillows from under the heads of sleepers. This is a very harmless occupation no doubt, but when the accounts of her playful tricks are related and magnified,

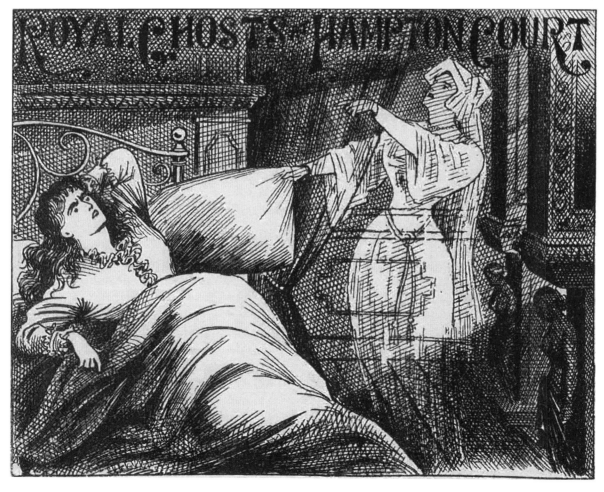

and servants begin to give notice, it is time that this contumacious spectre should be laid once and for all. But who can do it?

*Illustrated Police News.*

---

# 1893 – SUCH IMPERTINENCE!

We object to Royal Ghosts. Anne Boleyn, Jane Seymour, and a few others of Henry the Eighth's wives, are walking about Hampton Court Palace. What they want it is difficult to imagine. Surely, not a husband. History tells us that Henry was more than enough for one or several. But, here at the end of the century – the century of which we are all so professedly proud—ghosts have the indecency to open and shut doors as if nothing had happened since they were alive.

Royal ghosts especially are to be denounced. They had a good time; they lived their life while on Earth, and some of them (Jane Seymour, for instance) got more than enough of it. What a piece of impertinence that Anna Boleyn should be peering at our little happinesses!

The ordinary man's ghost can be forgiven; a fellow-feeling, even in ghosts, makes us kind. His ghost is to be pitied because, possibly, it dare not try the other world.

But Royal Kings and Queens noising about like rats in the wainscoting—it is too abominable.

There is great complaint made of Jane Seymour. She would really have to be up for "drunk and disorderly" if she lived in this year of grace Hannah Dominy. "Revelry sounds in the morning" (as it usually does) and for this Jane is blamed. Perhaps, after all, Henry VIII., was a moderate drinker wedded to an intemperate wife. "Her voice" (Jane's; not Mary Jane s) "is so often heard that it has become quite well-known to the living listeners, while her habit of pulling away pillows from under the heads of sleepers must go far to ensure her a hearing." We should think so, and, for ourselves, a response, Jane might not like. But Henry VIII., subject to this pillow snatching o' nights, might be forgiven for getting a divorce. It is quite clear that Jane Seymour was not better than she should be, even when alive. Now, that she is dead, it will be well for Henry if his soul rests in Heaven.

Anne Boleyn is more reserved and undemonstrative. But she "walks" —that nasty creepy walk along a corridor—which is more than enough for most of in the middle of the night. Anne does not pull pillows or make ribaldry. But she "walks." Here, too, is another dead woman not an angel, otherwise she would have wings wherewith to fly! "Anne Bullion" is driving away the cooks from Hampton Court with her walking, and the lady pensioners there are wishing (for the first time

perhaps) that they have their husbands back again. All this is very disgraceful, but that some of Henry's wives are still on Earth must tend to smooth and simplify matters Back of Beneath, wherever his Royal Holbein personage happens to be.

*Hull Daily Mail.*

---

# 1893 – THE COCK LANE GHOST – AN EIGHTEENTH CENTURY SENSATION.

The ghost of Cock Lane, says the *Daily News*, apropos of an article on the subject by Mr. Howard Pyle in *Harper's Magazine*, began to make more than a merely parochial stir in 1762. The lane, according to Mr. Pyle, was a dirty little slum at the back of St. Sepulchre s Church, between Snow Hill and Giltspur Street.

The house where the ghost disported himself was tenanted by Mr. Parsons, clerk of St Sepulchre's Church, who had a daughter aged twelve years, the "medium" in the case. To Mr. Parsons, in 1759, enters a Mr. Kent, or Kempe, who was living with his deceased wife's sister. Each of these interesting lovers made a will bequeathing his, or her, worldly wealth to the survivor. On a certain occasion Mr. Kent had to go to a funeral in the country, leaving "Miss Fanny" alone in Cock Lane. The young woman invited Parsons's little girl to share her bed, and both she and the child were kept awake all night by scratching and rapping noises. These phenomena recurred at intervals for some time, and were unexplained. Then the Kent's quarrelled with Parsons, and left the lodgings and the disturbance ceased. In her new lodgings, in Clerkenwell, "Miss Fanny" died, and then the trouble began again in Cock Lane, always attending Parsons's little girl. She became much alarmed and a woman named Mary Fraser was procured to attend her. Miss Fraser suggested trying to correspond by raps with the ghost, and the ghost chose to allege that it was Miss Fanny; that it or she had been poisoned by Mr. Kent, and that it wanted Mr. Kent to be satisfactorily hanged. Not only did it rap, but it filled the room with a sound of fluttering wings.

All London now flocked to Cock Lane. Horace Walpole went with Lady Mary Coke (the daughter of the Duke of Argyll who fought at Sherifmuir), and the Duke of York, whom Lady Mary loved with a ridiculous passion. Walpole saw and heard nothing, and of course ridiculed the whole affair. But the Wesleyans took up the ghost, the Church of England followed suit, Johnson investigated it, and the end came shortly. The ghost promised to rap on her own coffin in the crypt of St. John's, Clerkenwell, but when inquirers went thither the ghost did not come to scratch. Moreover, it became known that Mr. Parsons and Mr. Kent had a quarrel about money, and here was an obvious motive for the accusation of the ghost. The child was taken to a strange house; she was hung up in a hammock; she was told that if the ghost would not "manifest" her father would be imprisoned as an impostor. The unlucky child therefore took a little board of wood to bed and scratched on it. The old noises were not produced on it, but noises of a thoroughly normal character were produced. So all the Cock Lane people, including the Curate of St. Sepulchre's, were tried for conspiracy before Lord Mansfield, and were found guilty and punished.

Parsons was put in the pillory, but the rabble still believed, and collected money for him. The world then settled that the board of wood was the whole mystery, and Mr. Pyle seems to doubt the accuracy of the verdict.

*Glasgow Evening Post.*

# 1893 – THE PHANTOM PASSENGER.

When I was younger in my profession than I am now, Dresden was my favourite holiday resort. In the quiet and slow-flowing life current of the Old World, home of the fine arts, I frequently sought and found relaxation from the strain of work-a-day months in London.

One January night found me seated, cold, travel-stained and weary, in the train at Hamburg en route for my old resort. Experience had taught me that in Germany a fellow-traveller implies an instantaneous deprivation of the quantum of fresh air necessary to keep the lungs in play.

So, calling the guard, I requested that I might be secure from intrusion. Touching his cap with a laconic reply he pocketed a douceur and locked me in.

The train started. For a few moments we stopped at a wayside station. I consulted my watch.

How cold it grows as the day draws its last shivering breath. Strange at this hour the springs of being are at their lowest in all that lives, whilst, in mystic sympathy with the dying day, the life is spilt out of those in whose cup are only its lees. I wrapped my cloak around me.

Once more we were on the point of starting when the door I imagined securely locked was gently and easily opened. A lady entered and seated herself opposite me.

Below my breath I confounded the guard for a false "Deutsher," and reflected how extraordinary it was that the intruder should be a woman; for abroad the fair sex have special travelling compartments where no man dare put in an appearance and vice versa. In the confusion of starting she had doubtless mistaken her carriage, and now, perhaps, felt uncomfortable.

As the cold, each moment, increased I offered her one of my warm wraps, addressing a few conventional words to her on the topic of the weather.

"Thank you," she said, in a quiet and perfectly self-possessed voice, "but indeed I do not feel the cold you speak of."

A story is often told in the tone of a voice – and the tone of this one was peculiar. Unmistakably English and well-bred; but there was no ring in it, only a certain hopelessness sufficiently pathetic. She had evidently noticed some of my smaller professional belongings in the netting above me, for, as I silently pondered what manner of woman she was, she thus addressed me:-
"You are an artist?"
"I am."
"Could you paint a portrait from memory?"
"Most certainly."
She removed the thick veil that concealed her face and laid aside her bonnet. The light from the lamp fell full upon her. She had a lovely face but it was cold and white and still as chiselled marble. She encountered the bold, steady gaze of masculine eyes, yet no tinge of colour flickered on her cheek. A mass of ruddy-brown hair was coiled round her shapely head; large brown eyes, full of the dumb, questioning pain I have seen in the eyes of a hunted deer at bay, looked out from between dark lashes. Marring the stainless white of the left cheek, a livid mark ran from the temple into the neck – it almost looked as if a stinging riding switch had been drawn swift and sharp across the face, burning its brand into the delicate flesh. Her dress was of black velvet, and around the throat and wrists were ruffles of costly lace.

"Yours," I said, "is not a face soon to be forgotten. I could any day paint your portrait from memory."
"Will you do so?"
"Certainly, if you desire it."
"I do specially desire it."
I took out, my notebook and entered a memorandum.
"Promised to paint the portrait of a lady from memory, this 20th night of January, 18__."
She watched me make this entry, and resuming her bonnet and veil she fell into silence. As I sat opposite this beautiful, statuesque woman a strange sensation stole over me. Underneath that concealing veil there was a still, white face, with stricken eyes that haunted me and sent a chill to my heart. God help her, I thought, for life has been cruel to her. Then I mused on the singular promise I had made to paint her portrait from memory.

Would she come and claim the picture? Was I to send it to her? And where? I must come to an understanding before we parted. Meantime, in the first grey dawn, the train stopped at Berlin, where we changed carriages. For a moment I turned to gather my small impediments; when I resumed my position I was the sole occupant of the compartment. Hoping to encounter my sometime companion in the crowded station, I made haste to get out. My efforts were in vain – I was locked in. Presently the guard came and let me by out.

"There is trickery here," I said, in some heat. "A lady turned the handle of your locked door easily enough and has been my travelling companion since midnight."

"Impossible!" and the guard shrugged his shoulders incredulously. The key had been in his pocket all the time.

I shook my head, but there was no time for parley, and without another glimpse of the fair *incognita*, I resumed my journey.

Once more in Dresden, and amidst the realism of the old familiar life, the midnight episode of my journey began to fade into a trick of a fevered and over-wearied brain. And as I glanced at the entry in my notebook I reflected how completely a disordered imagination may fool a man. At the same time I resolved, some leisure day, to trace out my dream on canvas; but, absorbed in immediate study, I then postponed my intention,

Weeks rolled on, and I went to Berlin to look up a college chum, who was temporarily located in that city. When. I got to his quarters Unter der Lindeni, I found that some weeks previously he had been hastily recalled to England, and another Englishmen reigned in his stead. As I turned from the door, slightly chagrined, I encountered the tenant of Locksley's room, evidently returning from a stroll. A fine old man of the genuine type of courtly Englishman, now rarely to be met. He politely accosted me, and in a few words I told him of my disappointment.

"Do confer a kindness on me," he said, "and stop and dine. I am quite alone, and it is pleasant to hear one's mother tongue in this land of strangers."

We exchanged cards, and I accepted his invitation as cordially as it was offered. By degrees we fell into the most amicable relations with one another; and presently, he told me, with tears in his eyes, that within the last few weeks he had been bereft of a wife and daughter – all he had of best and loveliest, and was quite alone. Then I strove to turn his thoughts into another channel, and by and by we fell into art talk.

"Could you, Mr. Stanley," said my host, "paint a portrait from a minute verbal description?"

I feared not, but would try. On a whatnot at the other end of the room I found paper and colours, and I brought my materials to the table where we sat over our wine.

"Now, Mr. St. John, describe, and I will draw."

In a hushed voice he minutely detailed the items of a face, I made my sketch. No; it was rejected as unlike.

Another – alike unsuccessful, A verbal description failed to give my pencil the power of catching the expression of the dear familiar face.

"They tell me," said the old man, in a low, moody, tone, as if he unconsciously thought aloud – "they tell me that at the last she bore the mark of a cruel blow on her cheek. She, my tender, one ewe lamb, that I was fair to shelter in my bosom from every rough wind that blew."

Overwhelmed by a bitter tide of recollection, the old man covered his face with his hands and sank into silence. These few anguished words, dropping like blood from a wounded heart, I at once recalled the face of the unknown travelling companion of my midnight journey. Once more I saw before me the pale, perfect face, with sorrowful eyes and a livid mark on the left cheek. At last I fulfilled my neglected promise, and, taking my pencil, I rapidly sketched her portrait from memory. Silently I placed my work before Mr. St. John.

"It is she! It is Emmie – my darling, my darling!" he cried, and again and again he kissed the senseless paper on which were traced the lineaments of one who was very dear. "You have seen her then, for no such powerful likeness could otherwise be produced. You have caught the very trick of the half-drooping eyelids."

"Yes," I said, slowly, "I have seen her. And, what is more, on the 20th night of January last I promised, at her request, to paint her portrait from memory."

"Good God! It is impossible. On the 20th of January she died."

I felt like a man in a dream. With a slight shiver I recalled the pallor, the chill, the whiteness of the face of my travelling companion. Was this faithful sketch the vivid remembrance of a dead face? I took out my notebook and showed Mr. St. John the entry.

"Promised to paint the portrait of a lady from memory, the 20th night of January, 18__."

A deep silence brooded over us, As soon as possible I made my adieu. I returned to Dresden, and, once more in my studio, I hastened to paint a full length portrait of the mysterious presence that haunted me day and night. I should get rid of it that way. At the rapid rate I worked the picture was soon completed. I threw all the cunning of hand and brain into the task, and my knowledge of art told me that my labour had not been in vain. In each detail I painted the picture as I had last seen my mysterious sitter, save that in this portrait no unlovely scar marred the delicate oval of the cheek. Anxious to see it placed in Mr. St. John's possession, I had it carefully packed, and I myself took it to Berlin, I was fortunate enough to find the old man at home, and as I begged his acceptance of the work of my pencil his cordial satisfaction more than repaid me for the toil of the last few weeks .

"I think it is due to you, Mr. Stanley," he said, "that you should know something of the history of the lady whose portrait you have so admirably painted, and under circumstances so peculiar."

It cost him an evident effort to say these words, and I begged him to spare himself a recital that I felt must be painful, but he persisted in giving me the following rapid life sketch:-

"Emmie was our only child, and the fondest love of our hearts twined about her. During an autumn's wandering on the Continent we met Baron Wolfetein – gay, young, handsome, and knowing well how best to wile away a woman's heart – he won our Emmie's love. And we, who loved her better than we loved ourselves, gave her up, although we knew that in the very act we tore down our life's joy with our own hands.

Well, her lover was of good birth, rich, of excellent reputation, and as devoted to Emmie as she was to him. And for her sake we plucked our one sweet English rose from the parent stem, and Wolfstein bore her on in triumph to his chateau in the Black Forest.

The world called hers a brilliant part, but there was no brilliancy left for the mother and I. Without her, our house and heart were dark and chill. The events of our days were her letters – at first they were all sunshine and full of her husband's praises, After a while, we fancied they drooped a little in their cheery tone, her husband's name was more rarely mentioned, and at last he was quite ignored.

Time after time it was arranged that she should come to us, and time after time her visit was delayed on some paltry excuse. We had not seen the face of our darling for a year. We could bear the separation no longer. We should go to her. When so far on our journey as Berlin, my wife was seized violently ill. I wrote to Wolfstein and Emmie of our distress – no response came to my cry for succour.

On the morning of the 21st of January I bent over my wife to moisten her fevered lips with a little wine.

"Edward," she said, taking my hand in hers, "Emmie was with me in the night." "Darling, you were dreaming," I said, soothingly. "It was no dream, husband. She stood where you stand now. Her dress was of black velvet, with lace about the throat and wrists, She looked sad, and oh so cold, and down one cheek there was a horrid mark." "Mother," she said, "you have no portrait, not even a photograph, to remind you of poor Emmie. I shall send you one." "And before I could speak, or lay my hands on here, she was gone."

From her rapid pulse I knew fever was working in her veins, and, fearing this was the raving of delirium, I soothed her as best I could. Just then a servant entered the room; she held in her hand that which we had cause to dread – a telegram. I tore it open, and, as my eye learned its contents, a groan burst from my lips.

"'Emmie is dead,' said my wife, quietly. "I knew it, dear."

It was even so. This blow rapidly extinguished the flickering life of the mother, and she, too, quickly followed Emmie. After this sad event I arranged to go to Wolfstein's chateau. He had taken no notice of my various letters, but I concluded that, stunned by grief, the poor fellow was unable to attend to his ordinary duties of life. In this fellowship of sorrow, together we should mingle our tears.

On my way to the railway station I encountered Susan, Emmie's faithful maid, who had been with her young mistress before and since her marriage. The girl was weary and worn with fatigue, and her once bright English face was white and scarred. She stretched her hands towards me.

"Mr. St. John, Mr. St. John!" then she fell down in a swoon. I had her conveyed to my room, and after administering restoratives she recovered, and in a few terrible words she told me of my child.

For two or three months after marriage all was sunshine; then the fickle nature of the baron began to assert itself, and he became a very devil of causeless jealousy and malice. Every letter Emmie wrote was read before it left the chateau. She was debarred from going into Society – she was permitted to see no one save in the presence of her husband, who watched her as a tiger watches his prey. Then he took to drinking and playing heavily; but she, hoping to win him back to her, still compassed him round with sweet observances, and by her gentle goodness strove hard to exorcise the demon that possessed his heart. But it was no use. And then she told me how one night Emmie's husband returned from a boar hunt, and she ran to meet him in the hall, when he, in a fit of drunken fury, before servants and stranger guests, raised his riding switch and cut her across the face – the cowardly hound – and from that hour she never raised her head, but under the cruel indignity she slowly drooped.

On the night she died she moaned with pain that she could not see father or mother again, and they had no picture even to remember her by. "But they shall have one – they shall have one," and, thus saying, she died.

When the master of the chateau saw her dead remorse burned into his soul and drove him mad, and he was now a raving maniac. And at last Susan escaped from the chateau to tell the secrets of his prison house."

As Mr. St. John rapidly sketched these tragic outlines, great drops of anguish stood on his forehead, and, when I bade him farewell his hand was as cold as death. In the din and confusion of this great shouting world I lost sight of my friend, and some years after our rencontre at Berlin I was pained to read an intimation of his death in the paper.

Shortly after this melancholy announcement, a letter from the solicitors of the deceased Mr. St. John informed me that he had bequeathed me a full length portrait of his only daughter.

And this is the story of the picture of the lady with the pale, sad face that hangs in my library. But sometimes I think I only dreamed the tragic tale.

*Illustrated Police News.*

———◦◉◦———

# 1893 – THE SAILOR'S GHOST.

She was a Northumbrian, born and bred among the rough mining and seafaring folk of Tynemouth and thereabouts.

She once told me a curious ghost story, that must lose a good deal, I fear, translated from her vigorous vernacular, which I am not competent to use, and unhelped by her dramatic gestures.

"We think a deal more of New Year's Eve in my parts than you do here," she said; "and one New Year's Eve a queer thing happened that made me remember it, and believe in ghosts more than ever I did before."

I had a young brother then, called Walter. He was a seafaring lad, only twenty years of age, but married nearly a year to a girl of sixteen. He had been to sea best part of that time, but we had just heard that his vessel was come into port, and he had gone home to his wife at Tynemouth. That was on the Monday before New Year's Day, which fell that year on a Wednesday. My husband and I lived in a mining village, ten miles from Tynemouth, and my eldest brother, Jim, worked in a mine about a mile off.

We had a good few to supper at our place on Tuesday, New Year Eve, and my brother Jim was expected every moment from the mine he worked in. It was a very wild, stormy night, blowing a gale, yet bright moonlight now and then between the black, driving clouds.

We lived in a little street, with no way in or out of it but through an archway at one end. Our house was at the other end, where the street was closed up by the backs of some warehouses, painted black right across it.

We were all there that were expected, except Jim; all the family of us that could come, and friends beside. We did not think to see Walter, knowing he had only just gone home to his wife, and she not fit to come so far in such a rough night.

At last, just as someone finished singing a song – one of Bobbie Burn's, I remember – I heard footsteps coming down the street, and I said, "There's Jim!" and we looked to see the latch lifted and him come in. But it was a minute or so before he did, and then he burst in, and sat him down on the nearest chair as he could not stand, and we saw he was as white as my apron, and all of a tremble – and he a big, strong, high-coloured man, and one that was afraid of nought.

"Why, Jim," I said, "what's the matter with thee? Thou look'st as if thou had'st seen a ghost, lad" and he lifted his head from his breast, and he said; in a gasping sort of way, "Myriam, I have seen a ghost? I have seen Walter's ghost; he was there, by the warehouses, in the bright moonlight. I saw him as plain as I see thee. Walter's dead!"

Then he told us, when he could speak a bit better, that he had come through the archway, down the street, and had got to our door, when on a sudden the moon came out, and he saw Walter standing there close by, against the black warehouses in the bright light. "I saw his face as plain as ever I did," Jim said.

None of us had yet set eyes on Walter since he came back the day before, only we heard he had come. So Jim went up to him, calling out joyful, "Why, Watty, lad I art come to keep a New Year's Eve with Ma? Give us thy hand.". . . And Jim said, "I went up to him close, with my hand out; I should have touched him if he had been flesh and blood to touch . . . and then he wasn't there! . . He had disappeared right away! . . I've seen his ghost. Walter's dead," Jim said.

Well, we couldn't believe it. He was safe at a home at Tynemouth the day before, we knew. How could he be dead now, and we not know.

Next day, New Year's Day, my husband and Jim walked to Tynemouth, and went to Walter's lodging. His wife was there, but not Walter. She never owned as much, but it was easy to guess they had had a quarrel over something as soon as ever he came home. For, she said, he snatched up his kit, which he had not unpacked, and went straight out of the house again. And an old mate of his came up by-and-bye, and told her Walter had got a berth on board of a vessel bound for Christiansand, and would be off in her next morning.

Jim and my husband went down to the port, and found that was all quite correct. Walter had gone off to sea again the morning before, in the *Emma Jane*, bound for Christiansand. And down at the port the sailors were all saying she was too heavily laden, and low in the water, and they that had watched her sail away at sunrise, declared she would never live through bad weather – was certain to founder in a gale.

And it had blown a gale as I told you, that very night, which was New Year's Eve; and all that was ever known more of the *Emma Jane* and her crew was the body of her mate washed ashore a long way off, with a letter to his mother, ready to post at Christiansand, in his pocketbook in his breast pocket: and "On board the *Emma Jane*" writ at the top of the letter.

That is eleven years ago, and Walter's wife waited seven years, and then married another man, a tailor. One day a ship's carpenter met him in public, and told him he had seen Walter in some foreign port – I cannot mind the name – and had spoken to him.

This scared the tailor, who was a poor hare of a chap, and he kept thinking of it till he was always expecting Walter to turn up and pay him out for marrying his wife! though they had waited the full seven years, and so had law on their side, you know (commented this simple storyteller).

So one fine day the tailor bolted to America, leaving word he did not feel easy in his mind and could do no other. And now Walter's wife is laying by all she can. She keeps a lodging house for sea-faring men, and is a saving, industrious woman, and she says when she has got the brass together she shall take her boy (Walter's son), and make her way to that foreign port, and try to tract Walter out. She says she will search the world through to find him, if he's alive.

But my brother Jim has never doubted a moment that Walter went down in the *Emma Jane* on New Year's Eve, and that his ghost appeared to him to let us know.

And after all, most of the folk in our part disbelieve the ship carpenter's story, and think it was just a cram to frighten the tailor. And, indeed, one man declared he had heard the carpenter laughing with his mates over the yarn he had told."

"And what do you think about it?" I asked. "Well, I should believe for certain that Walter was drowned, only for this. . . . He was born with a caul, and mother kept it till she died, and left it to me. She had refused five pounds for it – that more than one sailor had offered her. And if Walter was dead it would have shrivelled up. And it hasn't."

*Victoria Magazine.*

---

## 1893 – THE SILENT LADY.

It was in the winter of 1838 that the occurrence which I am about to relate took place. I remember the time distinctly by the circumstance of my father being absent abroad. There was an old retainer of our family, who used, at that time to be very frequently about us. She had nursed my elder brother and myself, and the family felt for her all the attachment due to an old and faithful servant.

I remember her appearance distinctly; her neatly pleated cap and her scarlet ribbon, her white fringed apron and purple quilted skirt are all fresh in my memory as yesterday; and though nearly sixty at the period I speak of, she retained all the activity and good humour of sixteen. Her strength was but little impaired, and she was but slightly affected by fatigue or watching, she was in the habit of engaging

herself as a nurse in various respectable families in the neighbourhood, who were equally prepossessed in her favour.

It was about the middle of December when Old Nurse, as we always called her, came to tell us of an engagement she had obtained to attend a young gentleman who was lying dangerously ill in the great house, or Hall, of the picturesque though dull little town of Billericay, in Essex, where we lived. She mentioned that the local doctor, who had always been very kind to her, had recommended her to the London physician who had charge of the case. But as the patient was in a most critical state, the manner of her attendance was to be somewhat peculiar. She was to go every evening at eight o'clock to relieve another who remained during the day, and to be extremely cautious not to speak to the gentleman unless it was urgently necessary, nor to make any motion which might in the slightest degree disturb the few intervals of rest which he was enabled to enjoy, But she knew nothing of the person she was to wait on, not even his name, for the Hall, belonging to a non-resident nobleman, was at various times occupied by different members of his family, who, procuring their necessaries from London, rarely dealt with the local tradesmen.

There seemed something unusual in the arrangements, and I remember perfectly well my mother desiring her to call soon and let her know how she was getting on with her strange invalid.

Six weeks or more passed without our seeing or hearing anything of her. But on our return from a visit to town my mother resolved on sending to ascertain whether she was ill, and to say that she wished to see her again. The servant, on his return, informed us that poor nurse had been dangerously ill, and confined to her bed almost ever since her last visit, but that she was somewhat better, and proposed coming to see us on the next day. She came, but so altered, she was bent almost double, and could not walk without support. Her flesh and cheeks were all shrunk away, and her dim, lustreless eyes seemed almost lost in their sockets. We were all shocked at her appearance. It seemed that those few weeks had produced greater changes in her than years of disease in others.

But our surprise at the effect was nothing when compared to that which her recital of the cause excited. And as we had never known her to tell a falsehood we could not avoid placing implicit confidence in her words. She told us that in the evening, according to appointment, the London physician had conducted her to the Hall. It was one of those extensive square red brick houses which seem built for eternity rather than time, and in the constructing of which the founder had consulted convenience and comfort more than show or situation.

A flight of wide stone steps brought them to the door, and a dark oak staircase of immense width, fenced with balusters six inches wide, and supported by a railing of massive dimensions, led to the chamber of the invalid. This was a lofty wainscoted room, with two windows sunk a yard deep in the wall, and looking out upon what was once a garden in the rear, but now grown so wild that the weeds and grass almost reached the level of the wall which enclosed it.

At one end of the room stood an old-fashioned square bedstead, upon which the young man laid. It was hung with faded red tapestry, and seemed itself as large as a moderate-sized room. At the other end, and opposite to the foot of the bed, was a fireplace supported by ponderous stone buttresses, but with no grate, some smouldering logs piled on the spacious hearth. There was no door, except that by which she had entered, and no other furniture than a few faded velvet-covered chairs, and a table littered with medicines and glasses, beside a window. The oak which covered the walls and formed the panels of the ceiling was as black as time could make it; and the whole apartment, which was kept dark at the suggestion of the doctor, was so gloomy that the glimmering of the single candle in the shade of the fire place could not penetrate it, and cast a faint gleam around, not sad, but absolutely sickening.

Whilst the medical man was speaking in a low tone to the invalid, nurse tried to find out some particulars from the other attendant – a stranger from London – who was tying on her bonnet before going away to the principal hotel, known as the Lion, where she slept. She could gain no information from this singularly taciturn person. She did not know the gentleman's name, but believed he was a student from Cambridge; but no one save herself and the doctor had ever at crossed the threshold to inquire for him, nor had she ever seen anyone in the rest of the house, which she believed to be then uninhabited, but that was no affair of hers.

The household necessaries were brought down in plentiful quantity by a cart which accompanied the London doctor's chariot. Alter leaving a few unimportant directions, the physician and the day attendant left together. Nurse closed the door behind them, and, shivering with the cold frosty gust of air from the spacious lobby, hastened to her duty, wrapped her cloak about her, drew her seat close to the hearth, replenished the fire, and commenced reading a book which she had brought with her.

There was no sound to disturb her except now and then a blast of wind which shook the withering trees in the garden below, or "death watch," which ticked incessantly in the wainscoting of the room. In this manner an hour or two passed, when, concluding from the motionless posture of the invalid that he was asleep, she rose, and taking her light in her hand, moved on

tiptoe across the bare oaken floor to take a survey of his features.

She gently opened the curtains, and bringing the light to bear upon him, started to find that he was still awake. She attempted to apologise for her curiosity by an awkward offer of services. But apology and other were equally useless. He moved neither limb nor muscle, and made not the faintest reply, but lay motionless on his back, his bright blue eyes glaring fixedly upon her, his lower lip fallen, and his mouth open, his cheek a perfect hollow, and his long white teeth projecting from his shrunken lips, whilst his bony hand, covered with wiry sinews was stretched upon the bedclothes, and looked, more like the claws of a bird than the fingers of a human being.

She felt rather uneasy when looking at him, but a slight movement of the eyelids, which the light was too strong for, assured her that he was still alive, which she had been half-inclined to doubt, and she returned to her seat and her book by the fire. As she was directed not to disturb him, and his medicine was only to be administered in the morning, she had little to do, and the succeeding two hours passed heavily till about midnight, when the gentleman appeared to breathe heavily, and seemed uneasy.

As he said nothing, she thought perhaps he was asleep, and was rising to go towards him, when she was surprised to see a lady seated on a chair near the head of the bed beside him. Though startled at this, she was by no means alarmed, and making a curtsey, was moving on as she intended, when the lady raised her arm, and turning the palm of her hand, which was covered with a white glove, towards her, motioned her silently to keep her seat.

She accordingly sat down as before, but began to wonder within herself how and when this lady came in. It was true she had not been looking at the door, and it might have been opened without her perceiving it. But then it was so cold a night and so late. She turned quietly round and took a second view of her visitor. She wore a black veil over her bonnet, and as her face was turned towards the bed of the invalid, she could not in that gloomy chamber perceive her features, but she saw that the shape and turn of her head and neck were graceful and elegant in the extreme, and that her lavishly displayed shoulders were as white as marble, The rest of her person she could not so well discern, as it was enveloped in a green silk gown.

It occurred to her that it must be some intimate friend or relation who had just come in. But then the day attendant had told her that no visitors had ever come. She could not understand the matter, but determined to observe whether she went off as quietly as she had entered, and for that purpose altered the position of her chair so as to command a view of the door, and placed herself with a book on her knees, but her eyes intently fixed upon the lady in the green silk gown. In this position she remained some time, but no alteration took place in the room.

The stranger sat evidently gazing on the face of the invalid, whilst he heaved and sighed heavily, as if a nightmare was upon him. Nurse a second time moved onwards in order to hold him up in the bed or give him some temporary relief, and a second time the mysterious visitant motioned her to remain quiet, and unwillingly, but by a kind of fascination, she complied and again commenced her watch. But her position was a painful one; and she sat so long and so quietly that she at last closed her eyes for a moment, and when she opened them the lady was gone.

The young man was once more composed, and after taking something to relieve his breathing fell into a gentle sleep, from which he had not awakened when her colleague arrived in the morning to take her place, and nurse returned to her cottage. The following night she was again at her duty, but arriving somewhat late, she found the strangely taciturn day nurse already muffled up and waiting impatiently to set off to her cosy hotel, which was then, as it is still, one of the most comfortable in the county. Nurse lighted her to the stairs and heard her close the hall door, when on returning to the room the wind, as she shut the door, blew out her candle. She re-lighted it, roused up the wood fire, and resumed her seat and book.

The night was stormy, a crisp sleet hissed on the windows, and the wind moaned in heavy gusts down the spacious chimney, whilst the rattling of the shutters and the occasional clatter and banging of a door in some distant part of the house came with a dire and hollow clang along the dreary passages. She did not feel so comfortable as on the previous night; the whistling of the wind through the trees made her flesh creep involuntarily, and sometimes the thundering flap of a distant door made her start and drop her book, with a sudden prayer for protection.

She was thinking of giving up her engagement, when, all at once, her ear was struck with the heavy throes and agonised breathing of her charge, and, on raising her head, she saw the same lady with the gleaming shoulders and glittering green gown seated at the head of the bed, in the same position as the night before. Well, thought she, this is unusually strange; but it immediately struck her that it must be some inmate of the house, for what human being would venture out at so late an hour on such a dreary night. But then, her dress; it was neither such as one would wear in the street, nor yet such as they would be likely to have on in the house of an invalid. It was, in fact, the fashionable, very low-bodied ball costume of the period.

Nurse rose, made a curtsey to the lady, and spoke to her politely, but got no reply save the waving of her hand, by which she was silenced before. At length the agitation of the invalid was so increased that she could not reconcile it with her duty to sit still whilst a stranger was attending him. She accordingly drew near the bed in spite of the repeated beckoning's of the lady, who, as she advanced, draw her veil closer across her face, and retired to the table at the window.

Nurse approached the bed, but was terrified on beholding the countenance of the patient. The big drops of cold perspiration were rolling down his pale face, his livid lips were quivering with agony, and as he motioned her aside, his glaring eyes followed the retreating figure in the weirdly glistening green robe. She saw it was in vain to attempt to assist him, as he impatiently repulsed every proffer of attention, and she again resumed her seat, whilst the silent visitor returned to her place by his bedside.

Piqued at being thus baffled in her intentions of kindness, but still putting from her the idea of a supernatural being, the old woman determined to watch with close attention the retreat of the lady, and observe whether she resided in the house or took her departure by the main door. She almost refrained from winking in order to secure a thorough scrutiny of her motions, but it was all in vain. She could not remember to have taken off her glance for a moment, but still the visitant was gone. It seemed as if she had only changed her thoughts for an instant, and not her eyes, but the change was enough, and when she again reverted to the object of her anxiety the mysterious lady had departed.

As on the previous night, her patient now became composed, and enjoyed an uninterrupted slumber till the light of morning brought the uncommunicative woman who was to relieve guard at this bed of misery. Later in the day nurse met the London physician, with the determination of giving up the task in which she was engaged. He received her notice with regret, but was rather surprised when she informed him of the attentions of the strange lady, and the manner in which she had been prevented from performing her duty. He, however, treated it as a commonplace occurrence, and suggested that it might be some affectionate friend or relative, of whose existence he knew nothing. And, at his repeated request, nurse reluctantly consented to resume her duty for that night.

She accordingly went to the great house, arranged her chair, and seated herself to watch, not merely the departure, but the arrival, of her fair friend. As she had not, however, appeared till the night was far advanced, she did not expect her sooner, and endeavoured to occupy her attention till that time by some other means. But it was all in vain. She could only think of the one mysterious circumstance, fix her anxious gaze on the blackened work of the ceiling, and start at every trilling sound. Again her vigilance was frustrated, and as, wearied with thought, she raised her head with a long-drawn sigh and a yawn of fatigue; she encountered the glittering green garment of her unsolicited companion.

Angry with herself, and at the same time unwilling to accuse herself of remissness, she determined once again that she should not escape unnoticed. There hung a feeling of awe around her whenever she approached this singular being, and when, as before, the lady retired to another part of the room as she approached the bed, she had not the courage to follow her. Again the same distressing scene of suffering in her unfortunate charge ensued. He gasped and heaved till the noise of his agony made her heart sicken within her. When she drew near his bed, his corpse-like features were convulsed with an agony which seemed to twist their relaxed nerves into the most fearful expression, while his ghastly eyes were straining from their sockets. She spoke, but he answered not, she touched him, but he was cold with terror and unconscious of every object save the one mysterious being whom his glance followed with steady, fixed intensity.

Nurse was naturally a woman of very strong feelings, and now she was totally beside herself with anxiety. She thought the young man was expiring, and was preparing to leave the room in search of further assistance, when she saw the lady again move towards the bed of the dying man, She bent above him for a moment, whilst his writhings were indescribable, and then moved slowly towards the door.

Now was the moment! Nurse advanced at the same time, laid one hand on the handle, and with the other attempted to raise the stranger's veil. The next instant poor nurse fell senseless on the floor. As she glanced on the face of the lady, she saw that a death's head filled the large, old fashioned bonnet; its vacant sockets and ghastly teeth were all that could be seen beneath the folds of the veil. A loud peal of demoniacal laughter rang through the room, the lady disappeared and nurse remembered nothing more.

Daylight was breaking the next morning, when the other attendant arrived and found the poor old woman, cold and benumbed, stretched on the floor beside the door; and when she looked upon the bed of the invalid, he lay stiffened and lifeless, as if many hours had elapsed since his spirit had shaken off its mortal coil. One hand was thrown across his eyes, as if to shade them from some object on which he feared to look, and the other grasped the coverlet with convulsive firmness.

The remains of the mysterious stranger were buried in a vault made within the parish church. Gold was lavishly expended upon the arrangements for the funeral and its accessories. One gentleman, whose features are said to have strangely resembled a portrait on the coinage of the realm, with the London physician, alone followed the body to its last resting place, and the simple but exquisite white marble tablet sent down from town and placed upon the wall of the church during the silent hours of the night of the first anniversary of his death, bears the words-

Charles Leroy,<br>
Died 21st December, 1838.<br>
"Remember."

As for poor nurse, the events of those three terrible nights cost her her life, for she never recovered from the effects of the shock, and wasted away to the hour of her death, which occurred within three months.

The old Hall still dominates the main street of the interesting old town, but, modernised and renovated, its rooms bright with the glare of gas and the merry laughter of young children, few would imagine that so weird a tragedy had been enacted within its walls. Still, some of the older townspeople after sunset find an excuse to cross the road rather than pass beneath the ancient trees which shadow the entrance gates, And the great north-western chamber is desolate and deserted because no one is ever found willing to occupy it for a second night. No horrible sight has been alleged to have been witnessed in the room, but a strange feeling of awe and coldness falls upon the occupant, and some undefined presence seems to fill the apartment.

*Hampshire Telegraph.*

---

# 1894 – A GHOSTLY VISITANT.

A weird story is reported from a quiet little village on the slopes of the Mendips. Among the inhabitants rumours had been circulated that a ghostly apparition was to be seen after nightfall in the footway leading to the rural graveyard, and so gruesome were the tales told concerning the spectre that the path in question became deserted. At length the village patriarch started the theory that his grandfather had informed him, when a boy, that it had taken thirteen persons and a woman "to lay the spirit" of an old squire for 150 years in the Red Sea, that the time was expired, and that he had returned again.

Matters had reached this crisis when a local roysterer, after his daily peregrination, and having dined not wisely but too well, so far forgot himself as to endeavour to reach his home by the dreaded path. The following is the account he gave of his experience that night:—

"I were a coom just to the churchyard, when from under the gert chestnut tree thur coomed the most horrible site I ever seed, 'Twur a tall figgur, and his face and hands were a-shining just like a box of damp matches, and patches on him seemed to be all o a-flame. It frightened I mainlee; me hair was as stiff as brissels, and I should have bolted, only me legs wouldn't run. I wur sober enuff now, and he coomed towards I, and not a sound did hur make, and when hur weer coomed quite close, he spoke in a terrible tone the words, "Show me to my grave!" At that I found me feet, and hands, too, and I went for'n, and I found he was a main solid speerit; and didn't he holler for mercy, to be sure!"

The victor of this midnight encounter is now the hero of the district around, and he carries in his pocket a rubber tennis shoe as a trophy of his victory. The ghost has been confined to his house with a severe attack of influenza.

*South Wales Echo.*

## 1894 – BIGOTED INTOLERANCE.

The new volume of the Psychical Research Society, of which Mr. A. J. Balfour is the president, contains some very remarkable stories. Mr. Balfour's contribution to the volume is a closely-reasoned appeal to scientific men to drop the attitude of "bigoted intolerance" and face the mass of strange phenomena which the Psychical Research Society has gathered so conscientiously. Lord Beaconsfield was once "on the side of the angels," and spooks are similarly supported by Lord Beaconsfield's erudite and amiable successor. Mr. Balfour perceives that things do happen which cannot be explained away.

The Psychical Research Society has certainly made some very remarkable and infinitely suggestive discoveries. For the present only a gifted few are visited by ghosts. Naturally, like all good society, the best sets of ghosts are exclusive.

*Northern Whig.*

## 1894 – BACK AT HAMPTON COURT.

A few nights ago these Royal Ghosts again made their appearance. The oldest inhabitants of this palace tell me that these scenes are quite a revival of the ancient times, as nothing has of late been seen of these Royal Shades. A young girl sleeping (by choice) in the "Blue" or "Haunted Room" relates that about 1.15 a.m. she was awakened by a loud noise in the adjoining room. The folding doors between the two were violently shaken, the handles rattled, and she distinctly heard the sound of footsteps moving, and it seemed as if chairs were dancing a jig, while glasses jingled loudly. She was too much alarmed to move, and lay still in terror. There was no moon, but the room seemed filled with a pale blue ghostly light. Then a figure appeared to glide up and down past her bed, gently rustling, in a white dress; suddenly it stopped by her bed and leaned over her, and she felt an icy cold breath on her cheek, which might be best described as a blast of cold wind from a lonely churchyard. Gradually these noises ceased, the blue light faded, and she was left trembling with fright, in utter darkness, as before.

*Leicester Chronicle.*

## 1894 – THE DRUMMERS OF BLAIRGOWRIE.

The inhabitants of a section of a certain street in Blairgowrie have been greatly disturbed of late over mysterious sounds heard at nights. The sounds begin every night about eleven o'clock, with the exception of Saturday, when the mystery opens at midnight. It is heralded by a few slow raps, the sound resembling a muffled drum. After this prelude, the kettle drum, also muffled, takes up the strain, and keeps up the monotonous music for two or three hours. At first no notice was taken of the mysterious noise, but its regular repetition has caused a flutter of excitement. What it is, is as yet, a mystery.

The other evening the guidman of one of the disturbed households, with a bravery that is worthy of all commendation, stayed out of doors until the hour at which this drum concert usually started. He examined all around the house, but could find nothing, and, entering the house, told the guidwife the result of his quest. She answered that it had not yet started, but as soon as she said that the hidden drums were beat with unwonted vigour. One troubled lady gives the reason that she is certain there is someone tunnelling beneath her house; another that some coiners are at work somewhere below her dwelling. A peculiar feature of the case is that the members of each of the five households that have been troubled declare that the noise is immediately below the house in which they dwell. It is proposed to send up a requisition to Mr W. T. Stead or the Psychical Research Society, but while the sufferers hesitate which of these authorities to write to the music goes dolefully on.

*Dundee Courier.*

# 1894 – WRAITH SEEING.

The belief in the wraith – the exact counterpart of a person soon to die – has for centuries past been widely current in our own and other countries. Under a variety of forms, instances of this strange superstition may frequently be seen chronicled in the local Press, their explanation being regarded as unaccountable as the equally mysterious "second sight" to the existence of which Dr. Johnson professed himself almost a convert.

In the North of England the wraith is known by the peasantry as the "swarth," and in Yorkshire a common name for this uncanny apparition is the "waif," numerous tales of which are told in the traditional stories of that county. It is generally described as a mere shadow, but in every respect identical in appearance with the person whose death it is supposed to foretell.

A Wensleydale peasant one day related how he had seen an inhabitant of the next village walking on the road; "But," added he, "it was nobbut his shadow, and I don't think he'll live long." Cornish folklore tells how prevalent the belief in wraiths was in years gone by, and nowadays the seafaring community still cling to the old fancy. Mr Hunt, in his "Romances of the West of England," quotes several well-known cases, and adds, "I have never met with any people who so firmly believed in the appearance of the phantoms of the dying to those upon whom the last thoughts are centred as the Cornish did." The Devonshire peasantry dread the wraith, especially when the relative or friend happens to be abroad, or a long distance off. An interesting anecdote is told in Devonshire of Dr. Hawker, who, when, walking home one night, observed an old woman pass by to whom he was in the habit of giving relief. He put his hand in his pocket for a sixpence, but on turning round she was gone. Mentioning this incident to his family on reaching home, he was informed she had recently died.

Occasionally, it is said, the wraiths of persons dying are visible to one favoured individual only, and not to others present at the time, and, according to another popular idea, no wraith can appear except if the person is desirous of seeing his friends before he departs his life – in any case, he must have been thinking of them. Sometimes a person is supposed to see his own wraith, as is reported to have happened to Sir Robert Napier, an occurrence which is generally regarded as equally

ominous. On the other hand, the wraith is not always a prophet of death but is considered to have various reasons for appearing. Thus, the late Lord Dorchester is said to have seen his daughter's wraith standing at the window, his attention being attracted by its shadow which fell across the book he was reading. It seems she had accompanied a fishing expedition, was caught in a storm, and was distressed at the thought of her father's anxiety about her safety.

The belief in wraiths was formerly current throughout the greater part of Scotland, a superstition which has been prettily introduced in the song of "Auld Robin Gray." When the young wife narrates her meeting with her old sweetheart, she says, "I thought it was his wraith, I could not think it he," But, as in England, the seeing of a person's wraith was not always an omen of death. Mr. Napier tells us there were certain rules observed in relation to wraiths, by which their meaning could be ascertained but these rules varied in different localities. In certain localities, for instance, a wraith seen during the morning betokened that the person whose wraith was seen would be fortunate in life, or, if unwell at the time, would recover. But when the wraith was seen in the afternoon or evening, this distinctly betokened evil, or approaching death, and the time within which death would occur was considered to be within a year.

Sometimes the wraith of the person doomed to die within a short time was seen wrapped in a winding sheet; the idea being that the higher the winding sheet reached up towards the head, the nearer was death. The "'Statistical Account of Scotland," the writer, speaking of the parish of Applecross, in the county of Ross, informs us that, "the ghosts of the dying, called "tasks," are said to be heard, their cry being a repetition of the moans of the sick. Some assume the sagacity of distinguishing the voice of their departed friends." The same writer adds that the corpse follows the track led by the tasks to the place of internment, and the early or late completion of the prediction is made to depend on the period of the night at which the task is heard.

The literature of Scotland contains numerous illustrations of this belief, and in the introduction to the "Minstrelsy of the Scottish Border," it is spoken of as a firm article in the creed of Scottish superstition. It has been incorporated into many a tale of legendary romance, and holds a popular place in the household stories of the Scottish peasantry. In "Ritson's Songs" (I. 155) we find a curious allusion to the wraith:-

> "Scarce was he gane, I saw his ghost;
> It vanished like a shriek of sorrow.
> Thrice did the water wraith ascend,
> And gave a doleful groan through Yarrow."

And, indeed, numerous similar instances occur in old songs.

In Wales the wraith is known by the peasantry as the "Lledwith." It is locally described as the spectre of a person seen before his death; but it never speaks, and immediately vanishes if spoken to. It has occasionally been seen by miners, writes the late Mr Wirt Sikes, in his "British Goblins," previous to a fatal accident in the mine. The story is told of a miner who saw himself lying dead in a phantom tram car led by a phantom horse, and surrounded by phantom miners. A few days afterwards he was crushed by a stone, and was borne maimed and dead in the tram along the road where the ledrith had appeared.

Then there is the Irish "fetch," which is the exact counterpart of the wraith, and still retains its hold on the popular imagination. Like the ill-fated Banshee, it is oftentimes the cause of much alarm; and Mr. Wilde, in his "Irish Popular Superstitions," has given a good story illustrative of the terror occasioned by its presence.

Referring to wraith seeing abroad, it may be noted that it exists in New Zealand, where it is considered ominous to see the figure of an absent person, the common idea being that if it be shadowy, and the face not visible, his death may be expected before many days; but if his face be seen, he is already dead. The story is told of a party of Maoris who were seated round a fire in the open air, when there suddenly appeared, seen only by two of them, the figure of a relative left ill at home. On exclaiming, the figure vanished, and on the return of the party it transpired that the sick man had died about the time of the vision.

Cases of this kind might be easily multiplied, the popular theory being that the apparition presents itself to several of an assembled company, and that the person's death corresponds more or less nearly with the time when some friend perceives this phantom. On the Continent the gift of wraith seeing still flourishes, and, according to Dr. Tylor, "Folklore examples abound in Silesia and the Tyrol."

Again, it may be remembered how Catherine of Russia, after retiring to her private apartments, was informed that she had been seen just before to enter the State Chamber. She accordingly went thither and perceived the exact similitude of herself seated upon the throne. Goethe is reported to have seen his own double, or wraith, riding by his side under conditions which really happened many years afterwards; and we are informed how certain monks and nuns have, shortly prior to their death, seen the images of themselves seated in their chairs or stalls.

Wraiths, too, are not confined to land, but have been said to appear at sea. In Moore's "Life of Byron," an anecdote is told of a Captain Kidd, who maintained that the wraith of his brother, then in India, visited him on board ship and lay down in his bunk leaving the blankets damp with sea water. He afterwards found that his brother was drowned at that exact night and hour. Stories of this kind are very numerous, many interesting illustrations of which will be found in Mr Bassett's "Legend and Superstitions of the Sea."

*Evening Standard.*

---

# 1895 – STRANGE STORY OF A HAUNTED HOUSE.

Landlords and others who have the good or evil fortune to possess a haunted house cannot do better than send an early communication to the members of the Spiritualist body which has its headquarters at the Surrey Masonic Hall. If the spirits are of an irreproachable moral character, the ladies and gentlemen referred to will be pleased to make their acquaintance; if, on the contrary, they are of malignant description, given, for instance, to practical jokes with one's bedclothes, the same body will undertake not only to exorcise them but to bring them to a sense of their turpitude.

Such seems to be the moral of a remarkable story which was told the other night to an audience of the faithful gathered in the hall mentioned. Mr. Long, who acted as chairman or officiating minister, said that some time since they had brought to their notice a house at Blackheath which was said to be haunted. Strange noises and voices were heard in the silent watches of the night, furniture was moved without rhyme or reason, and the children could not sleep in their beds by reason of the manner in which their bedclothes were treated.

Undeterred by the fate which attended two former inquirers, who had been incontinently "chucked" by the spiritual forces, a deputation from the society resolved to visit the house, and what they saw and heard would forthwith be told. A Mr. Boddington then read a paper descriptive of the scene.

Eight individuals—three ladies and one gentleman—arrived at the house about nine p.m., and were introduced to a landlady of portly dimensions. Acting on the orders of "Douglas," "the spirit guide of their leader," one of the lady mediums accompanied the portly landlady to a cellar beneath the house. In two minutes the landlady returned in an excited condition, declaring that the lady had become possessed and was trying to bite off her ears. On the others going below they formed a circle in a dark and dismal dungeon, "Douglas" taking control of the proceedings. Almost directly three of the mediums became possessed by strange beings, and strove to maltreat each other. "Douglas" ascertained (so the story runs) that the spirits were four in number—an old man who had caused a girl to be murdered, two men who had committed the crime, and a woman who became an accessory after the fact. All were at loggerheads – the old man because he had not gained all he wanted, the men because they had quarrelled over the blood money, and the woman for some other reason.

"Douglas," by sheer willpower, forced the spirits to walk upstairs to the scene of their crime. They were mad because they had been trapped, but "Douglas" compelled them to admit contrition for their crime, afterwards putting them into a mesmeric sleep, during which they were safely conveyed from the premises. Mr. Beale, who was afterwards ordered by "Douglas" to revisit the dank and dismal dungeon below, was introduced as one who had a terrible tale to tell. All that happened was that he heard some knocks and was bathed in perspiration. He was, however, able to say that before the defaulting spirits were deported they were reconciled to each other, were induced to pray that God would have mercy upon them, and had been on their best behaviour ever since. Mr. Long then adorned the tale by remarking that the Blackheath experience showed conclusively that death was not the end of all, that disembodied spirits still frequented the scenes of their earthly career, but that there was still a road by which they could be converted and saved. This was the work to which spiritualists should devote themselves—a mission to unconverted spirits.

This ended the story of the haunted house and then, after singing in semi-darkness a hymn which sounded like an incantation to the spirits, the faithful among the audience waited in silence for a spiritual manifestation. A lady on the platform declared that she saw a beautiful young lady standing beside an elderly female and calling her mother. This might have been all right had not the latter lady declared that her daughter died in infancy some years ago. A similar attempt with regard to the spirit form of an elderly gentleman having fallen flat, owing to the individual whom he was said to be addressing, "Bob," not recognising the description, further manifestations were awaited.

*Chichester Observer.*

———⊷◉⊶———

# 1896 – A FATAL BED CHAMBER.

A new version of the haunted chamber comes from a small town on the Marne. At one of the inns at that place a bedroom is said to be fatal to any person who may spend a night therein. Attention was called to this fact a few weeks ago, when a visitor, who had retired to rest apparently in good health, was found lying dead in bed the following morning. A few days later a servant girl was sent to the chamber to spend the night, and as she did not appear next morning her master and mistress tapped at the door without eliciting any reply. She, too, was found to be dead. Nothing, it is added, was discovered in the room to account for the death of the girl, and locally the room is known as "the accursed chamber." A post mortem examination has been made, and the official inquiry as to the death may tend to clear up the mystery.

*Hampshire Telegraph.*

———⊷◉⊶———

# 1896 – A FATAL BED CHAMBER.

A new version of the haunted chamber comes from a small town on the Marne. At one of the inns at that place a bedroom is said to be fatal to any person who may spend a night therein. Attention was called to this fact a few weeks ago, when a visitor, who had retired to rest apparently in good health, was found lying dead in bed the following morning. A few days later a servant girl was sent to the chamber to spend the night, and as she did not appear next morning her master and mistress tapped at the door without eliciting any reply. She, too, was found to be dead. Nothing, it is added, was discovered in the room to account for the death of the girl, and locally the room is known as "the accursed chamber." A post mortem examination has been made, and the official inquiry as to the death may tend to clear up the mystery.

———⊷◉⊶———

# 1896 – A FEN GHOST.

A correspondent forwards the following extraordinary story: "The inhabitants of the fenny districts between Peterborough and Wisbech have been thrown into a state of great excitement of late by the report that an old farmhouse near Thorney was haunted, and that the residents, a farmer named Wilson and his wife, had been obliged to leave their abode. It appears that the inmates of the house were first made aware of the presence of the mysterious visitors by hearing several knocks on the door of the house, and this continued for some time, until matters got to be so unbearable, and the wife became so upset that, had she continued in the house, serious consequences might have resulted.

The "ghost" invariably commenced operations by a series of very gentle taps on windows and door, the force of the knocks gradually increasing until they finished up with a terrific crash, which shook the house. The fame of the "haunted" house soon spread, and thousands of persons have visited the place, including several spiritualists, one or two taking up their abode in the house for the night, but being obliged to leave it before morning dawned. A school inspector, who had been examining some children, paid a visit to the farm out of curiosity, and the knocks were heard as he held the door open. This gentleman became so deeply impressed that he wrote to the neighbouring clergyman that he was convinced it was a spiritual manifestation.

Another gentleman from Wisbech, said to have the strongest nerves in the Eastern counties, was obliged to take his departure from the house after hearing the knocks, and many people from long distances, bent on investigation, have been unsuccessful in their endeavours to lay the ghost.

*Illustrated Police News.*

———◆———

## 1896 – A GHOST IN OSBORNE STREET.

Last night about 9.30 I saw it. I say "it" because I cannot make up my mind whether the ghost was masculine or feminine. If I had known "it" were a ghost I think I should have tried to avoid it, but not until I bumped up against it was I aware of its presence. "I beg you par___," I began, but, seeing it more distinctly, I collapsed. Such a horrible face, with great empty sockets and a gaping mouth, which seemed for ever opening and shutting, resembling the snapping of a gigantic purse which was being opened and shut by a vicious owner, but I can't describe it, and even now in broad daylight I shudder at the memory of the sight.

There it stood barring my progress. I must do something so I commenced again. "If you please, can you tell me where Osborne Street is?" "This is Osborne Street," the ghost replied. "But where are the lights?" I asked. "Ah, there's the rub" replied the ghost; "There were some lights, a whole row of good gas lamps, and a certain tradesman paid for the gas out of his own pocket and never once asked the Corporation to share a penny of the expense. But the all-wise authorities thought that this generous tradesman ought to pay them rent for the lamps as well, and straightway charged him £5 5s per annum. This was too much, and our generous

friend (here the ghost pointed to a large establishment, which, until then, I had been unaware of) promptly told them to take the lamps away, and if they wanted them in future, they might light it."

"And now," went on the ghost, "you may expect mischief. Already I have had a hand in two free fights and…" – just then we heard a cry of "Murder! Police! Thieves!" "A bit more in my line," said the ghost, as it hobbled off in the direction of the shrieks.

After bruising myself against a wall, and taking the skin off my nose, I managed to feel my way into Anne Street, and thence proceeded homewards, marvelling all the while at the stupendous wisdom of the "authorities."

*Hull Daily Mail.*

———◆———

## 1896 – GHOSTS IN THE WITNESS BOX.

I am not aware that there is any instance on record of Counsel's cross-examination of a ghost but there certainly have been cases in which ghosts have figured as very material witnesses in courts of law, and in one case, at any rate, it was mainly on the evidence of a ghost that two men were convicted and hanged.

The two most remarkable of these cases I propose briefly narrating here.

In the year 1632 there lived at the village of Great Lumley, near Chester-le-Street, in Durham, a well-to-do yeoman named John Walker. He was a childless widower, and his house was kept by his comely young niece, Ann Walker. There were suspicions that the relations between uncle and niece were more intimate than they should have been. These suspicions were confirmed by the sudden departure of Ann Walker on a visit to her aunt, Dame Carr, who lived at Chester-le-Street. After a good deal of pressure Ann confessed to her aunt that her uncle, John Walker, was the author of her shame. Two days after this confession, one Mark Sharp, a collier, from Blackburn and an intimate friend of John Walker's, called at Dame Carrs and asked to see Ann. The girl went out with him and never returned nor was she ever seen again. To the enquiries of Dame Carr, John Walker replied by assuring her that Ann "was in safe hands," and probably no suspicions of foul play would have been excited had not the ghost of Ann Walker appeared about a fortnight after her disappearance to James Graham, a miller, who lived about two miles from Great Lumley.

James Graham was grinding corn about midnight when suddenly there stood before him "a woman with her hair about her head hanging down and all bloody, with five large wounds on her head." Asked who and what she was, the apparition replied that she was the spirit of Ann Walker, and she gave full details of her cruel murder by Mark Sharp, who had been paid by her uncle John Walker, to put her out of the way. She described minutely the place where the murder had been committed and where her body had been found buried, and further told the miller that "he must be the man to reveal it, or else that she must still appear and haunt him." But it was not until the ghost had thrice appeared to him and threatened him that James Graham summoned up courage to go to the nearest magistrate and tell the strange story. The magistrate, after taking the miller's depositions, caused a search to be made in the spot described by the ghost as the scene of the murder, and there, sure enough, the body of Ann Walker was found, buried on the moor, and on the corpse were five wounds, exactly similar to those exhibited by the apparition. John Walker and Mark Sharp were promptly arrested and committed for trial on the capital charge at the next Durham Assizes. The case was tried before Mr. Justice Davenport, and created extraordinary excitement in the district.

The principal witness for the prosecution was James Graham, the miller, who solemnly swore to the three visits of the ghost, and the revelation made to him. He was personally unknown, except by sight, to either of the prisoners, and it was never suggested on their behalf that he could have any possible motive in thus charging them with murder. Nor was any other way suggested by which the miller could have discovered the body of the murdered woman except through the revelation of the ghost.

Moreover, there was other supernatural evidence to connect John Walker with the murder. The foreman of the jury, Mr. Fairbairn, solemnly swore afterwards in an affidavit that during the trial he saw the "likeness of a child standing upon Walker's shoulder." And the Judge himself admitted that he saw something like the figure described by Mr. Fairbairn. The jury found both prisoners guilty and they were hanged in due course, but it is not on record that either of them confessed to the crime.

The official deposition of James Graham is preserved in the Bodleian Library at Oxford. There is also extant a long letter from Mr. Justice Davenport to his friend Sergeant Hutton, giving full particulars of the trial, whilst the facts are also vouched for in an affidavit of three most respectable gentlemen residing in the neighbourhood.

A not less remarkable instance of a ghost's testimony in a court of law occurred more than a hundred years later in Scotland.

Among the regiments entrusted with the task of stamping out the last sparks of the Jacobite Rebellion

of 1745 and maintaining order in the disturbed districts was one commanded by General Guise – generally known as Guise's Regiment. Among the non-commissioned officers of this regiment was a certain Sergeant Davies, a gentleman by birth and education, a man of splendid physique and dauntless courage, and the idol of his comrades.

On the morning of September 28, 1749, Sergeant Davies started off shooting alone over the moors surrounding Braemar, and was never again seen alive. His comrades scoured the district, but could find no trace of him living or dead. Five years passed, and the seargent's mysterious disappearance was almost forgotten when the interest was suddenly revived by the arrest of two Highlanders, Duncan Terig and Alexander Bain Macdonald, who were charged with the murder of the missing sergeant. It was entirely owing to the dogged, untiring patience and perseverance of Mr. James Small, an intimate friend of Davies, who had vowed never to rest until he had brought the murderers to justice, that the crime was traced home to these two Highlanders.

The fowling piece belonging to the murdered man had been found in the house of one of them, and trinkets and valuables known to have been the property of Sergeant Davies had been seen in the possession of both men. But there was a still a stronger and more damning proof of the guilt of these two persons which to superstitious minds carried overwhelming weight.

Alexander Macpherson, of Inverey, a farm servant, swore that one night in the summer of 1750, there appeared to him a man dressed in blue, who came to his bedside and beckoned to him to come out. Macpherson rose and followed the figure outside the door, whereupon the stranger turned and said, "I am Sergeant Davies," then pointing to a tract of swampy moorland known as Christie's Hill, added, "You will find my bones there; go and bury them at once, for I can have no peace, nor will I give you any, until my bones are buried; and you may get Donald Farquharson to help you." Having spoken these words very solemnly and earnestly, the apparition vanished. The next morning Macpherson went to the spot indicated by the ghost and discovered a body half buried in the moss. He dragged it out and found that though the flesh was almost entirely gone, the coat of blue cloth which the dead man had worn was almost entire. He laid the body on the upper soil, but made no attempt to bury it.

A few nights later the apparition again appeared to Macpherson and demanded angrily why the bones had not been buried. Then Macpherson plucked up courage to ask, "Who murdered you?" To which the ghost replied, "Duncan Terig and Alexander Macdonald." The next day Macpherson went to Donald Farquharson, told him the story of the ghost, and the two of them went together and buried the body. For four years they kept silence, till James Small, hearing rumours that these two men knew something about the fate of Sergeant Davies, questioned them closely, and drew from them the remarkable story of the ghost.

The trial of Duncan Terig and Alexander Bain Macdonald for the murder of Sergeant Davies took place before the Lords of Session in Edinburgh on June 11, 1754. Alexander Macpherson gravely gave his evidence as to the information given him by the ghost; and then the counsel for the prisoners, Alexander Lockhart, one of the most eminent advocates in Scotland, rose to cross-examine the witness. Macpherson could speak nothing but Gaelic, and his evidence had to be interpreted to the Court. The first and only question Lockhart asked the witness was, "What language did the ghost speak in?" To which Macpherson promptly replied, "As good Gaelic as ever I heard in Lochaber." "Pretty good for the ghost of an English sergeant," said Lockhart, and sat down amid roars of laughter from the court.

Despite the damning evidence of the dead man's property found in the possession of the prisoners, Lockhart fairly laughed the case out of court by the ridicule he threw upon the English ghost that spoke "as good Gaelic as ever was heard in Lochaber" and the jury found a verdict of "Not guilty"—though Lockhart himself afterwards admitted that but for that lucky joke about the ghost, and the capital he made out of it, he could never have secured an acquittal, for he had not the slightest doubt that the prisoners were guilty. That was, so far as I am aware, the last occasion on which a ghost figured in the witness box.

*Millom Gazette.*

—◦—

# 1896 – THE HAUNTED CHURCH.

The inhabitants of Boldon Colliery, Sunderland, are much excited (says our Sunderland correspondent) owing to a belief that Hedworth Church is haunted. It is stated that a ghost-like figure appears regularly at a church window. Various suggestions have been made to solve the mystery, but without success. The apparition is plainly visible to everyone in church, and has created much excitement amongst the superstitious section of the villagers who declare it to be a ghost. The figure has now been seen for over a month and is said to resemble a former vicar.

*Illustrated Police News.*

—◦—

# 1897 – A FARMHOUSE GHOST STORY.

A strange ghost story comes from Halton Holegate, a village near Spilsby, Lincolnshire. For some time rumours of human bones having been discovered under a brick floor of a farm near the village, of unearthly noises having been heard, and of a ghost having been seen, have been afloat. The farm in question stands back some distance from the high road, and is occupied by a Mr. and Mrs. Wilson and their man-servant. On being interviewed by a reporter, Mrs Wilson related the following story:-

"We came here on Lady Day last. The first night or so we heard very strange noises about midnight, as though someone was knocking at the doors and walls. Once it seemed as though someone was moving all the things about in a hurry downstairs. Another time the noise was like a heavy picture falling from the wall, but in the morning I found everything as right as it was the night before. The servant-man left saying that he dare not stop, and we had to get another. Then about six weeks ago I saw "something." Before getting into bed, my husband having retired before me, I thought I would go downstairs and see if the cow was all right, as it was about to calve . I did so, and when at the foot of the stairs, just as I was about to go up again, I saw an old man standing at the top and looking at me. He was standing as though he was very round shouldered. How I got past I can't say, but I darted past him into the bedroom and slammed the door. Here I went to get some water from the dressing table, but feeling that someone was behind me, I turned round sharply and there again stood the same old man. He quickly vanished, but I am quite certain I had seen him. I have also seen him several times since, though not quite so distinctly."

Mrs. Wilson next conducted her interviewer to the sitting room, where it appeared a gruesome discovery had been made. The floor in one corner, it seems, had been very uneven, and a day or two ago Mrs. Wilson took up the bricks with the intention of relaying them. No sooner had she done this, however, than a most disagreeable odour was emitted. Her suspicions were aroused, she called her husband, and the two commenced a minute examination. Three or four bones were soon turned over, together with a gold ring and several pieces of old black silk. All these had evidently been buried in quicklime, the bones and silk being obviously burned therewith. The search after this was not further prosecuted but a quantity of sand introduced and the floor quickly levelled again.

Asked what her own opinion was on the mysteries, Mrs. Wilson confidently asserted her belief that at some time or another foul play had taken place. She was fully persuaded in her own mind with regard to the apparition for though it was suggested she might have been mistaken, she disdained the idea as being beneath notice. Dr. Gay, to whom the bones were submitted stated that they might be those of a dog or a pig. Writing later, the correspondent says Dr. Gay, on further examination, states that the bones are undoubtedly human, but he believes them to be nearly a hundred years old.

*County Express.*

---

# 1897 – A GHOST APPEARS AT WOOLWICH.

Plumstead, near Woolwich, has for the past week been the scene of a ghostly visitation, in which the "spirit" has appeared enveloped at night in white array. Several children who saw the apparition were so alarmed that they have been laid up from the effects. Its haunts were principally the grounds of St. James's Church and schools, where lads to the number of about 100 assembled to waylay the ghost, who was seen flitting about. The assailants hurled stones by which several panes of glass were broken, and on the police appearing two of the ringleaders were arrested, but on being brought up at Woolwich they were discharged. One night the visitor visited the grounds of Mr. J. R. Jolly, J.P., and was seen in a tree, arrayed in white apparel. The freak referred to has been traced to an individual of solid flesh living in the neighbourhood, and the "ghost" has been put under restraint.

*Illustrated Police News.*

---

# 1897 – EXTRAORDINARY STORY OF A ROYAL GHOST AT WINDSOR CASTLE.

An extraordinary story is related to the effect that Lieut. A. St. Leger Glyn, of the 3rd Battalion of the Grenadier Guards, has seen what he believes to be a ghost in Windsor Castle. In the course of an interview with a reporter the Hon. Mrs. Carr-Glyn, the mother of the lieutenant, said:- "It is perfectly true that my son witnessed something abnormal. He was, he tells me, sitting in the library of Windsor Castle reading

a book – the "History of Dorsetshire," to be exact. As he read, he became aware of somebody passing in the inner library. He looked up and saw a female figure in black with black lace on her head, falling onto her shoulders. The figure passed across the library towards a corner which was out of view as my son sat, and he did not take much notice, thinking it was somebody reading in the inner room. This was just upon four in the afternoon and an attendant soon afterwards came in to close the place. My son asked who the lady was who was at work in the inner room, and the attendant replied that no one else was in the library. My son assured the attendant that a lady had just walked across the inner room. "Then where could she be?" asked the attendant having ascertained that nobody was in the inner room. "She must have gone out of a door in the corner," said my son, indicating the corner to which the figure had passed. "But there is no door," said the attendant.

My son said nothing about this incident, and did not think very much about it, I understand, until Mr. Holmes, the librarian, asked him about it, the attendant having mentioned the matter to Mr. Homes. Asked by Mr. Homes to describe the figure he had seen, my son did so, and Mr. Homes replied that my son had seen the apparition of Queen Elizabeth. Mr. Holmes added that there were records that this apparition haunted these rooms but Lieutenant Glyn was the first man in our time who had seen it.

The Dean of Windsor also asked my son about it, and several members of the Royal family have interviewed him on the subject. Mr. Holmes says that this gallery has had the reputation of being haunted by the ghost of Queen Elizabeth from time out of memory. His own recollection of the above dates from twenty seven years ago, and he has been in the habit of spending Halloween in the gallery for several years in the hope of encountering her deceased majesty. He had heard some rumour to the effect that the Empress Frederick had, when a child, seen an apparition in the gallery, and on her visiting Windsor hoped to secure some corroboration or denial of the rumour."

The Dean of Windsor somewhat doubts the alleged appearance of Queen Elizabeth; he had a stronger belief in the apparition, some years back, of King Charles I. The last person who is recorded to have been favoured with a manifestation on the part of the Royal martyr was Mrs. Boyd-Carpenter, wife of the present Bishop of Ripon, who was between 1882 and 1884 a Canon of Windsor.

*Illustrated Police News.*

---

A GHOST APPEARS NEAR WOOLWICH.
SCHOOLBOYS ENJOY THE SPORT OF PELTING IT.

# 1897 – HAUNTED HOUSES.

All houses wherein men have lived and died
Are haunted houses. Through the open doors
The harmless phantoms on their errands glide,
With feet that make no sound upon the floors.

We meet them at the doorway, on the stair,
Along the passages they come and go,
Impalpable impressions on the air,
A sense of something moving to and fro.

There are more guests at table, than the hosts
Invited; the illuminated hall
Is thronged with quiet, inoffensive ghosts.
As silent as the pictures on the wall.

The stranger at my fireside cannot see
The forms I see, nor hear the sounds I hear;
He but perceives what is; while unto me
All that has been is visible and clear.

We have title deeds to house or lands;
Owners and occupants of earlier dates
From graves forgotten stretch their dusty hands,
And hold in mortmain still their old estates.

The spirit world around this world of sense
Floats like an atmosphere, and everywhere
Wafts through these earthly mists and vapours dense
A vital breath of more ethereal air.

Our little lives are kept equipoise
By opposite attractions and desires;
The struggle of the instinct that enjoys,
And the more instinct that aspires.

These perturbations, this perpetual jar
Of earthly wants and aspirations high,
Come from the influence of an unseen star,
An undiscovered planet in our sky.

And as the moon from some dark gate of cloud
Throws o'er the sea a floating bridge of light,
Across whose trembling planks our fancies crowd
Into the realm of mystery and night,

So from the world of spirits there descends
A bridge of light, connecting it with this,
O'er whose unsteady floor, that sways and bends,
Wander our thoughts above the dark abyss.

Longfellow.

*Leeds Times.*

# 1897 – TALES AT THE TEA PARTY.

Among some tea party guests today we were presented to a lady who credits herself with "Second Sight." Though Southron bred, and not prone to this particular superstition, I confess to having felt some uneasiness in her presence, as part of her quality is to see people's faces more or less covered with a grey veil according to whether their death is nearer or further off. Sophia kept her own veil resolutely down, and I did not happen to interest her. Tom did, and though he avoided the good lady to the best of his power, and even at last took refuge in the smoking room, she tracked him thither and from what I could afterwards glean amongst his frequent exclamations of "Fudge!" the sibyl had given him a day on which he would be in peril of a watery grave. It would be interesting to see if he will up take up his cruise to Norway!

Another odd power possessed by this lady is that seeing one's head in an aura of other heads, these being the people who have most influenced one. I was delighted to learn that my own cloud of witnesses was nebulous as to be indistinguishable. Others may attribute this to my bad memory; I prefer to impute it to original genius. Eugenia's most prominent companion was a young person with what seemed to be a halo. Him she claimed as St. Aldate, the saint to whom she has peculiar devotion. But I tell you St. Aldate has been exploded by the Oxford historians; and the wraith is probably the master curate in his soft felt hat.

We were greatly pleased at the sibyl's success with Tom. "Only one head," said she, "is very plainly marked; and that furnished with a stubbly chin beard; and has something odd about the eyes, not a cast, nor a squint…"It is a glass eye, ma'am," said Tom, "you are describing my gamekeeper." Surely this is a rare thing, even in ghosts, the ghost with a glass eye!

In the evening we sat round the fire in the hall and told ghost stories, beginning with the ghost of the house of which I then learned for the first time. It haunts the corridors, which is perhaps considerate; though if I was a ghost I should haunt the dining or smoking rooms, not of course for the creature comforts, but for the society as Scotland has this great advantage over England, that is in any company there are sure be one or two persons who have seen a ghost themselves. One lady had seen several, but the particulars were not especially remarkable, except in the case of one which she saw in a street in Dresden pointing to a scaffolded house, which fell the next day, killing several persons.

Another lady was more sensitive with the ear than the eye. She was sleeping in a room at a girl's school opening into a large dormitory; at the door came several raps,

A Victorian Portrayal of Ghosts and the Unexplained

and opening the door suddenly, she found nothing at the other side. By post she heard that her aged father had been picked up fainting outside her bedroom door at home, at which he had knocked, forgetting her absence. In another house, the lower part of which had once formed part of a monastery, she was nursing her mother who was suffering with heart disease; and hearing suddenly the doors being unbarred, and suspecting burglars, she hurried downstairs with the plate that was brought to her mother's room every right, to bribe the thieves to part, fearing that the shock of their appearance would kill the old lady. But the doors were all fast!

*Manchester Evening News.*

---

## 1897 – THE BALLECHIN GHOST.

A late guest at Ballechin writes to *the Times*:-

As one of the guests at Ballechin a short time ago, I must demur the statement of our hostess in her letter which appears in your columns that all the guests came on the distinct understanding that they were bound in honour and courtesy to the owners of the house not to reveal its identity. In my case there was certainly no such stipulation, and had any condition of the kind been attached I should not have accepted the invitation sent to me. I went to Ballechin as an investigator, on the distinct understanding that I was to assume a critical and sceptical attitude, and was to have an absolutely free hand. There was, however, no call for either scepticism or criticism, as my experiences during the two nights I spent there in one of the haunted chambers were of the most common-place description. I heard no sough of the supernatural and saw no glimmer of a ghost.

What struck me as most extraordinary at Ballechin was that a so-called experiment had been carried on there for nearly three months at the time of my visit by the Psychical Research Society without any attempt at either experiment or research. Unscreened evidence of improbable phenomena had been collected in heaps, but the simplest and most obvious tests had not been applied. The residents and visitors, it seemed to me, had been sitting there all the time agape for wonders, straining on the limits of audition, and fomenting on one another's superstitions without taking any precautions to prevent deception or employing reagents to clear up turbid observations.

Our hostess, who had evidently an open mind and offered us every facility for our investigation, eagerly adopted our suggestions as to certain tests, but I regret to learn that there was no time to put these practice.

Practical joking, hallucination, and fraud will account for the bulk of the occult phenomena recorded at Ballechin during its occupation by the Psychical Research Society. What remains, if anything, may be explained by earth tremors (Ballechin is only 20 miles from Comrie, the chief centre of seismic disturbance in Scotland), by the creaking and reverberations of an old and somewhat curiously constructed house, or by some other simple natural cause.

I shall, however, defer comments on these occult phenomena until the Psychical Research Society has stated its case, or rather its two or three cases, for, if I am not mistaken, it is with reference to the Ballechin revelations a household divided against itself.

*The Times.*

---

## 1897 – THE HAUNTED CAB.

If one speaks of "haunted" cabs, one is likely to be greeted with a cynical smile. Nevertheless, in a certain mews in London there is an old and exceedingly dilapidated four wheeler, which is treated as a valuable relic, and spoken of with awe and deference by the cabbies who visit the yard. This ancient wreck is timeworn and worm-eaten. Its cushions smell musty, moths and mice have played havoc with its linings, and there is a vast hole in the roof that ventilates in a most uncomfortable manner its shabby interior. On certain nights muffled groans and harsh cries may be heard by those who are daring enough to venture near it after dark. And, if anyone is so foolhardy as to sit upon its dingy cushions, the whole yard shivers at the audacity and trembles for the consequences.

This cab is said to be the oldest four wheeler in existence, and the story concerning it runs as follows:-

One certain dismal night before Kensington was what it is now, the driver of the haunted cab was crawling slowly along, when he was met by a man who rounded a corner and jumped hastily in.

"Drive for your life!" he shouted, in a voice hoarse with terror. "Drive like the devil! I've got gold here —you shall have whatever you ask."

It took the cabby a second or two to collect his muddled thoughts and to remember that the fare had given him no direction. He looked round helplessly. To get down seemed a waste of time, and the fare had sunk back, apparently breathless, among the cushions. He therefore recklessly decided to drive anywhere, and, taking up the reins, whipped his tired horse into a feeble gallop. He had scarcely driven five minutes before his fare put his head out of the window.

"Go on!" he cried hoarsely. "For heaven's sake, go on. Don't you hear them? They'll catch us, you fool! Go on, go on, go on, I tell you."

The driver lashed into his horse, and the vehicle plunged forward. A little later the man's head was out of the window again.

"They're behind us" he cried. "I can hear them! Confound you, man! Do you want me to hang after all?"

The cabby looked round. The man was leaning out of the cab bareheaded, his face ghastly white, his eyes frantic with terror, and his hands clutched fearfully at the casement of the window. Behind them the road was clear and empty. Not a soul in sight; not a coach or a carriage to be seen. The cabby felt his blood run cold. Was his fare a madman or something worse? He strained his ears to listen, to catch any sound that might come from the distance, but he could hear nothing. He whipped at his tottering horse, and the beast started on again.

A little later he fancied he heard a faint sound borne on the breeze like the trotting of horses and the rolling of wheels, and he looked round expectantly. When he found that the road was still empty, a sort of terror seized him. He shivered involuntarily, and when his fare put his head out of the window again he started with almost a scream, and whipped and lashed at his horse until the animal grew terrified at the unusual treatment. How long they went on, how many hours elapsed until the horse fell exhausted by the wayside, no one knew; when the race came to an end at last, Kensington was left far behind, and before them stretched a long, uneven road, arched with trees and heavy with mud.

With the sound of the trotting horses still in his ears, the cabman descended hastily from his box. He looked back over his shoulder as he did so, and probably, to his distorted imagination, the road was filled with the figures of the pursuers. Heaven knows what terrors filled his mind as he sprang to the window and called out to his fare; but a fresh horror awaited him. The fare had made no sign. Instead of raving with impatience, as the driver expected, he was silent and invisible, and when the cabby looked into his vehicle he started back in affright. The man was lying on his seat with his head upon his shoulder, with his throat cut from ear to ear. A long stream of thick blood trickled slowly over his clothes, and his hand, clasping a short knife, was stained and red. As the driver looked, the suicide's eyes seemed to turn upon him. He shrank back with a cry, seized the reins, which had fallen to the ground, and clambered to his box again.

In the morning they found him whipping wildly at a dead horse! For the next few days he was kept in custody. Then he was discharged, as nothing was found against him, and a night or two afterwards he was found dead in his cab—strangled by the ghost of the suicide, they will tell you; but a little inquiry will ascertain the fact that he had been drinking all day, and that the events of the night of the suicide had so undermined his reason that he was quite likely to die of fright. Still it is a pity to spoil a good legend, and the cab, unless it has lately passed out of existence, is a picturesque object round which to weave a romantic history.

*Sheffield Weekly Telegraph.*

---

# 1898 – FAIR BEANO FOR BOYS AND GIRLS.

St. Peter's Church, De Beauvoir Town, has been a scene of great excitement the last few nights on account of a "ghost" that walks the churchyard.

"The children just come in hundreds from Hoxton and Kingsland, even Hackney and Homerton," said a communicative lady to a *Leader* ghost hunter. "And a rare noise and set out they make. I can't keep my own boys in after dark. They must be off to watch for the "ghost."

"Oh, yes, we've had extra police here, and on Friday night it was a fair "beano." There was a service at the church, and while they were lighting up inside there was an excited crowd of children and older people, who ought to have known better, rushing round from one side of the church to the other, imagining a ghost in ever ray of light that appeared in the church."

"What gave rise to the tale?"

"Well, they had a garden party at the vicarage, and were using a flash light, that's what I believe it was, but some people say that the vicar's daughter was riding round, dressed in white, on a bicycle, and being occasionally seen between the shrubs looked rather ghostly but it's wonderful what a lot some people make out of nothing."

"I heard some tale of the ghost coming down from the tower and walking round?"

"Yes, so have I, but seeing's believing, isn't it? And I haven't seen it."

The ghost seems to be quite a quick change artist, for the *Leader* man heard at least six different descriptions – green eyes, and flowing white garments was popular, but a death's head with a light round it ran it very close and one boy embellished his account with, "Yes and I saw red fire a-coming out of his mouth." There is a future for that boy as a historian.

The verger, on being interviewed, was highly indignant with everybody—boys, gossips, and ghosts. "I never did hear of such rubbish here they come and disturb the services, and make no end of bother about a light. I've no; patience with it."

The *Leader* huntsman was about to depart from the scene regretting that he had not happened on a healthy believer in the ghost, when fortune favoured him.

"The boys seem excited enough about the ghost in the daytime," he said to an old dame, who stood looking on at the children chalking up "Beware of the ghost."

"Yes," she said, slowly but when night comes they're frightened, most of 'em. I don't wonder, either. I wouldn't come round by myself at night, I know that."

"Surely you don't believe in it?"

"Well, I do. This is a haunted neighbourhood. Not so many years ago one of the houses in De Beauvoir Square was haunted. I saw that my own self. And I know someone who saw this one. At the church they pooh-pooh it, and the police say its rubbish, but I know somebody who saw it."

"What was it like?"

"A greyish white, with no face to speak of, a sort of cowl that hides the face, and I wouldn't go round there at night for anything. Ah! You may laugh, but I wouldn't."

*South Wales Daily News.*

---

# 1898 – PHANTOM REGIMENTS.

Many curious cases are on record of phantom regiments appearing in the clouds, which have assured the most sceptical that such things are quite possible and not unfrequently happen, especially in mountainous districts. They are nothing more than the shadows of what is really taking place in another part of the country, although it may be miles away. These shadows are reflected by the sun's rays, and are seen to perfection in misty atmospheres, such as are prevalent in the North of Scotland.

Many strange rumours passed over the country with regard to spirit armies after the civil war of Charles I.'s time. Battles, says a military paper, were seen to be fought again in the clouds, the absence of noise alone proving that the eye was deluded. Later on, in 1650, it is alleged that a spectre drummer boy was seen going along beating the Scottish and English marches by turns, and is said to have been summoned to a conference of spirits at Edinburgh Castle. It seems strange, however, that just afterwards Colonel Dundas surrendered the castle to Cromwell on being bribed with gold. At the same period, too, the hum of cannon shot is said to have been heard in the air.

Such apparitions, of course, terrified the inhabitants of the districts in which they appeared, and the traditions were handed down for ages.

*Buckingham Express.*

---

# 1898 – A HEADLESS GHOST IN BUCKINGHAMSHIRE.

The people of Buckingham and neighbourhood are troubled at the appearance of a ghost, the truth of which is vouched for by a well-known farmer living in the neighbourhood.

About six miles from the outskirts of the town there stands a weather-beaten hand-post at the corner of four crossroads, and also a small plantation of young oak saplings at the terminus. Near to this spot some few nights ago the farmer referred to, accompanied by a friend, was driving his horse and trap along the roadway. The night was well advanced and dark, when suddenly the farmer saw standing a few yards in front of him a black object. "What's that?" he said to his friend, and aloud to the figure, "Hullo there; move on, please." There was no answer, and the figure remained almost motionless. It was completely enveloped in a long black sheet, and had the ghastly appearance of a headless woman. Simultaneously the horse saw it, and trembled like a leaf, as if paralysed with fear.

Again the farmer cried, "What do you do there? Move on, please." But there was no response, and the apparition remained still. The horse became restive, and commenced backing into a ditch. At this stage the driver's companion got down and took the reins, and endeavoured to back by the spot. Then for a minute or so their queer visitant disappeared. As the trap again faced the roadway the occupants were greatly alarmed at the further appearance of the black, sombre figure a few yards ahead of them, in the same motionless position as before.

Their situation was now getting positively serious. The farmer, whose presence of mind had stood him in good stead, now finding his nerve on the point of giving way, asked the apparition in the name of God to speak. Then it was that the spectre slowly glided away, and appeared to float through the thick-set bordered hedge. The animal at once galloped off at a rattling pace towards the village they were bound for. Other people in the district have related their experiences, and the belief now prevails that there is a ghost to be seen, and not a little surprising the spot referred to has been less frequented of late.

*Illustrated Police News.*

A HEADLESS GHOST IN BUCKINGHAMSHIRE.

# 1898 – THE SCOTCH M.P. AND THE GHOST.

"Lloyds" tells a story of a haunted house in Euston and a daring ghost disillusioner in the person of a well-known Scotch Member of Parliament noted for his courage and the possessor of a fine bulldog. The M.P. offered to spend a night in the house. About one in the morning there were distinct sounds of someone walking about in the room above. Presently the noise grew louder, and seemed to be getting nearer. Barney, for such was the dog's, name, emitted an irrepressible growl, and for an hour or so the sounds ceased.

During this time the M.P. examined a small casket which lay at the foot of the stairs, and had apparently been noiselessly precipitated. The box opened upon a smaller box, and yet another, till in the bottom part lay the photograph of a quaintly attired gentleman, an Egyptian he seemed. "Who finds this finds the supposed ghost," read the legend on the back of the card.

The M.P. put the box into his breast pocket. Then the servant jumped downstairs at break neck speed and banged out at the front door gasping something quite unintelligibly. His exit was simultaneous with the sharp report of a pistol. Then all became still again. Steadying his nerves, the M.P. resolved to go upstairs and look for the dog. He found the animal all of a heap on the stair landing dead. Yet there was no one to be seen.

On again returning to the room of his night watch he found his hat and stick gone. Obviously the ghost had been looking for him also.

The sequel to the adventure is hardly less exciting. Some few nights afterwards the M.P. was a guest at an evening in Belgravia. He came late, and on entering made straight for a laughing group of ladies and gentlemen who were being vastly amused by a leger-demain of a professional conjuror. "The face is familiar," thought the M.P., "and the fantastic attire I have seen it all somewhere. "Yes, yes, I know, the photograph!" Quickly he sought out the head of the house and told his story, winding up with the injunction. "You must have him arrested." But lo! the conjurer had disappeared.

*Falkirk Herald.*

---

# 1899 – A SCOTTISH GHOST STORY.

The ghost story from Lockerbie which has been published, bears a family likeness to a great many narratives of the same subject, and when one reads of the terrified young man fleeing from the supposed apparition it is impossible not to think of some lines of Scotland's national poet which need not however be applied to the hero of the incident in question. But really this "tall and white ghostly figure" appears to be a very ordinary kind of spook, notwithstanding the "luminous halo which seems to surround it."

There was, some years ago, a similar apparition at what was then the quiet village of Ilford in Essex. For two weeks the villagers were nocturnally frightened by a tall object with glaring eyes and clothed in white, which used to nightly to promenade the neighbourhood, appearing when the clock struck midnight, and vanishing precisely at one, to the great terror of Ilfordians. A bold youth swore that he would capture the "ghost" and went one night to the spot with a loaded gun. He fired, and the spectre dropped, whereupon the youth administered some severe strokes with the butt end of his weapon, which laid the ghost groaning and bleeding, at his feet. So vigorous had been the blows that the apparition's assailant had very nearly made a ghost of him, but a medical man being called, the spectre was brought round after some hours.

It would be interesting to experiment with the ghost at Lockerbie, which appears at its own risk, and ought not to object to such a test of its good faith. But it may be that there was no spectre at all, and that the man who was so alarmed only imagined that he saw one. He would not be the first who had been deceived in this way, and when there are ghosts in the air, it is not a very uncommon thing for people to report, like Caesar's officer in Gaul, that they had seen that which they had not seen.

Trees have been taken for spectres before now, and even horses, cows, and donkeys, but whatever it was that the young man saw, it will take a good deal of evidence to convince the British public that it was a spirit. We have read so often in the dull season of the sea serpent and the big gooseberry, that we ought to be grateful for a new sensation. Probably we shall read of more ghosts before the summer is over, and indeed we have an embarrassment of riches in the recently published book of Miss Goodrich Freer and the Marquis of Bute, who evidently think that there is something in the ghostly visitations at a cottage at Falkland, Fifeshire, although it is a little disappointing to find that they "offer no conclusions" on the subject.

The most enterprising spectre in this case appears to be that of a dog, which has been known to act in rather a strange way for a member of the brute creation. But there are any number of precedents for the appearance of canine spectres. Sir Walter Scott almost founded his "Lay of the Last Minstrel" upon such an incident, and he tells us in his interesting notes thereto, of a large black spaniel with curled shaggy hair, "its appearance being indubitably attested by an old soldier who had seen it oftener than he had then hairs on his head." It would seem frivolous to suggest that the old soldier's head was as bald as a billiard ball, but this story--of which the scene is not laid in Scotland—finds a parallel in many Scottish legends of spectre hounds. This particular spaniel seems to be rather a substantial ghost for we are told that it has a way of falling against doors with a bang, producing such a "loud inexplicable noise" as to trouble even the mind of a good priest who heard it. Then the latter writes that, being awoke when he was sleeping the sleep of the just, he "held the clothes round his neck with his hands, but they were gently lifted in spite of his efforts to hold them." This was rather a strange thing for a dog to do, and it is equally surprising to read that the priest aforesaid, not only heard sounds resembling falling quadrupeds, but screams, shrieks, spirit raps, and noises, like the explosion of petards.

These two stories belong to Scotland but the North has no monopoly of such legends and many similar narratives might be related which have had their origin in England, Ireland and Wales. It is even said that the ghost of Queen Elizabeth has been seen in the library at Windsor Castle and if recent reports are to be believed, strange things happen at times within the precincts of the House of Commons.

*Millom Gazette.*

# 1899 – HANDEL'S WRAITH.

The Psychical Research Society, if that institution be still in existence, should instantly despatch a deputation to Liverpool. Ghost stories, as a rule, are eminently unsatisfactory. There are plenty of persons who have an acquaintance with ghostly visitants—but only second hand, and the difficulty of procuring witnesses ready to aver that they have seen a ghost with their own eyes must have considerably hampered the investigations which at one time the Psychical Research Society so diligently pursued.

The story of the appearance of Handel's wraith at Liverpool is distinctly the best ghost story presented to the public for years. According to the version presented "M.A.P.," Miss Regina de Sales, the well-known singer, while rendering the principal part in the Messiah at Liverpool a fortnight ago, considerably disconcerted the conductor by adopting her own time, an explanation subsequently tendered being that "Handel himself was present in the hall, and gave her the correct tempi."

As this story stood it might have been taken by the incredulous and the ungallant as an unusually elaborate attempt to cloak an inexplicable eccentricity on the part of the artiste; and without on our part insinuating that Miss de Sales' word stands in need of corroboration, it is perhaps as well that additional testimony is forthcoming. Handel appears to have been restless after the performance, and in the middle of the night Miss Edith Thomas, the well-known harpist, who was staying at the same hotel as Miss de Sales, was awakened by a loud cry of "Brava," exclaimed by a burly man, attired in full-bottomed wig, lace, frills, and wristbands—Handel himself conducting with a roll of music an imaginary performance. That is the story, and the public may make of it what they please.

Can it be that Handel, disgusted by the mutilations and variations to which the "Messiah" has been subjected, has determined to come back to demonstrate how his masterpiece should actually be performed? The matter is one of serious interest for Sheffield. The "Messiah" is down for performance at the forthcoming local musical festival, and according to present arrangements Mr. August Manns will wield the baton. With every respect for the talents of the Crystal Palace conductor, this part of the programme might be advantageously altered.

If only Handel's wraith could be captured and installed in the conductor's chair! It is safe to predict that in such an event the Festival would assume an interest and importance before which every other musical festival in the country would yield. The executive of the Festival should lose no time in appointing a Psychical Research Committee, entrusted with authority to proceed to Liverpool, and to offer Handel—when successfully interviewed—his own terms!

*Sheffield Evening Telegraph.*

# 1899 – NOT DEAD YET!

During the last few days a story has been going about that the rooms—situated in the Speaker's Court—of Mr. A. J. C. Milman, Assistant Clerk of the House of Commons, are haunted.

The apparition, it was stated, took the form of Mrs. Milman, and always appeared in her absence.

"The funny thing about the story," said Mrs. Milman, "is that it is perfectly true. It has been going on for years. People are constantly telling me that they have seen me in places where I have certainly not been at the time they mention. One of my hobbies is book binding. I have a binding room at the top of the house. One afternoon a friend was assisting me, and on taking his leave found me again on the other side of the binding room door! Quite taken aback —he said—he stood aside to let my double pass in.

I have never seen my double myself, but I have heard it. One night when I had just retired to my bedroom I heard a noise outside the door, and was sure there was something there. I went out and found all the doors on the landing open.

I went back and fastened my door by means of a night bolt, which is worked by a rope from the bed. The handle of the door was immediately turned, and the door pushed open again, the bolt being shot back. I again went out and found nobody there.

Then I rang for two of the servants, my maid at the top the house, and the butler at the bottom. As they came to me I knew that they must intercept anyone on the stairs. My maid had seen nobody, but the butler had just met me coming through the folding doors of the bottom corridor!

One of my governesses some time ago left simply because of meeting this strange sight so often. Only today a young lady who is staying at the house told me she had seen me somewhere where I had not been."

"Are you not nervous with such a peculiar visitor about?" Mrs. Milman was asked.

"Not a bit," laughed Mrs. Milman. "It doesn't make the least difference to me. I have got used to it. In fact I have often tried to waylay the stranger, waiting for footsteps to come along."

*Illustrated Police Budget.*

---

# 1900 – A GENUINE HAUNTED HOUSE.

The "*Temps*" relates a curious story concerning an alleged haunted house in the Rue de Bourgogne. It says that since October last the inhabitants of No. 57 of this thoroughfare have been perturbed at hearing the persistent cries of a child, though there are no children in the house. To such an extent have these cries troubled one the inhabitants, Mdlle Marie Breton, that she made a complaint to the local Commissary of Police. According to her statement, she heard the voice of a child groaning and saying, "Mamma, you are burning me." Two detectives, sent by the Commissary, also heard the cries, but they were unable to discover their origin. The police Commissary then took the enquiry, and has visited the neighbouring houses, but without result; and

M. Cochefort, the well-known head of the Detective Department, who has unravelled more than one so called ghost story, has undertaken to make a personal investigation.

*Cheltenham Chronicle.*

---

# 1900 – A HAUNTED HOTEL.

A correspondent writes:—A series of remarkable incidents, which are popularly supposed to be due to supernatural causes, have occurred recently at a Brixton hotel. The most extraordinary of these occurrences is the ringing at intervals of the whole of the bells in the house, and this is invariably preceded by other noises resembling the battering of a heavy object against some obstacle from the direction of the cellar, or occasionally from some other part of the house. In addition to these indications of the supposed supernatural tendency of the hotel such visual signs as the passage of unsubstantial shapes along the corridors and up the staircases are said be present, and it is also alleged that locked doors have been opened during the night, and that gas jets have been lighted by the same inexplicable means, and even that the balls and cues, notwithstanding that they had been locked up in a drawer, have been found upon the billiard tables as if someone had been playing overnight.

About a month ago a barmaid employed at the hotel was startled into hysterics at being suddenly waked while in bed and finding the door of her room, which she had locked, to be slowly opening. She at once left her situation, and nothing will induce her now to return. Other assistants, among them the manageress of the house, have also resigned, being too frightened to remain. One of the barmen employed at the hotel, who is a soldier just returned from active service in South Africa, states that the ringing of the bell communicating with the bar occurs frequently, and he has so far investigated the cause. He is perfectly certain that the bells are not rung by human agency, and would appear that the ringing of the bells is of too violent a nature to be caused by rats, as has been suggested. An inquiry into the cause of the phenomena is to be made on the premises by the Psychical Research Society.

*Derry Journal.*

## 1900 – A PARLIAMENTARY WRAITH.

A famous Parliamentary ghost is known as Big Ben. More than a dozen people have declared that they have seen it at different times, some of the occasions being very recent.

This spectre is that of an old man who, near midnight, comes along the river from the Surrey side, near Westminster Bridge, in an old-fashioned boat. His oars are held still, but the boat glides on without sound, passes through the third arch of the bridge, and then, just as Big Ben begins to strike the midnight hour, vanishes into the stone wall of the Terrace of the House!

It is declared that on these memorable occasions Big Ben has struck, or has seemed to strike, thirteen to the dozen, and that the circumstance has boded ill-luck for the Royal Family. Thus the ghost appeared at midnight on January 13th, 1892, and the Duke of Clarence died the next day.

A remarkable and very circumstantial story is told of the appearance of the spectre on this date. It is to the effect that it was seen by a river police boat, which hailed it. Of course no answer was given, and the river police thereupon gave chase. It was a fruitless chase. The ghost, as usual, passed through the third arch and made direct for the Terrace wall, the police boat in mad pursuit, so mad indeed that when they reached the wall and the spectre vanished within, they dashed into the stonework with such force that their boat was almost wrecked!

*Bromyard News.*

---

## 1900 – A SCIENTIST'S EXPERIENCES.

Dr. Elliott Coues, the famous ornithologist and member of the American National Academy of Sciences, who died recently, was long recognised as the foremost advocate of belief in the existence of ghosts. He had promised several of his friends that, if able to do so, he would appear to them after his own demise, and now they are waiting with no little interest to see if he will carry out the agreement. Himself a born ghost-seer, as he used to say, he enjoyed discussing the subject of phantoms with the same method of cool-headed analysis as he would apply to the classification of birds or any other matter susceptible of approach by rational argument.

"I have myself seen the ghosts of a good many dead persons," said the doctor to a friend one day. "I remember one occasion when I had just gone to bed, the light being turned out, I was composing myself to slumber, when I suddenly became aware of a presence in the room. The impression conveyed to my mind was that it was the presence of a certain person lately deceased, with whom I had been on very intimate terms. In fact, I felt an overpowering sense of the nearness of the individual in question. At about the same moment there arose slowly from the floor a nebulous mass of what looked like a shining white vapour, which began to take shape, as did the smoke from the casket opened by the fisherman in the "Arabian Knights" tale. Gradually it assumed a more distinct outline, until it presented a radiant image of my friend. The lips appeared to move, and from them came an unintelligible utterance – a message, in short, from the departed."

"I can assure you that the vision was no dream, and the nature of the message was such as to eliminate, to my own satisfaction, at all events, the theory of hallucination. What, then, was this shape of shining white vapour? Was it a human soul'? It is a question pregnant with much interest."

The doctor took another pipeful of tobacco, lighted it, and, with a reflective puff or two, continued:-

"Every afternoon at about five o'clock I lie down on the sofa in my library for a brief rest before dinner. Occasionally, while enjoying this repose, though perfectly wide awake, there comes upon me the peculiar sensation of the ghost chill, which I will presently speak of. I wait with much attention and interest to see what is going to happen, and presently I find my own consciousness projected objectively, as it were, so that my conscious self stands out in the room and views my body lying on the lounge. About the latter is a bright light, which grows gradually until it has filled all the room, and my conscious self finds itself surrounded by phantoms, most of them of persons who appear to be strangers to me, while others resemble acquaintances who have long been dead. They seem to walk about and converse in the ordinary way, though not audibly. All the time I am clearly aware of the situation and make a useful mental note of whatever I observe, until after a few brief moments the spectacle vanishes and I feel myself on the sofa again."

"It is obvious, if ghosts exist at all, that they must be made of something. My belief is that they are in a sense substantial, and possess a semi-material structure. If you ask what I mean by 'semi-material,' I will refer for illustration to the ether which is understood to occupy all space. It has waves of known lengths and measured velocity, which strike upon the retina of the eye and produce impressions of light. In short, we know a good deal about this ether, but nobody ever saw a particle of it, inasmuch as it has not the molecular constitution of ordinary matter. It is semi-material. I have no notion of the nature of the substance that makes a ghost, but I suppose that when a man dies it separates itself from the grosser particles that it compose his physical organism. The latter decomposes, but the spiritual part of the individual does not necessarily share that fate, being composed of finer stuff."

"Did it ever occur to you that we ourselves may be moving in a world of unseen spectres and are continually surrounded, whether at home or on our walks abroad by invisible phantoms of the dead? It has been estimated that for every human being now living thirty thousand have died on this earth, so that, if the spiritual bodies of all preserve existence here after death, we survivors are but a comparative few, passing a brief term of years of what we call life in the flesh amid a vast impalpable swarm of beings incorporeal. Indeed my own notion is that it is only the very rare and exceptional ghost that makes itself visible to the living, and that such a phenomenon is to be regarded as wholly extraordinary."

"We have reason now to think that there is no such thing as the highly conventionalised ghost represented by tradition and described in popular fiction – the corpse-like apparition which enters by preference at the stroke of midnight, dressed in a winding-sheet, smelling of the grave, and dragging a clanking chain through the sliding panel just by the door, while the candles burn blue and the dogs howl dismally. According to my own observation, and to the testimony of many other reliable persons who have observed stich phenomena, the real spectre of a dead person shows few signs of life, resembling a magic lantern picture more than anything else to which it is so readily comparable. It does not speak, nor use its limbs, its method of locomotion, when it moves, being a gilding. It is clothed not in a winding sheet, but in garments such as were worn in life by the individual of whom it is the eidolon or image. It appears by daylight as it often as at night, but never with any purpose in its actions that is at all comprehensible. Occasionally it is self-luminous. In most cases it disappears through a door or wall, but often it simply fades away in shadowy mist. Sometimes the phantasmal figure is seen as though illuminated on a dark background; sometimes the contour is indistinct and resembles a luminous cloud; sometimes there is no figure at all, but merely a diffused glow."

The doctor's pipe had gone out. He took a match from the skull of an Indian chief, which served him as a matchbox, and lighted it again. Said he:-

"Each of us, I believe, has in him a ghost, which ordinarily is confined to the precincts of the body. When I die my ghost leaves my body permanently, and, having done so, perhaps it may continue to be the vehicle and means of expression of conscious will, memory, and understanding. St. Paul says, "There is a natural body

and a spiritual body." It is of the spiritual body that I am speaking."

"Our senses take cognisance of no forms of matter except those which are in a certain degree of condensation, but, as I have already said, the spiritual body may be of a more rarefied and tenuous substance. The non-appearance of ghosts to us may be a question, not of the existence of spectres, but of the acuteness of our perceptive faculties. My own experience is that the coming of an apparition is always preceded by a curious sensation which I call the "ghost chill." When this symptom arrives the threshold of consciousness seems to be shifted to the extent of rendering possible a perception of something ordinarily invisible. The change is usually very brief, lasting only a few seconds, during which the manifestation occurs. The evidential value of these experiences is wholly personal, of course, inasmuch as they are not subject to the ordinary processes of verification."

"I have spoken of the permanent separation of the ghost from the physical body as implying the death of the latter; but there is plenty of evidence to show that it sometimes leaves the corporeal tenement for a brief time, presently returning. I myself have seen phantoms of living persons on more than one occasion which looked and acted precisely as the individuals themselves might have done. They looked like figures thrown upon a screen by magic lantern, usually bring recognised for a few moments and then disappearing; but it some cases they had every appearance of solidarity, to the extent of hiding objects behind them. I never heard any of them speak, but on two or three occasions they gave intelligible messages by their attitudes and gestures. There is no essential difference between the spectre of a living human being and the apparition of a dead person, so far as appearances go. Each of us, as I have said, carries his own ghost with him, which ordinarily is under the control of the possessor, but sometimes appears to act independently. As a rule the projection or a phantom by a living person is an involuntary act, resulting ordinarily from great mental perturbation, with the cause of which the individual to whom the spectre appears is in some way connected. The most startling instances of this kind occur a little before or shortly after the death of the sender, and such ghosts are known as "death wraiths.""

"One reason, I have for believing the evidence of my own senses in this matter is that on several occasions the apparition of my own personality has presented itself to other persons in places where my body was not at the time, Some years ago I was in Chicago, at an ordinary evening party with about 49 friends, when an individual in Washington, who did not even know where I was, was visited by my phantasm, and received, from it a brief message, stating where I was at the time, and giving the names of two or three of the guests present – persons with whom the observer was unacquainted. This was one of those rare cases where a ghost made itself audible."

"You ask what would happen if one should approach a ghost such as I have described and try to touch it. My reply is that there would certainly be no danger in doing so, for spectres never do anybody any harm, the fear of the entertained by most people being simply a dread of that which is unknown and not understood. Whatever is unknown in always terrible, but the phantom is composed of matter tenuous to present any obstacle, and I do not doubt that it would dissolve and disappear if you attempted to walk through it."

*Hampshire Telegraph.*

---

# 1900 – A SHOEMAKER'S FRIGHT.

In our bonnie Borderland, high up where the moorland slopes imperceptibly into the Cheviots, lies a lonely little churchyard, wonderfully graced by the ruins of a very old church.

Little now remains but a gable, ivy draped, an arched window and doorway, and some bits of broken walls; but modern graves have crept within them, and modern masonry supports and points not untastefully the crumbling old stonework, and a poet's monument is there. All is open to the sunshine and the butterflies, and it looks a sweet and sheltered spot in which to lay the dead.

Yet fifty years ago that old church was reckoned haunted by ghosts and goblins, feared and dreaded for miles around.

A new church having been built at a more convenient distance from the village, the old one was deserted but not demolished, and as the churchyard around it was still the burying place of the neighbourhood, people came and went by it continually.

The pews and its pulpit stood empty, but untouched, its doors and windows were left open, and up among the rafters hung the old hinged coffin used in olden days for pauper funerals; and as years went on dust and decay reigned within, till the auld kirk looked more forlorn and desolate than any roofless ruin could have done, and tales that it was haunted began to grow and magnify. Lights were sometimes seen within it and noises heard, but the startled passer-by had no wish to pry upon the witches at their revels, and only hurried on the faster.

Adjoining the Laird's pew a door led into his family vault, and tradition said before the death of one of that house occurred, the door opened of itself, and the ghost

came and sat in the pew, waiting to receive their new companion.

One wintry night, as the village cronies crawed crouse around the fire of the village inn, the tales grew weird and yet weirder, till one told of the fearsome sights to be seen when the Laird's vault opened, and declared it was to risk his life for anyone to venture into the Laird's pew after dark.

The lights were bright and the room was cosy, so the shoemaker's courage rose high, and vowed that neither ghost nor goblin, witch nor fairy, could frighten him. But the blacksmith scorned his valour, and defied him to venture alone that night into the auld kirk and stick his awl into the floor of the Laird's pew, where next morning all might see the clear daylight.

The shoemaker had not meant his boast to be brought home to him in this manner, but, surrounded by his cronies, he could not now withdraw, so the whole company started to see the deed done.

It was a gusty, gurly night; the wind sighed and moaned through the bare boughs like a thing in pain, and the dead leaves made disagreeable rustlings as the little band trudged along the dark lanes. Arrived at the little lonely church, the escort halted at the churchyard gate, and the valiant ghost-defier had to do the rest alone. He shivered and shook as he passed the tall tombstones that surely had more fearsome shapes than daylight showed them. A screech owl hooted at him; his heart was in his mouth; he would have turned and fled; but his companions barred the way. With careful, noiseless steps, as if he feared to awaken the dead, he ventured on. They watched him push the church door open, and then the darkness swallowed him up, and, in silence that could be felt, they waited breathlessly for his return, when an awful scream appalled them.

Scared half out their wits, yet anxious for their comrade, they scuttled in a body to the church door, when another yell dispersed them. As they tumbled over one another, someone caught the rope of the old church bell and set it clanging. Its clamour added to their fright and confusion, but brought help too. The unusual noise roused the neighbourhood, and some poachers "burning" the river down below rushed up with their lighted torches in their hands, and being more accustomed to deeds of darkness than honest village folk, headed the rescue party into the church.

Neither sight nor sound of ghost or goblin was to be seen or heard, but the shoemaker lay like dead on the floor of the Laird's pew. Willing hands stretched out to raise him, but they could not do so; though inert and motionless, he resisted all their efforts. It speaks well for their courage and their real kind hearts that they did not turn and fly and leave him lying there, but making yet another effort, and stooping closer, by the aid of the smoking torches' somewhat murky light, found out what held him. It was his awl. Poor fellow, when in his haste and fright he drove his awl into the haunted floor, he drove it also through his stout leathern apron, which, when he tried to rise, held him fast to the place, and resisted all his efforts to escape.

No wonder he thought the powers of darkness had him in their clutches, and yelled in his despair. He did not die of his fright. Medical aid restored him; but never again did he care to listen to ghost stories.

*Motherwell Times.*

<hr />

# 1900 – A TRUE 1900 GHOST STORY.

"What up Trereife a ghost? No, I really can believe it!" "Well, you just go up and see for yourself, any time between 10 and midnight." "What's the ghost like then?" "Oh, it's a terrible thing—about the size of an elephant and with eyes like carriage lamps." "Do it harm one?" "Oh, yes, very dangerous they say as some has been knocked down, trampled on, and nearly killed." "Oh my!"

The foregoing was the conversation overheard by the writer in the Green Market, Penzance, a few days ago. Now I must confess that ghosts have a horrible fascination for me—not that I had ever seen one, but I was always hoping I should. Wait a bit. Well, I at once decided that I would go and prowl around Trereife, see some of the servants at the big house, and try to hear if it was at last a ghost!

There was no doubt about it. Several of them had been attacked, and not even the bravest of the brave at Newlyn would venture up to Trereife after dark. Now I am a brave man, and to prove it I very nearly volunteered for service in South Africa. The only thing that stopped me was an uncomfortable feeling in the region of the stomach when I thought how I should be such a good mark for a Boer bullet, because I have such a red nose caused by indigestion. But a ghost! Now that is the thing to bring out the mettle of a man. My plans were quickly laid. That very night I would set forth, after a hearty meal with just a drop of something to steady my nerves. I started my preparations. In each of my trousers pockets I carried a six-chambered revolver; and, in case I was surprised, and had no time to shoot, I carried my sword stick. Thus equipped, I sallied forth.

The very night for such an expedition – a low moaning wind and the moon obscured by heavy black clouds. Out through Alverton, "as brave as a lion," strode I, and up St. Just hill fairly well. Then into Trereife fields.

And I must now confess a creepy sensation began to come over me.

Now, in case of accidents, I had placed a flask of whisky over my heart, to turn the bullet if the ghost shot. So I had a good long pull and felt much braver.

Right through the fields and down as far as the mansion, and no sign of a ghost. I began to think it was old women's gossip, but I suddenly remembered the ghost was always seen (so said one of the informants) between where I was and where the four roads meet – an ancient haunt of the restless spirits of buried suicides. Another good long pull at my flask and on I went.

I was just thinking all was well when a horrible creepy sensation came over me; my knees knocked together; and all of a sudden there came a great mighty rushing wind, with fumes like lyddite, and, before I had time to take one more pull at my flask, to steady me, I received a fearful crushing blow behind the ear, which evidently knocked me over the hedge, where I was found next morning and carried home more dead than alive.

When sufficiently recovered I went to see the Editor of *The Cornishman*, to tell him my adventures. A beautiful smile spread over his features, and he told me a very curious thing. It appears there was an owl, with its nest, in an elm tree, by the side of the road running from Trereife down to the Land's End road, and, still more curious, that owl had attacked several people; in fact it had become such a nuisance, not to say a danger, that Mr. Rowe had to shoot it, and it is now being stuffed by Mr. Rowe. "After this," said Mr. Editor, "I don't think your ghost story will wash." This I thought very rude of him, more especially as I am such a brave man; and that is my first and I sincerely trust last meeting with a ghost, say nothing of an unbelieving editor.

*The Cornishman.*

<hr />

# 1900 – ANN CONNER'S GHOST.

One of the "best authenticated" ghost stories I have ever heard was told to me by an old farmer, with whom I once boarded for the summer.

He was an old Englishman, and at the time the events here narrated took place, resided in the northern part of England with his wife and children. He was then a young man, and one who had had a fairly decent bringing up. He could read, write and cipher, and he went regularly to church. He read the daily papers, but had never perused a work of fiction in his life. Anything of the supernatural order he classed under the head of "Old woman's nonsense." And he was probably, at that date, too healthy and too happy to be the victim of optical illusions or clairvoyant experiences.

It was towards the close of a warm midsummers day that a certain buxom servant girl, in Mrs. Gwill's employ, came to her mistress, as the latter stood beside her husband, admiring the antics of a young colt, who was trying its legs in the meadow for the first time, and said, in a very earnest way:-

"I'd like leave this afternoon, Missus, if you please. Kitty says she'll get the tea, and I haven't seen my mother this three weeks."

"You may go, Ann," said Mrs. Gwill, kindly, "but you'll be sure to be home tonight, for tomorrow is baking day."

"Oh, I'll be home, ma'am," said Ann. "And to tell the truth, ma'am, I want to go, because I hear she's behind with the rent, and I want to take her my wages. It's been hard for her since father died, with all those little children."

"Yes, poor soul, it must have been," said Mrs. Gwill; "and you may take her a dozen new laid eggs, and the pat of butter in the stone jar, and a loaf of our cream bread for her tea."

And Ann, with a grateful, "Thank you, Missus," ran away to get herself ready for her walk, and soon reappeared with a black straw basket on her arm.

In this, as her fellow servants knew, she had her quarter's wages in a handkerchief. They paid servants by the quarter in that part of England and above it the good things her mistress had sent to the widow.

"That's a good girl," said Mrs. Gwill, as she watched her on her way up the road. "It isn't everyone that would save for the mother's sake as Ann does. I'll give her a new stiff gown for her Christmas present."

After that no more was said of Ann Conner. The family had tea, and after it was over a friend dropped in. When he had gone the children were put to bed, and the servants were heard trudging to their garret overhead. All was dark, for the moon rose late that night; and Mrs. Gwill, as she looked at the clock and saw that its hands pointed to the hour of nine said, "Ann's a foolish girl to stay so late. She'll hardly find her way over the road by this light."

"Maybe she'll wait for moonrise," said Mr. Gwill.

"Then she'll be out later than a decent woman ought," said the wife; "and I'm too tired to wait all night for her; and I won't leave the door unlocked. She can just wait on the porch until day breaks."

"Don't be cross, mother," said Mr. Gwill, good-naturedly. "Go to bed. I'll just sit up a bit, and read the paper, and she'll be along in no time."

And Mrs. Gwill took her lord's advice, and went to her room, where she was soon asleep and snoring. He, for his part, lit two candles, seated himself in a big arm chair, opened his paper, and went asleep over it.

"When I wakened up," he says, as he tells the story, "it was with a start like. I'd been asleep a long while. I could see, for the candles were burnt clean down to the sockets; and there was the moon, big as a bushel basket, and yellow as gold, staring in at the window. I felt queerish, as if I'd had a bad dream that I couldn't remember; and while I was rubbing my eyes and shaking myself, the clock began to strike. It struck twelve."

"Ann is never coming home tonight," said I, "I'll go to bed;' and with that the candle wicks dropped both together into the hot grease, and began to fry. I snuffed them out, and went to the window to draw the shutters to and bar them, and just as I'd got my hand on one, our old dog that always slept across the door on the porch, set up such a howl as I never heard him give before. You know they say, in our part of the world, a dog's howl is a sign of death. I don't believe such stuff, but I thought of the saying, somehow, and it didn't make me comfortable. I felt angry at the dog, and I was making ready to throw a bit of stick at him, but before I could cast it from my hand, I saw Ann Conner standing close beside the dog, who was crouching low and shaking all over.

"The next thing I'd have hit you," says I, putting down the stick. "You're late enough tonight; what happened to you?"

For somehow she looked white and strange in the moonlight, and I thought she might have been ill. Then I took my head in from the window and opened the door, and Ann came in across the sill; and I remember just how she stood in the white moonlight, white as snow herself, and how the dog lifted up his head and, trembling all over, howled again—three long, awful howls that made my blood run cold.

"Well, Ann, what's happened to you?" I says again, and I felt stranger than I ever felt before that minute. Queer little prickles flew all over me, as they do when you catch hold of that electric machine some doctors have. And I was frightened—I couldn't say at what, unless it was the dog.

"Haven't you a tongue in your head, Ann?" says I. "What's the matter?"

"The matter master?" says she, looking into my eyes. "Oh master, don't you know I'm dead. The man that killed me is Jack Hazzard and you'll find me behind Carston Cliff."

"You're a pretty sort of dead person," says I. "I never thought you'd take to drink, Ann Conner. Go to your bed now and I'll talk to you in the morning when you're sober."

She passed by me as I spoke, and I turned to bar the kitchen door, and when I'd done it she was gone—to her own room, I supposed, and I went to my bed and went to sleep—thinking what a fool I was to feel half frightened by the howl of a dog and the words of a tipsy woman.

"Your fine Ann came home crazy drunk last night," I said to the mother, when I got up the next morning, "and told me she was dead and buried behind Carston Cliff and that some Jack Hazzard or other killed her."

"But you shouldn't have sent her away in the dead of night like that, good man," says the wife.

"I sent her to her bed," says I.

"She's never touched it," says the wife. "She's not in the house."

She was not; and none of us ever saw Ann Connor alive again. She had not been to her mother's; and they found her body jammed amongst the rocks at Carston Cliff next day. The loaf of bread, and the eggs, and the pat butter were in the grass. The basket was floating in the water below. They thought she'd fallen over the cliff at first; but the coroner's inquest showed she'd been murdered for the money she had with her, most likely; and the queerest part is to come. They found the man that did the thing, chiefly through marked money that my wife had paid the girl with, and a ring she had—a gold ring that her sweetheart, who had gone to sea, had given her; and the fellow's name was Jack Hazzard, and nothing else.

"It's not for me to say I saw Ann's ghost," said Mr. Gwill, in conclusion. "I'm bound to believe there's no such thing as a ghost, for better learnt people than I am say so. But what I did see that night is more than I can tell. If it weren't a ghost, what was it!"

*West Briton and Cornwall Advertiser.*

———◆———

# 1900 – BRIXTON GHOST'S TRICKS.

A contributor to the current number of *Light*, the organ of the psychologists, evidently anxious like the fat boy on Pickwick, to make all people's flesh creep, rakes up the ashes of the Brixton ghost.

That ghost, as was described recently, has been performing during the past six months at the sedate hostelry known as the Gresham Hotel, its chief indulgences being bell ringing all hours of the day and night, midnight billiards, and unauthorised interference with the gas lights in the house.

A week or two ago a séance was held, and the ghost on that occasion dropped a hammer or something of the kind down a flight of stairs. It must have been the ghost, for nobody but a ghost would be guilty of such facetious conduct while Spiritualists were holding a solemn investigation under the same roof.

The *Light* contributor clinches the matter by saying, "This affair, which has unfortunately got into the papers

too early, is undoubtedly the work of some supernormal agency."

"A séance," says the correspondent, "was held by Mrs. Brinckley, who gave her services. There were only two Spiritualists in a circle of nine. The conditions were naturally most difficult for any medium. However. Mrs Brinckley was soon "influenced," and made much ado about one who had dropped down dead in the house. A man died in the bar singing, "Those bells shall not ring out," some few months ago. This fact was absolutely unknown to the medium, who was a stranger to us and the district. In the various rooms into which we followed the medium, deaths were described, and she pointed out one particular window through which, she said, a coffin had been lowered. This was all subsequently verified."

But the ghost refused to come out of his lair, and the actual causes of the phenomena have still to be discovered, which is a distinct victory for that very elusive ghost.

*Sunderland Daily Echo & Shipping Gazette.*

———◆———

# 1900 – CHRISTMAS SPIRITS.

It seems somewhat of a paradox that Christmastide should be the special season when weird stories of ghostly horrors are most in request. But superstition and custom based on the traditional and legendary lore of the past must be considered in a great measure accountable for this peculiar feature of our Yuletide festival. In the early days of Christianity it would appear that the supernatural element was supposed to enter largely into the observance of Christmas; and, despite the fact that Shakespeare has alluded to an old belief that at this sacred time no spirit dare stir abroad, there can be no doubt that both the seen and unseen world, as well as the animal and vegetable creation, were thought to be compelled to do homage to the new born Christ.

Indeed, some have maintained that so blessed and beneficent is the present period that even ghosts, who are not permitted at other times to walk on earth, are now licensed to do so; although it must be confessed – judging from the many ghost tales issued at this time of the year – their visits are far from being always of the most happy or desirable kind. From the strange and uncanny stories told of haunted Christmases both in our own and other countries, it may be gathered that ghostly visitors take an ill-natured delight in their efforts to mar the pleasures of the family party, oftentimes by their eccentric movements and persistent presence raking up from the buried ashes of the past the dread memory of some deed of darkness – secretly committed, it may be, centuries ago – of which they were the ill-fated victims.

And thus, although the Yuletide log may burn cheerily on the hearth, the wassail bowl go merrily round, and the well-spread board resound with shouts of revelry and mirth, yet over all there hangs a cloud of fear, a sense of mystery, which says, as plain as a whisper in the ear the place is "haunted!"

Occasionally the skeleton plays a prominent part in stories of haunted Christmases, Suggesting by its grim demeanour Longfellow's well-known lines:-

> The stranger feasted at his board;
> But like the skeleton at the feast,
> That warning timepiece never ceased,
> "Forever-never!
> Never-forever!"

Hence, although years have passed after the unexplained disappearance of a certain family connection, the skeleton at length breaks the long silence, and tells its own tale.

A romantic and tragic story is related, for instance, of two skulls which have long haunted an old house near Ambleside. A small piece of ground, known as Calgrath, was owned by a farmer, Kraster Cook, and his wife Dorothy. But, their little inheritance was coveted by a wealthy Magistrate, Myles Phillipson, who, unable to induce them to sell it, brought a false charge of theft against them. Such an offence was then capital, and as Phillipson was the Magistrate, Kraster and Dorothy were sentenced to death. Before her death, however, Dorothy exclaimed. "While Calgrath walls shall stand, we'll haunt it night and day. Never will ye be rid of us!" Henceforth the Phillipsons had for their guests two skulls, which never failed at Christmastide to appear at the head of the staircase. Again and again they were buried, but to no purpose, for they persistently appeared at Christmas, while old Dorothy's weird imprecation went on to its fulfilment until the family sank into poverty and disappeared.

Many an old castle, also, with its historic romance, has its phantom skeleton. Instead of the silk-rustling of some "white lady," the uncanny rattling of bones has been heard at Christmastide, the apparition of an unavenged death.

But it is not always in the same way that these so-called "spirit-members" of the family intrude their presence on their relatives in the flesh, if we are to believe the host of tales illustrative of haunted Christmases which have been handed down. That terrible scare, the family ghost, which throws into a state of temporary panic the Christmas household, appears in a diversity of forms, as it visits the old homestead and catches a glimpse of the feasting and merrymaking, in which

it has no longer the power to participate. Thus, some years ago, a famous ghost made her Christmas serenade habited in black satin, with white kid gloves, while of others it may be said that they come at this season, "some in rags, and some in jags, and some in silken gowns" – according to the position they held in life. The ghosts which haunt Christmas generally contrive, however, to maintain the phantom grandeur of their earthly existence, hoping thereby, perhaps, to be more easily recognised.

Some ghosts of a more modest and retiring nature are content to remain unseen, intimating their arrival at Christmas by sundry sounds of a more or less creepy kind, each as a lengthened sigh, a deep sob, and other mysterious noises and rumblings, the exact whereabouts of which it is no easy matter to locate. On one occasion the miscreant ghost of some wicked person, as was generally supposed, startled the Christmas household by imitating the sound of dripping water; and on another, for some hours at intervals, by peals of laughter. But there can be no doubt that many of the unearthly noises heard in our old baronial halls might easily have been explained on natural grounds, the real culprits for disturbing the hilarity of Christmastide oftentimes being the rats and mice with their appetites sharpened at the savoury smell of Yuletide fare. And, as it has been frequently suggested, many a haunted Christmas in past years, especially in lonely and isolated houses on the coast, was produced by an illicit class of spirits, that is, through the agency of smugglers and other interested persons, in order to alarm and drive away all others but themselves and their accomplices from some particular house.

Stories of haunted Christmases – or supposed to be such – might easily be enumerated, which, under one form or another, have long been current, imparting a dramatic element to the festive observances of the season. At the same time, it is noteworthy that they have evidently considerable fascination for the majority of persons, if we are to rely on the prominence assigned to the sensational ghost tale in our hit Christmas annuals.

But it is on the Continent that due ghostly honour is done at Christmas, where the most extravagant and fanciful tales of every description are circulated at this season. Not only now are spirits supposed to walk the earth and mingle with mortals, but supernatural agencies to be actively at work. According to a pretty and rustic tradition in Russia, all sorts of hidden treasures are now revealed. And at midnight, on Christmas Eve the heavenly doors are thrown open, the new born divinity descends from heaven and wanders on earth, the radiant realms of Paradise in which the sun dwells disclose their treasures; the waters of springs and rivers become animated and receive a healing efficacy, and the trees put forth blossoms. Ideas of this kind, we are told, were common in Russia, and at the present day songs are still sung at Christmastide which embody the belief.

German folklore tells how the inhabitants of the fairy world play all kinds of mischievous pranks on Christmas night and a Swedish tale records how, as a lady was sitting in her mansion at this time, a loud noise was heard in the grounds adjoining it. A servant was despatched to ascertain the cause, when he found some of the fairy tribe dancing. A beautiful young lady stepped forth and presented him with a drinking horn and a pipe, which taking, he spurred his horse and returned to the mansion. Despite the threats if he did not return the pipe and horn; he delivered them to his mistress, and it is said they are still preserved at Linnby as memorials of this supernatural Christmas event. But the same legend adds that the servant died three days afterwards. Nor did the lady escape with impunity, for the mansion has been twice burnt, and the family have never prospered since that fatal Christmas day.

*Hampshire Telegraph.*

———❖———

# 1900 – FAMOUS GHOSTS IN THE CAPITAL.

Doubtless, if a chronicler can be found to unearth the reports from among old newspapers, countless stories could be told of alleged hauntings of the type which has lately been titillating West Kensington nerves, and giving the police a deal of extra point duty in Edith Walk. Nevertheless, the haunted houses in London which have achieved anything more than merely transitory and vulgar notice appear to be but few and far between; while of duly authenticated ghostly visitations the Metropolis boast practically nil. Of course, what is still the most famous London ghost story, the notorious Cock Lane affair of the last century, was a bogus spirit altogether.

### The Cock Lane Ghost.

Almost every one of us, young and old, has heard how cunning "Fanny," with her mysterious knockings, contrived to hoax wonder loving Londoners, until at length the cheat was discovered and its chief contriver brought to condign punishment. Dr. Johnson solemnly investigated the affair, sitting up through the night of February 7th, 1762, in the vault of St. John's Church, Clerkenwell; and Goldsmith wrote a pamphlet on the subject for which Newberry paid him three guineas. The whole was a plot, devised by one Parsons, the parish clerk of St. Sepulchre's, and carried out by his daughter, a girl of twelve, the object being to malign

a gentleman of Norfolk, who had sued him for debt. This gentleman was a widower, who had taken his wife's sister as a mistress (the marriage being forbidden by law), and had brought her to lodge with Parsons, from whom he had removed her to other lodgings, where she had died suddenly of smallpox. Parsons' object was to obtain the ghost's declaration that she had been poisoned by his (Parsons') creditor. The knave was subsequently tried and sentenced to the pillory and one year's imprisonment; but even after the exposure the London mob still believed in the Cock Lane ghost, and freely subscribed for a testimonial to its originator.

### The Tower Bear.

The Tower of London, which ought to be haunted if any place is, once boasted an awe inspiring spectre that assumed the shape of a bear. Before the burning of the armouries there was a paved yard in front the Jewel House, from which a gloomy ghostlike doorway led down a flight of stairs to the Mint. Strange noises used to be heard in this gloomy corner, and on a dark night in January, 1816, the sentry saw a figure like a bear cross the pavement and disappear down the steps. This so terrified him that he fell, and in a few hours, after having recovered sufficiently to tell the tale, he died. This unfortunate affair, which was fully investigated by an official inquiry, is believed to have arisen from phantasmagoria, and the Governor doubled the sentry and used such energetic precautions that no more ghosts haunted the Tower from that time. The soldier bore a high character for bravery and good conduct, and the affair created a considerable stir at the period.

### The Berkeley Square House.

The most famous modern example of how stories of this kind can be manufactured even in our day out of hearsay and third hand statements is that of the haunted house in Berkeley Square, which seems to have received its popularity and fame from being identified through some accidental circumstance as the scene of a similar story in Temple Bar for 1868 by Miss Broughton of a house in the country. The house in question belonged to an eccentric gentleman. He was in good circumstances, but chose to spend no money on it. For many years soap, paint, and whitewash were never used, and then by degrees began the most outrageous stories of servants and visitors going out of their minds after sleeping one night in one particular room, while some imaginative individual was so carried away with unwholesome excitement that he stated that the very party walls of the house, when touched, were found "saturated with electric horror!" That mysterious noises were heard at night by neighbours, thus giving rise to the apprehension that the house was being used by a gang of coiners, is probably true, for it subsequently appeared that the occupant's eccentricity took the form of wandering up and down the staircases and passages during the small hours. The lease had still six years to run when the unfortunate gentleman died, whereupon the action of his sister, to whom the property passed, in refusing either to let the house or live in it herself, caused the ghost stories concerning it be circulated more freely than ever. Finally this lady sold the lease, and on the house passing to a sceptical firm of house agents, the exterior and interior were put into a thorough state of repair. Tenants were then speedily forthcoming, and as these, needless to say, neither saw nor heard anything abnormal, the haunted reputation soon became a thing of the past.

The manner in which the series of outrageous spook stories had grown to be connected with it was very cleverly and indefatigably exposed by the correspondents of *Notes and Queries*. Only one point remained to be cleared up when the house was renovated —namely, whether it had possessed the reputation of being haunted before the eccentric gentleman's tenancy. Fortunately, the butler of the previous occupier was discovered, and he solemnly stated that during the years he had been in the house, often alone, and at all hours, he had "never seen any bigger ghost than himself." The moral, if any is, keep the exterior of your house in good repair, otherwise a ghost may be appropriated to you with as little show of evidence, authority, or justification as is the case of the so-called Berkeley Square mystery. The house was quite the London ghost sensation of the "seventies," though it is said a certain house in Sloan Street then possessed, and may still possess, a far more substantial horror, an apparition which could squeeze you as if in an iron vice.

### A Chelsea Apparition.

One of the first cases of a haunted house which the Society for Psychical Research was asked to investigate was in Chelsea, where an artist's studio was the scene of weird visitations. An apparition was seen by the artist in broad daylight, and appeared to him constantly during his three years' tenancy. The circumstances were such as to preclude all possibility of deception, and the figure itself was so distinct and lifelike that he succeeded in producing a portrait of it. A rough sketch of this portrait, which is now in possession of the Society, represents a young man about 25, with the right arm torn away from the shoulder, and a strangely mournful pleading expression in the eyes. The Society examined the house, and found its then tenant, who had replaced the artist, had seen nothing. It was discovered, however, that a distressing suicide had taken place in the house shortly after it had been built (and about 40 years before the date of the vision alleged have been seen by the artist), but it did not seem possible to connect this in

any way with the latter. And there the matter ended. This is the last *bona fide* case of a London haunted house which we have been able to trace. The West Kensington one reads spuriously, though the reputation had really originated in the tempting target which a long empty and derelict-looking house always offers to the stone throwing propensities of the small boys of the neighbourhood. Nevertheless, it is only fair to add that, according to some accounts, this unfortunate villa has suffered its uncanny distinction for 16 years past.

*Sunderland Daily Echo & Shipping Gazette.*

———◦◦◦———

## 1900 – HAMPSON'S GHOST.

We sat in a cosy corner of the Journalists club room, and yawned over our pipes. Hampson had contented himself with listening only, which was strange. Generally speaking, he is quite picturesque in his reminiscences. As he sat puffing at a long clay pipe an amused smile came over his features, and, looking up, he asked:-

"Ever heard of the ghost hunt I had when I was on the *Blankshire Express*?"

We hastily disavowed all knowledge of the event, and begged he would relate the episode, each of us, I believe, registering the mental proviso that to listen to was not to accept. We knew Hampson!

"You must understand," he prefaced, drawing a little nearer the fire, "that what I have to tell you is not anything in the way of a yarn; it is merely an incident. Still, it has the merit of truth."

"Hampson," exclaimed Lonsdale, "you will greatly oblige us if you will stow that and get to the yarn." Hampson laughed, and related as follows:-

At that time I was chief reporter on the *Blankshire Express*. One night—it was in the late autumn, I think—I had been doing an election meeting, and when it was over I returned to the office to write up ready for the next day's paper. We published weekly. There was nobody but myself in the building, which was, for a newspaper office, exceptionally large and roomy.

I had been writing some time when I heard footsteps in the composing room, which was directly overhead. Imagining it was the tread of Lomax, the chief compositor, I started upstairs with the intention of handing him the first portion of my copy; so that he might have it in readiness for his men on the following morning. Opening the door at the top of the stairs I entered the room, exclaiming, "Working late, Mr Lomax? Here's the first___" I got no further with my remarks, for I perceived that I was alone in the moonlit room.

Somewhat mystified I went back to my work, fully convinced that I had really heard footsteps, and that it was no freak of disordered imagination. Two or three minutes I worked on uninterrupted, and then once more I heard the steady pat, pat, pat overhead.

I began to feel a bit shaky, but throwing off the feeling I went up the stairs and carefully looked around the room—it was certainly unoccupied. I called out, "Who's there?" in as loud a voice as I could command, but the reverberation of my own exclamation was the only sound I heard.

The thing was growing uncanny, I admit that, unbeliever though I was, I almost decided to funk the business and complete my work at my diggings. However, I went downstairs again, and, feeling a little more composed, started writing, hoping to finish without further disturbance. Vain hope! Scarcely had I put pen to paper than the measured tread recommenced overhead.

It was just at that moment the memory returned to me of a story which had been told me when I first joined the staff of the *Express* of a mad compositor who had hanged himself in the room above, and whose ghostly form was, it was averred, accustomed to sit all night setting up ghostly type with melancholy monotony.

Pat, pat, pat came the echo from above. I sat back in my chair and absolutely trembled.

A few moments I sat inert, terrified, and then I pulled myself together, and vowing silently that neither ghost nor spook should best me, unlocked my drawer, and took out a revolver. It was loaded in one of its chambers.

Thus armed I started up with the intention of searching the whole building before I would give in. As I passed out of the room I noticed that an old file of the *Express* lay open on a desk by the door. Something impelled me to glance at it, and as I did so a thrill of horror struck through me as I noticed right before my eyes the account of the making of the ghost I was seeking to lay. Could this merely be coincidence?

Every nerve in my body was sharp set as I started up the stairs and entered the silent composing room, which was dimly lighted by the pale moonlight. I advanced a few steps and peered into the gloomy shadows thrown by the compositors' frames.

Bang! I started; a shiver ran down my back, but I had only been startled by the door behind me banging to, and satisfied there was no one but myself in the room I went across it, down into the printing room, and into the machine room, searching every nook and corner, but nowhere could I find sign of natural or supernatural visitor.

Once more I moved forward in my quest, through the dark basement and the publishing department, around the offices and upstairs again to my own room. After all it was only morbid fancy. I was, as I had been convinced, alone in the place, and having settled that to satisfaction, I prepared to depart. I put on my hat, took down my coat, when—tap, tap, tap, I distinctly heard in the room above.

I was decidedly annoyed, and grasping my revolver I rushed upstairs, and banging into the haunted room gazed intently around me.

By this time the moon had waned considerably, and only a faint, eerie light came through the skylights.

As I looked into one comer of the room I gasped, for there I beheld a long, white, ghastly form, which, as I looked upon it, moved slightly. Were such things as ghosts and spirits realities then?

No; it was impossible. I thrust the thought from me. Someone was playing tricks upon me. And so, in the sternest tones I could muster, I called, "I am covering you with a loaded revolver. I shall give you until I count to three to step out of there. If you do not come, I shall then fire."

"One."

No reply.

"Two."

Still no movement.

"Three."

I hesitated an instant, and then fired. As I did so the ghost fell with a curious clatter—to my disordered mind it seemed like the collapse of a skeleton—to the floor.

I stepped forward, and saw to my chagrin, that the ghost I had laid was a big, white apron which one of the compositors had left hanging beside his case.

A great bare patch on the wall showed me that, beside the ghost, I had succeeded in "laying" a large amount of plaster.

"But, man," disgustedly exclaimed Hayward, as Hampson ceased speaking, "what about the footsteps? How do you explain them?"

"Well, old chap," replied the veracious Hampson, "of course it takes a lot of shine out of the yarn; but really, the solution of that part of the business was equally commonplace. It was this way—a new roof ventilator, which worked with a silk flap escapement, had been fixed in the room above to me. As the air escaped from the room the silk flap rose and fell, and its being now caused the tapping sound which I had mistaken for footsteps." And Hampson yawned.

Lonsdale mumbled something as he gazed meditatively into the fire, and I caught the words:-

"And it's a true story. Shades Ananias!" Then Lonsdale looked and turning to Hayward and me, said dryly, "Say, you fellows, let's start a Liars' League, and make Hampson President!"

*Shields Daily News.*

# 1900 – HAUNTED APPLE TREE.

"It is probable that to the town of Douglass, Mass, alone belongs the reputation of having a haunted apple tree," writes Samuel S. Kingdon, in "*The Ladies' Home Journal*." "The tradition of the town is that a foul murder was committed in the orchard many years ago, and that since then it has been haunted by the spirit of the victim. As the story goes, a peddler, whose custom it was to sell goods from house to house from a pack, lay down to rest at midday under a tree in the orchard, and before the day was ended he was found with a cruel gash in the neck from which his lifeblood had ebbed away.

Suspicion rested on the owner of the orchard, and he was said to have been constantly followed by the spirit of the victim. In an attempt to escape from its dreadful presence he moved away. Then the apparition became a terror to all who had occasion to pass over the road at night. So potent was its influence —standing, as it had a habit of doing, under the apple tree, with one hand at its throat and the other extended as though seeking aid, and uttering shrill cries that could be heard half a mile away—that the location of the highway was changed and it is now a long distance from the orchard.

The old trees still bear fruit, and the apples from the one beneath which the peddler was killed are said to be streaked with red, resembling blood, the streaks extending from skin to core."

*Cork Examiner.*

———◦◉◦———

# 1900 – HAUNTED RAILWAY ENGINES.

There are, on nearly every railway, locomotives that are known as "Jonahs". Some years ago an engine on a Scotch line blew up, cutting the stoker's head off with a segment of boiler iron. The engine was rebuilt and made as good as new, but no driver could be found to run it more than one trip. It was soon whispered about that it was haunted; that the headless stoker had an unpleasant habit of appearing on the tender and insisting on firing up. One night a driver and his stoker deserted the locomotive when out on a run. For a month the engine lay in the shop. Then a driver who was compelled either to take it out or lose his place, mounted it. Before it had run a dozen miles it went through a culvert, wrecked the train, and killed nine people. It was never rebuilt.

*Forfar Herald.*

———◦◉◦———

# 1900 – HAUNTS OF GHOSTS.

Thanks, perhaps, to the labours of the Society for Psychical Research, there has of late been quite a marked revival of interest in supernatural affairs, and especially in ghost stories. The majority of these so-called supernatural disturbances are, of course, capable of some simple and oftentimes amusing explanations, though there are others which have never been satisfactorily cleared up. Scattered about, up and down Great Britain, there are many ivy-covered old halls and castles about which weird tales are told; where at the midnight hour strange sights and sounds are said to be seen and heard, the rattling of chains, and the wailing of perturbed spirits – perhaps revisiting the scene of some foul crime committed in days gone by.

Ghost-lore flourishes with peculiar strength among the ancestral halls of Scotland; but of all its haunted dwellings none seem more troubled than the glorious old Castle of Glammis, the ancient Forfarshire home of the Lyons family. Here, according to tradition, Duncan was done to death by Macbeth; and many another blood curdling tale is told of the historic old pile – the knocking and hammering of spectral carpenters; ghastly faces which look in at the windows; horrible shrieks which rend the midnight air; and a ghostly man in armour who patrols at night as if to guard the secret chamber, which is supposed to be hidden somewhere in the ancient part of the Castle, where this gentleman delights to wander. This haunted room, about which so much has been written and so little is known, is supposed to contain some terrible secret which is very jealously guarded by the family. It seems, however, tolerably certain that there is a secret concealed somewhere within the depths of the old Castle which is known only to three persons – the Earl of Strathmore for the time being, the heir apparent, and one other individual whom they think worthy of their confidence. Thus is the mystery handed down from Strathmore to Strathmore. Various wild tales are, of course, told concerning this ominous chamber; but even its locality is unknown save to the three, and access to it is said to be cut off by a stone wall.

"There is no doubt about the reality of the noises at Glammis Castle," writes a correspondent of Dr. Lee. "On one occasion, some years ago the head of the family, with several companions, determined to investigate the cause. One night, when the disturbance was greater and more violent and alarming than usual – and, it should be premised, strange, weird, and unearthly sounds had often been heard, and by many persons, some quite unacquainted with the ill-repute of the Castle – his Lordship went to the haunted room, opened the door with a key, and dropped back in a dead swoon into the arms of his companions; nor could he ever be induced to open his lips on the subject afterwards."

There is a local tradition which might explain the horrible sight his Lordship is supposed to have seen. In the olden time a party of the Ogilvies, flying from their enemies the Lindsays, begged shelter from the Lord of Glammis, which was granted; but, under the plea of hiding them, he secured them in the ever-afterwards haunted chamber and left them to starve; and there, it is averred, their bones lie to this day.

Another version of the mystery is that the beautiful and unfortunate Lady Janet (the widow of the sixth Lord), who was burned as a witch on Castle Hill in 1537, was in league with the Evil One, and that her familiar demon, an embodied and visible fiend, endures to this day, shut from light in the mysterious chamber of Glammis Castle!

An altogether different tale, given by Howitt, is re-told by Ingram. The famous "Earl Beardie," popularly known as "the wicked Laird," was playing at cards in the Castle. Being warned to give over, on account of his heavy losses, he swore an oath that he would play until the Day of Judgment, whereupon the Devil suddenly appeared and took charge of old "Beardie" and all his company, who were never seen again. Nor has the room been discovered; but many people firmly believe that old "Beardie" and his company are still playing on, and will continue to play until the end of time, and that on stormy nights the players are heard stamping and swearing with rage over their play.

Instances of supernatural warnings are by no means uncommon in the history of ancient castles and halls. Such a tale, and a very terrible one, is told of the ruined Castle of Berry Pomeroy, in Devonshire. Whenever death was about to visit the inmates of the Castle, the spectre of a lady, richly dressed, and wringing her hands as if in the deepest distress, was seen to wend her way towards a certain apartment. Here, it is said, the daughter of some former Baron of Berry Pomeroy had strangled her own child.

Another tale of a supernatural warning is told in connection with Netley Abbey, the lovely ruins of which lie some eight miles from Southampton. In 1704 Sir Bartlet Lucy sold the materials of the Abbey to a carpenter, of whose death Browne Willis, and others after him, have left us the following account. While the purchaser was treating with Sir Bartlet about the Abbey business, he was much terrified and frequently haunted in his sleep by the phantom of a monk, who foretold some great evil would certainly happen to him if he proceeded with the transaction, One night he dreamed that a large stone fell from one of the windows and killed him. A friend to whom he related all this advised him to drop the undertaking, but, others advising him not to lose such a profitable job, he struck the bargain.

However, it proved fatal to him, for, as he was endeavouring to take some stones out of the bottom of the west wall, not a single stone only, but the whole of the window fell down upon him, killing him on the spot.
*Hampshire Telegraph.*

---

# 1900 – HAVE YOU SEEN THE GHOST?

Having heard so much about the Blairgowrie ghost, we thought it might be a rare opportunity for testing the abilities of our new Demonology Man, so gave him orders to take the first train to Blair, and run the bogey to earth. He is a first class expert in this line of business, this D.M. Of that we have had repeated assurances from himself, and no one should know better, of course. He is the possessor, also, of a first class certificate from either the Psychical Research Society or the Ghost of Ballechin, the staff has never been quite sure which, and is understood to have taken a leading part with Miss X., Mr. M___, Lord B___ , and the other psychological celebrities in that famous investigation.

Whether ghost, or ghost hunter, has always been a moot point; but that is a detail. It is quite clear, at any rate, that he was just the man to lay the ghost which had been troubling decent people in Blairgowrie this sometime back, or to perish in the attempt. He returned last night in a very exhausted condition. His nerves, in fact, seems to have been completely shattered by his terrible experience. So bad was he, the porters had to carry him from the train to a cab, into which he was bundled rather unceremoniously (he is to make a case of this, we understand; he declares they did the same thing on the last occasion), taken home, and put to bed not, however, it may be mentioned, with his boots on, which he was for insisting upon with considerable vehemence for a while. To attempt interviewing the poor fellow then was, of course, out of the question. It might have proved fatal to one of such a highly strung temperament. Besides, it was of no manner of use, for we tried it. All we could get out of the beggar was some disjointed scraps of rhyme, which, when pieced together, seemed to run as follows:-

The spirits o' Blair, the spirits o' Blair,
They're everywhere, in street and square!
Ye're hardly oot in the open air
But ye're nabbed and grabbed,
Bamboozled and tousled,
By the terrible, horrible spirits o' Blair!

We are not sure "horrible" is the right word here; it sounded rather more sulphurous. It shows, however, what a sensitive soul this fellow must be. This morning, it was gratifying to note, the demonology man was much better; except for a splitting headache, he explained, he could have got up. He was always the same after these spirituous experiences. He was prevailed upon, with remarkably little trouble, however, to remain where he was, and give the following narrative:—

The first thing I did on landing at Blair Station was to put the momentous question to one of the porters, "Have you seen the ghost?"

"Which ghost?'" asked he.

"The Blair ghost, you fool," said I, in my politest tones.

"Fool yourself," replied he, quite rude; "there are at least 27 ghosts going about here just now."

"Great Scot!" exclaimed I, "you say so? What luck! Could you put me on the track of any of them? I should like to bag, say, half a dozen before the last train."

"Where's your bag?"

"Oh, well, I've a bottle here," said I; "but it's full just now."

"A' the better o' that," said he, with great gusto, and the cork was drawn.

After that he explained that he was one of the ghosts himself—the Welton Road one, where two ploughmen had nearly fainted one evening at dusk as they came suddenly upon him at the unloading bank. Perhaps it was his white, newly-washed face they saw gleaming in the dim light; anyhow, they got a fright, and had the "ghost" for little badly.

The next to come into line was the Ardblair ghost, and this was a very important fellow. A farmer, driving home last market night, was near Ardblair when the object of terror sprang up beside his pony's head, and gave the animal such a fright that it bolted, the farmer said, never slackening rein until was well past the Sprot. The ghost appeared to be only partly clad in white. The following evening a similar figure suddenly appeared from a raspberry field amongst some boys, who were concluding a game of football on the public park. The same night a gentleman driving towards Blairgowrie, on the Coupar Angus Road, is said to have been met by the apparition, who, or which, when asked his place of abode, indicated in sepulchral tones the nether regions. It is not certain that the gentleman in question did not tell him to go there, but it is said that he helped that direction by applying his whip vigorously round the demon's ears—or horns, and there was an end of him for the time.

A few hours later —about 1 a.m.—when it was very dark, a gentleman who had to walk from Rosemount to Blairgowrie saw two very strange lights in the middle of the road in front of him. They were yet a considerable distance off, but appeared too low for vehicles or bicycles, and too steady for either, or to be carried by hand; besides, the roads were too bad for bicycles, not to speak of the late hour, and there was no noise which could account for the mysterious lights. The mystery, however, was solved on coming up to them and discovering they were attached low down to two furniture lorries which were "flitting" someone.

A little further on there was noticed next a ghostly shimmer light on the opposite—Altamont—side of the road, which could not be accounted for at all for a while, there being no house or other likely cause. On turning the road, however, the brilliant lamp at the end of Emma Street, at the entrance to the town, and which cast its rays far along one side of the road, while the other was left in complete shadow, explained the phenomenon. As the gentleman referred to had not heard of the "ghost" at this time, he had no occasion to feel nervous.

Before giving what appears to be the real solution of the whole business, the other "appearances" may be enumerated. The most notable was on the Oakbank Road, which is decidedly "eerie" at parts owing to the overhanging trees from the brae, on the top of which may be seen sharply outlined against the sky the striking spire of the Parish Church, with the auld kirkyard its foot.

One night recently, there seems little doubt, a woman was coming down the road, when "something" suddenly came up to her, and for a while kept pace with her without speaking. The woman, although terrified, made some remark about the weather, but, without deigning reply, the figure suddenly disappeared up the Cuttle Burn, where there is a deep ravine leading to Burnhead Road. Then there is also the appearances on the Haugh Road, Coupar Angus, Alyth, Newtyle, Meigle, Kirkmichael, and there is no saying where else. At Meigle "it is said'," that a girl who went to draw a blind was startled by seeing a ghostly figure with phosphorescent face gliding past the window, so that she had to go to bed; and there was even a rumour that she had since died, which needs confirming.

It seems to be quite settled now as an article of public belief that the ghost is a young man who, for a wager of £1,000, has undertaken to scare the whole of Perthshire undetected. Whence the story has originated it would be very difficult to say. If, however, other flotations are true, the £1,000, even if he won it, will have been discounted considerably before the end by the liberal bribes he is said to have been forced to give in order to free himself after having been captured. For captured, repeatedly, the public will have him; Coupar Argus is, where he had to give £10 to a ploughman; at Newtyle, where he was mulcted in £20; at Alyth—fine unknown; and, only on Tuesday night, at Kirkmichael, where he got off once more—for what amount of rumour saith not.

To explain the whole affair; some young men have been out recently at nights running as "harriers." On the market night when the farmer was returning home, it is a fact that two of the "harriers"—one dressed in a white shirt—came up suddenly upon the dogcart, and undoubtedly frightened the horse. The farmer struck the disappearing figure with his whip, and the young fellow thought, not unnaturally, that this was because of the fright he had given the horse. His amazement was equalled only by his amusement, however, when he learned be had been taken for a "ghost!" He had a companion with him in black, which is probably why he was not detected at the time.

The other mysterious appearances in the district are all attributable to the same cause. In many cases, however, there have been none whatever; simple imagination being the only ghostly thing about it.

It is very amusing to hear the other "ghost" stories which this scare has evoked. One of them relates to another scare which spread over the district a number of years ago. Just then one of the inmates of Murthly Asylum had escaped, and was supposed to be in hiding in the vicinity of Blairgowrie. It happened that, about the November term, a ploughman was loading a lorry with furniture not far from the Dunkeld Road, and was getting near ten o'clock—"closing time"—and loading furniture, even on a dark November night, is such dry job. Anyhow, our friend felt thirsty, and as time was precious he made a bee-line, as near as might be, across the fields, for the Stormont lnn. Wearing, as he did, a white shirt, several people who happened to see him scudding along under full sail for the closing "pub." jumped to the conclusion that this was the escaped lunatic everybody was after. Why they did not follow him up history explaineth not. There were others who met the individual, however, knew who he was, knew also his errand – sympathised with and joined in it; for when the police were set on the track of the "escaped lunatic," they were compelled, somewhat reluctantly doubtless, to admit the force of the evidence which was brought to bear on the identity of the individual in question.

Another story is of a more gruesome character, but quite true. It dates back a considerable number of years but it is vouched for by a pleasant spoken Irish woman staying at Oakbank, who has her own ideas regarding the present "ghost scare." It seems that she and a companion were visiting Murthly Castle —the "new" one and were being shown round that wonderful edifice, which was then in a much better state of preservation than now, when they came to a door which was closed. On turning the handle and pushing the door open, the girls' horror may be imagined when it is stated that a "strong and active" skeleton suddenly sprang out and clasped her firmly in its grisly arms! The efforts of the girl to free herself were in vain till someone else came on the scene, and operated on a spring which caused the bony bogey to loosen his hold. The girl was in a dead faint by this time, and it was many weeks before she quite recovered from the shock. So far as could be learned, this skeleton is still about Murthly, but most probably at the old Castle. It is supposed to have been brought from abroad.

And the last word regarding the Blairgowrie Ghost is "Requiescat in pace," which, being translated, means there "never was no such thing!"

*Dundee Evening Telegraph.*

———•◦•———

# 1900 – LEGENDS OF THE SKULLS.

Legends of haunting skulls abound, and they are necessarily droll, more or less. Indeed, the public did not take them quite seriously even in "the Ages of Faith." One of the best authenticated has its scene at Tunstead, in Derbyshire. There is the evidence of an eyewitness that the skull lay upon the window sill of a farmhouse there so late as 1807, and this witness, the respectable author of "A Tour Through the High Peak," reports that it had certainly lain there for 200 years. Many times had it been removed, and, once at least it had been buried in the churchyard, but such tremendous manifestations ensued that the farmer dug it up by stealth and replaced it on the window sill. An object of which these uncanny tales were current should be regarded with awe. But the neighbours called it "Dicky" or "Dicky of Tunstead," as they do in this unbelieving age.

A skull with a like story is kept at Bettiscombe, near Bridport, called the "screamer." This case is worth the attention of the Psychical Research philosophers, for we have read that Dr. Richard Garnett, of the British Museum, found the skull *in situ*, as one may say, as late as 1883. It stood upon the step of a winding staircase leading to the roof, and the farmer's wife declared that it had been there "for ages" – certainly it was very old and weather beaten. Dr. Garnett recognised the Negro type at a glance, and the woman, much impressed, told her story. At an unknown date a Roman Catholic priest lodged at the farm with a Negro servant, whom he murdered, because the man threatened to reveal certain secrets.

Then there is the grand example at Burton Agnes, seat of the Boynton family in the East Riding, where the skull of a lady reposes in a box upon a table in the

old hall—so at least it is reported in the neighbourhood books. But people persist in calling it "Awd Nance."
*Evening Standard.*

# 1900 – OUR HAUNTED SUBURBS.

Locbee has during the past week been extremely quiet at nights. The suburbanites retire early o' nights, and the quiet, secluded promenades on the Birkie Road are as deserted as the Sahara, save for the occasional tread of the policeman going his round. And all this has been caused by the cantrips of one who apparently recognises not the sway of poor mortal beings.

Despite the precautions taken by the Lochee people to keep clear of the path of the nocturnal prowler, there are one or two persons in the suburb who boast (when they are safe at the fireside) of having a nodding acquaintanceship with the dread visitor.

It was only the other night that a young maid of some twenty winters was tripping merrily along Perrie Street bent on some domestic errand. When some distance along the thoroughfare she came to an abrupt standstill. In front of her stood an awful vision, dressed in white. (Notice how exactly the descriptions the habiliments of the visitor coincide). His hat was ablaze with light, and, as the breeze blew the folds of his garments aside, it disclosed vestments of a flaming red. The visitor may have appeared for the amicable purpose of presenting the compliments of the season to the fair maid, but she apparently would not hear them. Uttering a piercing shriek, she fled down the street, and into the house of a friend.

The further movements of the apparition that night cannot be traced with accuracy, but the following story embraces a theory:- A certain young worthy, whom we shall call "Brannigan," is employed as message boy to a baker, and one dark night he was sent on an errand with a heavy basket. The road was dark and dreary, and Brannigan armed himself with a small lantern. Along the road he went, whistling with all his might and main a few bars of the "Lass of Killiecrankie," just to keep his spirits up.

Now, it so happened that there was coming along the road a youth employed on a farm in the vicinity, and who, as the day had been very wet, had a sack over his head, with the body of it hanging down his back like a cloak. Soon the two representatives of the rising generation met on the narrow pathway. The farmer lad looked at Brannigan, and Brannigan, with terror-struck face and lantern in his hand stood

gazing at his visitor. For some minutes both stood staring at one another, and then the humour of the situation struck the bucolic youth, and he ejaculated "Boo!"

This was too much for the baker boy. Dropping his basket and lantern, he ran down the road calling for help and mercy.

From Lochee to Downfield is not a far cry, and a well-equipped spring-heeled Jack could readily cover the distance of an evening. At any rate, the people have had a taste of the thrilling sensations experienced by the dwellers of the "dark suburb" for the past fortnight.

Last night, just when most people were thinking of retiring to rest, the hue and cry was raised in the northern part of the village that his ghostship had appeared, and was holding high jinks in a field in the vicinity of the Downfield tennis courts.

The apparition was seen by quite a number of people, and is described as being of the phosphorescent kind – a fact which points to his being either the Lochee ghost himself or a twin brother.

After the first sensations had subsided, the affrighted inhabitants held a council of war, and a strong force of stalwarts was speedily organised, armed with sticks and bludgeons, to hunt down the nocturnal visitant.

The pursuers had no difficulty in locating his whereabouts, but as they advanced across the field he showed his "slimness" by vanishing into the Camperdown Woods.

Needless to say, the appearance of the ghost has created something like a reign of terror among more timid residents, and the "'stalwarts' ' vow that the hunt will be made hotter for him if he should again honour the village with a visit.

While the "ghost" has been advertising himself throughout Perthshire and Lochee, Arbroath had, up to last night, been exempt from such visitations. The men in blue had apparently been making matters just a little too hot for his liking in Lochee, and, having raised a hornets' nest about his ear, he decided to seek fresh fields and pastures new. The good folks of Arbroath are not just what you would call timid, but the town had apparently taken the ghost's fancy, and last night revealed himself in all his ghostly array on the High Common.

Ranged along the top of the common are a number of seats, and about nine o'clock last night seated on the farthest seat were a youth and a maiden. Chancing to look round, the girl was horrified to see what she took to be the head of a man peering over the wall, and with a shriek, she rushed along the footpath. Her unusual conduct had apparently startled her knight, who made off as fast as he could after her. Once when he ventured to look behind him, there stood the ghost—a tall figure, clad in white, waving its arms. Fear lent speed to the lovers' flight, who, on meeting others, told them what had occurred.

On arriving in town, the story of the appearance of the ghost was told, and shortly after eleven o'clock a number of young men, armed with sticks, proceeded to the Common prepared to give him a warm reception should he appear before them; but though they waited long and patiently, nothing rewarded their search.

*Dundee Evening Post.*

---

# 1900 – PEPPER'S GHOST.

The once familiar phrase, "Pepper's Ghost," has got a new meaning, for Professor Pepper has just died. But indeed it is to be feared that to the rising generation Pepper's Ghost has little meaning, for the ghost was virtually dead before the professor who created it. Yet the ghost is little more than thirty years born from the teeming brain of Professor Pepper, and for a ghost such a term of years is commonly regarded as toothless infancy. People of thirty years and upwards well remember what a sensation Pepper's Ghost created at his first appearance at the Panopticon in Leicester Square; how people quivered with excitement at the mysterious exits and entrances, and how the rival attractions of the diving bell in a tank and the electric eel instantly yielded to the ghost.

Presently the entire Three Kingdoms were haunted by Professor Pepper's scientific spectre. Blood-curdling five act tragedies of "The Haunted House," "Murder Will Out," and "Sold to the Devil" were built round the ghost, as someone describes a cannon as a long steel tube built round a hole. Ghost stories were no longer legendary and second hand; you could see one any night at any price from sixpence to five shillings, according to your place in the theatre, with all the most blood-curdling attributes. There was no deception about the ghosts Professor Pepper introduced to the public. They held all the trademarks of the genuine article. They vanished into thin air and emerged from it. They floated and sank like goldfish in a bowl. They made their exit through the wall or the roof or the floor with equal ease. Like spirits of another kind, they readily blended with each other, completely changing their identity. No wonder the public, old and young, were half mad with the new wonder.

Yet it was an old wonder after all. People had seen ghosts of the same family long before Professor Pepper appropriated them by Royal Letters Patents, Whenever you look through the window of a lighted room into the blackness of the night you see a "Pepper's Ghost" of fire and candle blazing cheerily in empty space. In the tramcar and the railway carriages there are Pepper's ghosts of trees, houses, and traffic, and the mingling of the shadows and the substance is infinitely bewildering. But Professor Pepper first taught the spirits to come when he called them. He made them obedient to command and from his unsubstantial troupe he reaped a substantial reward. For patented ghosts are a profitable commodity. To borrow a slang phrase, at all his performances in town and country, "the ghost walked." Time out of mind it has been the function of ghosts of all ages and sexes, down to our diminutive Irish Leprechaun, to find buried treasures for their fortunate masters.

But Peppers ghosts' excelled in the art. It was not ghosts merely, the Professor raised, but the wind as well. He used his patents as freely as Aladdin used his lamp to keep them going. Those unfortunate apparitions were as hard worked as the trained dog in the circus. They had to learn new tricks every day. They had to learn to shift from one form to another, to show their body without their head or their head without their body. All modern illusions are but the perfected performances of the highly-trained ghost of Professor Pepper. He was the first that held the mirror up to magic, and all the modern magicians have profited by his example.

*Freeman's Journal.*

---

# 1900 – THE AGE OF SUPERSTITION.

Evidently the age of superstition is not dead yet in England. Education, and the failure of a well-behaved ghost to appear before sceptical mortals, have not made people less ready to believe in these apparitions. Thousands of people journey nightly to a south London suburban road in the hope of seeing a real ghost, of which they have heard various reports. It is only said to have been seen by one person, and that individual has not been seen or heard of since, but the vehicles are crowded each night by people journeying to extend welcome to the "spirit," evidently thinking that the unearthly shadow will be tempted to give a gratuitous performance for their edification in order to receive the applause of the admiring multitude. As the publicans are doing a brisk trade some malicious person has set it about that one of them invented the ghost for trade purposes.

*Taunton Courier and Western Advertiser.*

———◦◉◦———

# 1900 – THE KENSINGTON "GHOST."

The recurring reports of the appearance of a "ghost" in a house at Edith Villas, West Kensington, caused an extraordinary amount of excitement in the neighbourhood. One night at least 1,500 people were assembled in the vicinity of the house, closely watching the window at which the spectre is alleged to have appeared, and, despite the efforts of the police, the crowd increased rapidly, until the street became entirely congested. A force of twenty constables was required for the protection of the "haunted" house, the outside wall of which has been torn down, and bricks from the debris thrown through the whole of the windows. The "ghost" is alleged to have been seen twice this week by returning visitors to the Exhibition, and the apparition is described as resembling a death's head appearing indistinctly in the aperture of a narrow window.

*Lakes Chronicle and Reporter.*

———◦◉◦———

# 1900 – THE VAGARIES OF A GHOST.

Harry Smith and his wife have moved from the Foy homestead, in Church Street, Mount Holly, New Jersey. They say they were forced to move because a ghost objected to their presence in the house. They tell a weird story of their experience. Dish rattling was one the accomplishments of the ghost and, according to the Smiths, their crockery was kept on the jump night after night in the efforts of the ghost to furnish music for his amusement and the terror of the family. Night after night, and occasionally while the sun was shining, the dishes would commence their rattling. Apparently it was a muscular ghost, for in some cases dishes while piled in the closet would have chips broken out of them.

The spirit, according to the Smiths, did not like pictures, and frequently they would be dislodged and come crashing down to the floor. Strong wire and cord added not to their security. The Smiths are confident that six-inch steel cable would not have held their pictures upon the walls of that house. Doors opened and shut

without visible cause. The ghost liked noise, for when he had occasion to pass through the house he would bang the doors as hard as he could. And he passed at will through walls brick and stone, plaster and laths. Anyone who would have the hardihood to tell Mrs. Smith there is no such thing as a ghost would be politely told he did not know what he was talking about. Did she not wake up one night at an hour when ghosts are supposed to be abroad and see the ghost "weeping good hard weeps" at the foot her bed?

Mr. Smith is equally positive, although he never saw the apparition. He says he heard it, and that was enough for him. A child who saw the ghost in the cellar spoke to it. Instead of responding it went through the solid wall of the cellar. The Smiths say the ghost has played more pranks in one night than they could tell of in a week by talking in relays.

Their tale is not the first told of the ghost. He has been around the Foy homestead for a long time, if the stories of the neighbourhood are true. He is a bold fellow, too, for a year or so ago he got tired of the solitude of the then empty house, wandered into the yard to seek human companionship, and made himself visible to pedestrians passing along Church Street. Timid persons hurry past the house after nightfall.

*Cheltenham Chronicle.*

———◦◉◦———

# 1900 – UNEARTHLY NOISES.

A superstitious belief in ghosts has been dissipated from the imagination of a number of Guildford people in a very prosaic fashion. During the last few months stories of spectral visitants and unearthly noises have been connected with an unoccupied house off the road known as the Hogsback. The police began to watch patiently at night in the neighbourhood. At last one of the supposed ghosts emerged—with a feather bed on his back. The rest was soon cleared up. The house was merely in the process of being steadily robbed of all its furniture. Four persons—William Smithers and his wife, Thomas Brown, and William Glue—are now awaiting trial for being concerned in the robbery.

*Mail.*

———◦◉◦———

# 1900 – WAYS OF GHOSTS.

Hundreds of ghosts which are being annually brought to light in the dragnets of scientific spook catchers conform to no general rules as to appearance or behaviour. Ghost land must, in truth, be a realm of spicy variety and absolute independence. A well-known psychic researcher has lately permitted access to his voluminous records of 1,000 or more of the most vivid phantoms experienced here and abroad within the last ten years. Among their number are the most respectable and best authenticated shades haunting our sphere during this *fin de secole* decade.

Grey, rather than black or white, appears to the prevailing colour worn by these latter day ghosts. Two houses, one in England and the other in Ireland, are persistently haunted by what are called "grey ladies." The Irish spook of this category recently stood in front of a bust of Shakespeare, hidden by her form. A pair of shoes, thrown at her opaque substance, penetrated it completely and crashed against the marble bust. A third grey ghost, haunting the ancient dormitory of an English College, is, on the other hand transparent. The panels of windows can be seen through its form. A fourth grey ghost appears as a shadow, singularly distinct, and showing all of the lines and features of a human being. Still another spook, that of Colonel Av-Meinander, seen in St. Petersburg, is a grey shadow. In fact, there are too many grey ghosts for enumeration.

The "sheeted dead" appear to be in a small minority nowadays. Even black ghosts seem to outnumber them. The black shade of an ancient clergyman often seen in daylight upon an English country road, sometimes wears a white film of vapour enveloping his sable raiment. The phantom of another clergyman, seen in church, is described as "a black, clear mist, with the outline of a man." That of "a little old woman in brown" has long haunted the front yard of a certain cottage, while that of "an old lady in green" bothers a minister of the Gospel.

Many ghosts are peculiarly luminous. One is especially so when the moon shines on it. Blue lights have been often seen after dark along the country haunts of a daylight ghost of black hue. Blue light surrounded also the ghost of a dead parent who came to inform his daughter that she had lost a favourite aunt. The spook of a dead friend appearing to another woman illuminated her apartment at night until it was as bright as day.

Haunted people experience various sensations while touching ghosts. The rough clothing of an invisible spook is felt to brush against the skin of a young woman. Another spectre had an icy hand when grasped by a terrified woman. One woman on going upstairs at night saw a tall man directly in front of her. Recognising him as a dear friend, she reached out to touch him, but her hand simply penetrated a space. Later she received word from India that this friend had died on the date of the experience. Another woman who seized a ghost in her room says that it felt "soft, like flimsy drapery," and seemed to be dragged from her by some invisible power as it sank into the floor by her bedside. One ghost is accompanied by a wave of cold air which chills those who draw near it; another is apparently warm. On hot nights he is seen to mop his face with a handkerchief.

A spook which lay down by a friend in bed placed its "frozen lips" against her cheek. That some phantoms have appreciable weight is perhaps indicated by the case of a certain woman visited by the shades of two dead friends. They appeared behind her while she was seated at her tea table, and leaning upon her shoulders, rendering her immovable. She was unaware of what had happened until her daughter, across the table, cried out and gave the names of the intruders.

Ghosts differ quite as widely in facial expression as in other characteristics. One always has a long clean shaven, physiognomy, cadaverous and pitiful in expression. Another clean shaven spook wears his hair on his head and has a "generally distinguished and gentle air." One of the percipients of a woman ghost, though frightened by its first appearance, afterwards anticipated pleasure in the hope of seeing the kindly-disposed face. "Its eyes were green and glistening, but the rest of its face was muffled up," is recorded of another "haunt." A tall black ghost, frequently seen upon rural roads, paralysed some children with fright when they looked up and beheld the "awful expression" of its countenance. Women who saw its face at other times described it as thin and deadly pale. The face of a young man's spook haunting a modern city house is pale and luminous. His eyes are downcast as though in deep thought.

The majority of ghosts appear to look sad and deathly pale. A conspicuous number among the masculine persuasion are clean shaven; yet many are adorned with the shades of moustaches and beards worn in real life. To those who were near to them in life they usually appear in their normal form. Sometimes to those who have not seen them for long intervals they exhibit changes experienced before death, but not previously observed. A little girl of three years, for instance, went to the dining room to get some cakes. Suddenly the household was startled by her screams. She insisted that she had seen "Poor Papa" sitting in his armchair, and that he had put out his arms "for baby to kiss him." "But Baby wouldn't," she said, "'cause he looked so funny. He had black whiskers." The child's father was, unknown to her, dying at this moment in a distant place. Since leaving home he had, also unknown to her, grown a dark beard, though his hair and moustache were blonde.

Few if any of the phantoms now being ferreted out by the professional hunters of such uncanny game appear to "squeak and gibber" like those of ancient Rome. A great majority of those actually seen are silent, so far as conversation is concerned. Many are unscrupulous as to the noise which they make in moving about. Some make their presence known by a rustling sound. The footfalls of others are loud and so heavy as to make houses tremble. An outside ghost announces his presence to persons wandering about in the country by producing an uncanny thud or thump on the ground beside them. A majority of the Spooks with audible voices appear to have invisible forms.

Fashion in dress appears to cut no figure in spook land. The majority of late arrivals adhere to styles prevalent at their time of death. A grandmother's ghost appears in her customary gown of black silk, and holds up her skirts while going up and down stairs. A phantom priest haunting the English estate of Lady Stafford appears in ecclesiastical robes and a red sash. A ghost which peers and occasionally enters through a window opening upon a churchyard and wears a ruffled shirt front and knee-breeches. Another dons tattered clothing from head to foot, and "looks like a scarecrow." It haunts the room occupied by a suicide who jumped from his window and tore his clothes to shreds while meeting death.

The phantom visitor of a druggist and his brother, rooming together, habitually parades in its nightshirt. One seen by a lady dwelling in another place wore a long, grey dressing gown with a long pointed collar which exposed a "finely formed throat." A stiff brocade skirt, rustling when she moves, is always worn by a well-known ghost haunting an ancient garret. A shade in knee-breeches and otherwise old fashioned costume was discovered in Charles Lamb's old cottage, Edmonton, by Mrs. Thompson, its present occupant. Later, while studying a portrait of the great writer, she identified the shade as his.

A vanishing ghost haunting lonely lanes in daytime wears a long coat, gaiters, and knee-breeches, all black, but a white cravat, such as seen in old fashioned pictures. An old lady haunting a farmhouse adheres to her white cap, white handkerchief, and white apron.

A ghost in a drab cutaway coat frequented the same house. Some years afterwards it was learned that a former owner was an ancient Quaker who wore such apparel. Several officers of British cavalry seated at a table in the barracks at Aldershot saw the ghost of a young woman in a soiled bridal dress glide slowly past the window in front of them. The window was twenty feet from the ground. The spook's face was later identified by the photograph of an unknown woman found in the room of a veterinary surgeon dying, at the moment of the haunting. In another part of the building, the feminine ghost dresses like a nun, but in grey. Another is seen in a plain shawl and grey-black bonnet.

A ghost with the power to multiply itself and appear in the same place and at the same time as three complete counterparts of its form, as remembered in life, is indeed a wonder. Yet a Liverpool man lately beheld three distinct spooks of his lame uncle, hobbling one behind the other. He mentioned the experience to a brother and sister accompanying him. When they arrived home they learned that the same uncle had died at the time of the phantom's appearance.

Another spectre haunting an American lady and her daughter annoys them by rattling their toilet articles and pulling at their dresses. Another arouses its sleepy victims by placing its icy hand on their faces. The ghost of one man's sister-in-law pushes him about, hits his legs, shakes his door, and blows cold air on him. The phantom of a friend visiting a young lady on the day of his death appeared to her first as a hand waving to her. Later, while she was taking down her hair, it appeared to assist her. After she retired it lay down beside her, kissed her and said "Goodbye."

*Hampshire Telegraph.*